AF660458

Governance Issues in India from Grassroots Perspective

About the Author

Prof. G. Palanithurai, Rajiv Gandhi Chair for Panchayati Raj Studies and Dean, Students Welfare, Gandhigram Rural Institute, Gandhigram is an academic activist. He is specializing in grassroots governance and development. He closely works with local, regional and federal governments. He actively collaborates with civil society activities to strengthen Panchayati Raj System in India. He has developed a leadership school in Rajiv Gandhi Chair. To his credit he has sixty-five books, eighty three monographs, seventy six popular articles, one hundred and thirty nine research articles in his area of specialization. He is a visiting professor in Cologne University, Germany. He extensively travelled abroad in academic assignments. His action research activities were supported by the Ford Foundation, the Population Foundation of India, DANIDA, Rajiv Gandhi Foundation, UNDP, The Hunger Project, UNICEF, The World Bank, State Planning Commission, Action Aid International, Swiss Development and Cooperation, Toolkit Foundation, Netherland and a few other agencies. He is the coordinator of the UGC Sponsored Innovative Programme and UGC Special Assistance Programme of the Department of Political Science and Development Administration, Gandhigram Rural Institute.

Governance Issues in India from Grassroots Perspective

G. Palanithurai

CONCEPT PUBLISHING COMPANY PVT. LTD.
NEW DELHI-110059

© Author

All rights reserved. No part of this work may be reproduced, stored, adapted, or transmitted in any form or by any means, electronic, mechanical, photocopying, micro-filming recording or otherwise, or translated in any language, without the prior written permission of the copyright owner and the publisher. The book is sold subject to the condition that it shall not, by way of trade or otherwise, be lent, resold, hired out, or otherwise circulated without the prior publisher's written consent in any form of binding or cover other than that in which it is published.

The views and opinions expressed in this book are author(s) own and the facts reported by him/her have been verified to the extent possible, and the publishers are not in any way liable for the same.

ISBN-13 : 978-93-5125-011-1

First Published 2014

Published and Printed by

Concept Publishing Company Pvt. Ltd.
A/15-16, Commercial Block, Mohan Garden
New Delhi-110059 (India)
T: 25351460, 25351794, *F*: 091-11-25357109
E: publishing@conceptpub.com, W: www.conceptpub.com
Editorial Office: H-13, Bali Nagar, New Delhi-110 015, India.

Cataloging in Publication Data--*Courtesy:* D.K. Agencies (P) Ltd. <docinfo@dkagencies.com>

Palanithurai, G. (Ganapathy)
Governance issues in India from grassroots perspective / G. Palanithurai.
p. cm.
Includes bibliographical references (p.) and index.
ISBN 9789351250111

1. Local government—India—Tamil Nadu. 2. Panchayat—India—Tamil Nadu. 3. Tamil Nadu (India)—Politics and government—20th century. 4. Tamil Nadu (India)—Social conditions. 5. India--Economic conditions. 6. India—Economic policy—1991- I. Title.

DDC 320.8095482 23

TO

DIVINE MOTHER

Preface

From 1991 onwards I have been discussing in many fora that globalization is governability. Even before the onset of globalization of economy in India, India had increasingly been facing the problems of poverty and governability. The governing system created in this country in free India did not have the needed capacity even to manage the socio-political crisis in India. But the new economy introduced in the year 1991 had compounded and complicated the governance process and intensified the socio-economic crisis and to solve the above problems suitable remedies have to be taken. The globalization process had started affecting all aspects of the society. Understanding the whole process of transformation due to globalization is very difficult and it has to be done. By doing so, one has to visualize what opportunity comes and what threat comes out of globalization and suitable solutions have to be found out to make use of opportunity and to avoid the threats.

Further as a student of political science I look at the whole process of transformation from the perspective of governance. Because the state has to take enormous responsibilities to regulate the market to deliver goods properly to the people. In the context of growing aspiration of the people towards the material comfort and to enjoy democracy made the state more responsive and responsible for the people. In the same way the state has to enable the market forces to create wealth for the nation. In this context the state machinery should have adequate capacity and capability to manage the new kinds and volumes of economic activities. State requires more self-regulation to regulate the market and the society. What we witness in the globalised world is more of default rather than order and regulation. As a result large scale misuse of power, scams and scandals by using the public offices. It becomes culture and order of the day.

Efforts were on to reform governance and administration to

enable the market to unleash the potentials. In the same way reform initiatives had been taken to make governance process more transparent and accountable. In order to enable the people to participate in the process of governance and development decentralization of powers was initiated. Yet things are complicated and complex. To understand the current crisis in governance and administration and to help institutions, organizations and policy makers India needs more number of people who are thoroughly oriented and framed in the new process. Hence, a small initiative was taken at our institute to introduce a new master's programme on governance and development. It was supported by the UGC under innovative programme. Under this innovative programme we have to do research on the area chosen. We have conducted several such studies in governance and administration for the past two years. The articles and papers which have been published in different journals have been edited and made it as a book under the title "Governance Issues in India from the Grassroots Perspective" for the publication.

In this volume I have touched upon certain important themes such as the Anti Corruption movement in India, a new framework for governance, governance from the perspective of Gandhi, Corruption at the grassroots, visionary framework for managing crisis in governance, accountability and transparency in development activities at grassroots, role of ICT in data generation and management at the grassroots, status of Dalits and Dalit representatives at the grassroots, democracy, development and conflict at grassroots, local governance as a factor in Centre-State relations in India, and restructuring local governance in globalization. Totally all the above issues have been looked at from the grassroots perspective and that too from the perspective of the poor and the marginalized. While analyzing the above problems specifically ways and means were found out to remedy the maladies in the existing governance arrangements. Further all the articles packed in this volume opened more avenues to the research scholars in social science to move deeper into the issues which I have touched. I have thrown light on certain key aspects of governance and administration from the perspective of the grassroots and the poor. This has to be followed. All the above articles came out from my research meant for the UGC programme on Governance and Development.

G. Palanithurai

Acknowledgements

Though I was a student of history, I evinced keen interest in politics and as a result I did yet another master in Political Science and joined as faculty member in Political Science Department of Annamalai University. Even in Politics of late I started working in grassroots politics substantially after joining in Gandhigram Rural Institute. Having done substantial work in this area of decentralization, democratization and governance Rajiv Gandhi Chair for Panchayati Raj studies has been created in our department. UGC has provided substantial grants to the tune of Rs. 80 Lakh for the introduction of M.A. Governance and Development as an innovative programme and for special assistance programme to improve the quality of research, teaching and outreach programme. To get such recognition of UGC, we have worked in the same area for the past fifteen years with the support of the Ford Foundation; Rajiv Gandhi Foundation, Population Foundation of India, World Bank, Ministry of Panchayati Raj, Government of India, Ministry of Rural Development, Government of India, State Planning Commission, DANIDA, UNDP, UNICEF, the Hunger Project, PRIA, Institute of Social Sciences, Action Aid International and a few other small agencies. Without the support of above agencies we could not have to come to this level. Series of monographs, working papers, books and articles have been written and published in the earmarked area of specialization. Hence, I record my profound sense of gratitude to the above organizations. In the same way I record my profound thanks to UGC for sanctioning the project on innovative programme in specialized area which enabled me to write all the articles which have been included in this volume.

Thirdly, my project staff who worked in the projects has done commendable work by which the Department and the Rajiv Gandhi Chair have acquired enormous data and resources in the areas of governance and administration. Their hard work has to be appreciated and recognized and for which I place on record my appreciation to all of them who worked in different projects in different periods.

Further my colleagues in the Department have concentrated much in teaching and learning the enormous research space for me and, hence, I concentrate much on research , policy advocacy and outreach programmes. Hence, I register my thanks to them in immeasurable terms as they are always very positive and supportive to all my academic, research and outreach activities.

Fifth, my family members who substantially supported my activities by allowing me freely without drawing my attention to the family responsibilities. I have been doing injustice to them by not attending my family responsibilities and yet they are tolerating me and keeping me in good humour. I thank my wife, my daughter, son-in-law and my son profusely.

Sixth, the community from which I hailed deserves my appreciation. Though I am not attending any social call, the members of my community have tolerated me by seeing my activities in the field. But at the same time the members of my community extended all their help to me and to my family to remain in community life.

Seventh, my kith and kin who never expect anything expect my participation in their programmes and functions. But I could not do this also and yet they are not taking it seriously. They are always affectionate to me and for which I am thankful to them.

Lastly, the publishing company — the Concept Publishing Company Pvt. Ltd., New Delhi deserves my appreciation as it emerges as specialized agency publishing continuously books on grassroots studies and more specifically on grassroots governance. There are companies publishing books on decentralization but the Concept Publishing Company Pvt. Ltd., New Delhi continuously publishing books based on field notes. Mr.Ashok Kumar Mittal and his sons deserve appreciation. Without taking much time they publish the manuscripts continuously by maintaining quality. I thank the editors of various journals who have published my articles in their journals in different periods.

Gandhigram
27.11.2011

G. Palanithurai

Contents

Preface vii
Acknowledgements ix
List of Tables, Figures, Diagrames and Charts xiii

I. Introduction 1

II. A New Framework for Governance 5

III. Anti Corruption Movement in India 30

IV. Governance from the Perspective of Gandhi 58

V. Corruption at Grassroots 73

VI. Visionary Framework for Managing Crisis in Governance 88

VII. Accountability and Transparency in Development Activities at Grassroots 96

VIII. Role of ICT in Scientific Data Generation and Management at the Grassroots 119

IX. Problems and Scope in Handling RTI: A Grassroot Perspective 132

X. An Analysis of the Status of Dalit Gram Panchayat (Local Governance System) Leaders in Tamil Nadu (India) 150

XI. Democracy, Development and Conflict at Grassroots 180

XII. Local Governance as a Factor in Centre-State Relations in India 197

XIII. Restructuring Local Governance in Globalization 214

XIV. Conclusion 231

Bibliography 233

Index 241

List of Tables, Figures, Diagrames and Charts

LIST OF TABLES

7.1: Organizational Structure of Various Departments 101
7.2: Governance Structure 107

10.1: Types of Discrimination and Atrocities committed against dalits in the Panchayat Areas which are Governed by Dalit Panchayat Leaders in Tamil Nadu 159

Annexure Table 10.1: Affidavit Filed by Gram Panchayat Dalit Leaders for Public Hearing 179

LIST OF FIGURES

4.1: Dynamics of State Society Market Relationship 60
4.2: Difference between the existing Framework and Gandhi's Framework of Relations 62

7.1: Administration 106
7.2: Flow of Fund 113

8.1: Data Generation Mechanism 125
8.2: Basic Data 126
8.3: Data Details 127

9.1: The Structure of State government 139

LIST OF DIAGRAM

4.1: Rational Governance Model 63

LIST OF CHART

9.1: Organogram of Government Department Delivery System 140

I
Introduction

World has witnessed unprecedented change and transformation both positive and negative in the last two decades. On the one hand, wealth has been created in unfathomable measure and equally mass deprivation has increased enormously. It is always a myth why the created wealth in the world has not percolated down in the society for the well-being of the people. People's anger against governing instrument has been increasing as the state machinery failed to fulfil the basic needs of the people and yet it facilitated the wealth makers to make wealth unbelievably in higher quantum. But in poverty reduction and attacking mass deprivation the state has failed miserably. As a result the people started questioning the ability and capability of the governing institutions. In the new context the state has slowly withdrawn from some basic responsibilities and allowed many agencies to perform the role of the institutions of the state. Corporate and civil societies have become part of the governing institutions. Now government's responsibilities are being shared by many agencies. In this regard, governance acquires importance. Governance is more a process and government has a role. In this context governance becomes much complex and multidimensional. The existing governance arrangement needs a thorough change to suit the new requirement. The whole world is facing the problem only in contextualizing and repositioning the governance institutions with the aim of establishing good governance. But unfortunately it is not emerging. All the governments are facing intense problems in managing the institutions. How this problem is tackled is the indicator by which the nature of governance can be gauged. How governance and governance mechanisms can be made more friendly to poor and amenable and manageable to the poor.

In Indian context, the above problems are visualized and explained in different write-ups done by me. In the first article on "A New Framework of Governance" the existing governance issues have been analyzed from the perspective of the rural masses and more specifically from the perspective of the poor. In the process of analysis decentralization of powers has been identified as a framework to empower the poor and the marginalized and to make them to participate in the process of governance and development. A major shift can be made for the people from political mobilization to development mobilization. An alternative politics could be found out and that will be "Peoples Politics". Party politics has reached its lowest ebb and it has to be replaced by people's politics. But the new polity has to evolve from grass roots politics. Ultimately it will end up in development Politics. Ultimately it will end up in development politics. Substantial analysis has been made on the practices of the current politics and governance.

The second article entitled "Anti Corruption Movement in India" has analyzed extensively the movement launched by Anna Hazare. The whole movement has been analyzed through its process. While analyzing the movement the failure of the political parties and potential danger to the representative institution have been indicated. At the same time the article pin pointed the people's aspiration and mood towards cleansing politics and governance in India.

Next article entitled "Government from the Perspective of Gandhiji" visualized the whole problem of governability from the perspective of Gandhi on governance. His conceptualization of governance arrangement and the existing paradigm of governance have been analyzed. The key elements which have determined the bases of governance have been analyzed from the perspective of their suitability to the existing context. Gandhian framework of Governance is highly relevant and yet the problem lies in operationalisation. Many of the key elements of Gandhian Framework of governance are in operation. In this article relevance of Gandhian framework has been highlighted. The fifth article entitled "Corruption at Grassroots" is the outcome of an action research. In this article practices of corruption at the grassroots and their causes and courses have been analyzed and explained.

Remedies have been suggested as to how corruption could be controlled and eliminated in the process of development at grassroots. Useful suggestions have been made based on the analysis of the issue.

The sixth article on "Visionary Framework of Managing Crisis in Governance" tries to explain the operational framework evolved by R. Venkatraman and followed subsequently by Shankar Dayal Sharma and K.R. Narayanan as Presidents of Republic of India to manage the crisis which emanated due to coalition politics. This article highlights the emergence of certain institutions in Indian democracy namely the Election Commission and Supreme Court during the time of crisis in governance.

Article seven entitled "Accountability and Transparency in Development Activities at Grassroots" brought to light the intricacies and complexities in administration and delivering of services to the people. This chapter highlighted the gap between the people and the administrative arrangements. Further it focuses its attention on the information distance between the people and the governance mechanism.

The next article "Role of ICT in Scientific Data Generation and Management at the Grassroots" indicated the drawbacks in data generation and data management at grassroots for decision making. It projects a framework for accurate decision making at community level. The whole framework is evolved in the backdrop of the New Panchayati Raj System.

The article entitled "Problems and Scope in Handling RTI: A Grassroots Perspective" brought to light how it could be effectively used to check corruption at the grassroot level in all development activities. It also highlighted the problems involved in handling of RTI. The whole issue is being analyzed from the perspective of poor and the marginalized at the grassroot.

Article ten deals with the issues of exclusion. But the whole issue is looked at from the perspective of the space created for the *dalits* and the women. The whole analysis has been made with the assumption that the critical mass formed because of the reservation of seats for *dalits* and women, will perform critical function. The impact of *dalits* in local governance especially on the life of the *dalits* in the rural areas.

In yet another article entitled "Democracy, Development and Conflicts at Grassroots" another has analyzed the democratization process at the grassroots. Through this study the author has brought to light the increased conditions for more of conflict than harmony as communities have not been democratically oriented. In the absence of a democratic culture at the grassroots, new governance process has created conflict at the community level. Constitutional values and community practices are at clash at the grassroots wherever the communities are not modernized and demonatised.

In the thirteenth article "Local Governance as a Factor in Centre – State Relations in India" the author has critically looked into the relationship between the State and Centre while operationalising the New Panchayati Raj System as per the 73rd Amendment to the Constitution of India. Tamil Nadu State has been taken as a case analysis. In this article how deliberately keeping the Panchayati Raj institutions weak in the name of state autonomy has been captured and analyzed.

In the final article "Restructuring Local Governance in Globalization" the author has pointedly focused his attention on the context and its backdrop in operationalising and process of decentralization of powers. The current wave of decentralization has to be seen in the context of globalization otherwise many of the vital links will be missed. The author suggested as to how grassroots democratic institutions have to be evolved to manage globalization.

II

A New Framework for Governance

Introduction

In the history of mankind, the changes and challenges we have been seeing and responding in the process of development in the last three decades are unprecedented and unexpected. They are of both highly rewarding and devastating for the human society and nature. People of different groups look at changes and challenges from their own perspectives and understanding based on the reality. Moreover, people take positions and argue from their own position and perspective. Against this background I look at the crises of governance and development objectively from the perspective of the poor and the marginalized as they are three-fourth of the world population. Unless their lives are transformed there is no meaning in claiming that we are living in the world as a civilized individuals or collectivities. Our happiness in life should not be at the cost of others and more particularly by exploiting the poor and the marginalized in the world. We should live happily and we should allow and enable others to lead life happily and with self-respect. We should not achieve prosperity by exploiting the masses. While looking from the perspective of the poor and marginalized I am not making an argument that all the poor are in distress all the time and they are not coming out from poverty. But at the same time I am not bringing an argument that the life of the poor is fine. I do not close my eyes while seeing the opportunities for the poor to redeem their conditions and to improve their life. I always feel that opportunities are sky high for the poor to redeem their conditions provided they understand the process of development and governance and take part in the process of governance and development. Here it is to be noted that to make use of the opportunities, poor need enabling conditions and otherwise they can see and feel the opportunities and they cannot go beyond it to make use of the opportunities. People, those who are aware of the opportunities and institutions which work for poor, will make use of the opportunities and institutions to alleviate poverty and achieve prosperity. Millions of people came out from poverty and achieved prosperity only through this way over a period of time. But, in reality, majority of the poor are clueless without having direction and support and they are in struggle. The struggle is also not for progress or development alone but also for survival. Their survival in the development process made them to lose their self respect, self dignity and self confidence. The institutions which had been created for the purpose of facilitating the poor are neither in performing the facilitation role nor playing the supportive role. Hence, we face such a crisis in development scenario throughout the world which ultimately reflected in governance[1]. Because ever since nation-state was formed, the state took the responsibility of protecting the people and facilitates them to achieve development. Now the humanity is struggling to come out from bad governance to just governance and to move on to good governance[2]. Against this background I look at the Indian development scenario and the governance problems.

The problem we face in India is out and out not material but moral and ethical in nature. Further, it is mostly governance related. It had been always in discourse whether India is governable[3]. It was the British who brought an administrative state but after the British exit Indian elites had adopted a sophisticated governance mechanism namely representative democracy. The governance mechanism – representative democracy – was an evolved one in the west and for that purpose the western society had waged a relentless struggle over centuries. In this process the western societies had acquired the needed skills and maturity to handle the same. For its smooth functioning equity and equality were achieved to some extent in the western society whereas in India the two are the major tasks before the democratic governance[4]. Hence, questions have been raised whether India is governable and if so, can it be done through the representative democracy.

The representative democracy expects adherence to rule of law and it has to be evolved as a culture[5]. Will it be possible in India to have such a culture in the context of vast differences and disparities[6]. India is a land known for its *dharmic* practices in public life, yet we not even follow rudimentary accepted moral values in public life at present. Violations are made not by ordinary citizens of this country. But they are being done by the people who are in the helm of affairs in governance and administration. They are supposed to make laws and they are the models. They are the leaders to lead the society. This kind of violations at a higher level made the ordinary citizens of the country to lose faith in the present system of governance and administration[7]. Leaders of the Political System and Administration have lost their respect of the people. People who have been showing respect to the party leaders are the party men and brokers who expect spoils from the leaders when they are in power. We witness a total anarchic condition today in India. People are in disarray and they are disillusioned. But in anarchy India functions as a system. India is functional because of the high level of peoples' tolerance and endurance and for which our religious and cultural practices have contributed substantially. Otherwise the political, governance and administrative system would have come to a complete halt long back. The secularization and modernization process have not substantially transformed the people. They are in tradition with modernity. Since 71 per cent of the people are living in the rural areas with traditional outlook and institutions and of the total population 58 per cent of the people relying on agriculture for livelihood, one cannot expect a total transformation adhering to the norms of mainstream development. Really it is a struggle for development. The existing conditions could be tackled and corrected provided our leaders have will power and determination. The present day leaders are not having that much leadership skill and will as we had during the period of freedom struggle. Now many of our leaders are only having managerial skill and ability and, hence, they manage and not transform. India had demonstrated to the world through its non-violent freedom struggle that the colonial societies can be freed from the clutches of the colonial yoke. It was the remarkable achievement made by our leaders' through their transformative leadership skill. But now the problem we face is the non-availability of transformative leaders in the society and politics. But we have enormous business leaders to generate wealth. When we are able to make unbelievable wealth by using globalization opportunities, why we are unable to tackle poverty by using globalization is the basic question. One unequivocal reason is that the aspiration of people to amass wealth and to possess material advancement to unfathomable level legally and illegally has increased exponentially. The moment opportunities are provided people who have got skill and capacity make use of the same and create wealth and whereas the poor could not do anything and they expect everything from the state. The state is spending its time in enabling the wealth makers to make wealth and the poor to come out from poverty. The capacitated have unleashed their energy and potentials and they have exceeded their limits by crossing the regulations of the state for making wealth and thereby created unprecedented problems for governance. But the poor could not identify any of the opportunities to achieve prosperity. They continue to rely on state and its welfare programmes. When the poor are agitating against the state for their rightful claim of their entitlements they are being controlled over by the state ruthlessly. Whereas the rich violates all established norms while making wealth, the state has not done anything. The above impressions have been created among the people in India. The state authorities are not in a position to regulate the market forces when they are erring. How market forces could be controlled by the state is a big discourse all over the world. The fault lies not in the system but in the system operators. Further people who hold power adopt all kinds of fraudulent means and as a result they are slowly becoming unpopular and losing influence over the society. In order to retain their influence over the poor segments of the society, populist measures are being announced and implemented. Unfortunately populist programmes and schemes are considered or termed as welfare measures. Populist measures are almost corrupting the society. Nobody has scrutinized and questioned the process of fraudulent wealth making process in the government and hence wealth making exercise has gone to the maximum level unchecked. When the whole process of wealth making exercise has over thrown millions of people from their livelihood options and from their settlements, what the state is doing? is yet another question. Even the state (government) machineries are used to displace people from their settlements for the benefit of the market. Instead of providing better opportunities and options for the poor people to lead life with needed facilities and convenience, state along with market made the poor peoples life miserable. State is in the fold of the market forces.

In India, we are not facing the problem of scarcity of resources. We have resources, good policies, enabling laws but they are not reaching the target population. Because we are very weak in implementing the enacted laws, evolved policies and taken decisions. The targeted groups are not in a position to claim their entitlement as they are ignorant and far away from access to power, resources and information. They are in such disability. Hence, it is the role of the government to reach out to the needy masses. Now all crises we face and see in India are the crises of, growth and development. When many of the groups are able to get and achieve prosperity, it is natural in a democracy the deprived mass will also develop such aspiration to achieve the same. When they are not able to achieve the aspired development, they tend to accuse the state as state has not facilitated them to achieve development. As a result the crises are linked to politics, governance and administration. Unless we address the above problems one cannot dream of a just social order, good governance and efficient administration in India[8]. India's governability is always being questioned as the social unrest is always antithetical to democracy. In this context how democracy will deliver goods is the basic question everyone raised.

India is unique and cannot be compared with any country in the world as commonalities for comparison of India with other countries are rare. India's vastness, inequalities, size of population, differences, and diversities make it unique and distinct. Managing more than one billion populations with extreme inequalities, disparities and differences through democracy is not a small exercise. Despite these differences, inequalities and disparities, making democracy to work is really a stupendous task and it is being seen as a paradox popularly called "Indian Paradox"[9]. With all the drawbacks and shortcomings India has achieved unprecedented economic growth in the recent years. Further during the slow down of economy the recovery of Indian economy from recession is also remarkable. Yet the achieved growth has not helped the community to achieve equity and alleviate poverty to the level of our expectations[10]. The two miracles namely democracy and growth have not done the third miracle of improving the quality of life of the people more particularly the poor and the marginalized. For the success of market, government facilitates, the stakeholders utilize the opportunities and effectively they take part in the whole process of the market activities. For the activities of the state people give their full powers and responsibilities to the state and participate in the electoral process whereas for development of the poor, neither the stakeholders participate in the process nor the state facilitates the stakeholder's participation. Against this background how to make the third miracle of eradicating poverty to happen is the basic question in India[11].

Background

One has to understand the ground reality at the grassroots. In the six decades of experience in democratic governance in India we have seen that our representative democracy through its governance has created the vast gap between the masses and the ruling elites in the country in terms of living conditions and economic prosperity. The gap between the ruling elites and the masses has reduced the citizens into beneficiaries, petitioners and voters and not as stakeholders or active participants in the process of democracy and development. The existing social hierarchy based on the caste system, the economic inequality and patriarchy which ought to have been tackled through democratic governance were not tackled effectively over a period of sixty years and as a result the democratic institutions have been largely damaged[12]. The democratic institutions which are in vogue are being manipulated by a few sections of the people for their own material advancement. Both democratic institutions and development institutions are very much helpful only to the capable individuals and groups. The democratic institutions have not given confidence to a major section of the society that it would provide opportunity for many to come up in life and to mitigate all social ills which have afflicted them. It is to be noted here that the existing social realities are antithetical to democracy. The conduct of election and handing over of power and responsibility to the party or parties which got elected are considered as success of democracy in India[13]. Beyond that democracy does not percolate into the Indian society as a culture.

The finer values of democracy did not even influence the political institutions which manage the governing institutions in India. Because the very basic conditions of India do not fit into the theoretical framework of representative democracy[14]. Democracy will not deliver goods in a conflicting situation. This is the theoretical position and yet Indian democracy works slowly. The lifeline of Indian democracy lies in general election where every citizen is playing his / her role decisively and hence poor has got a stake. This is the only way by which poor can make their demands legitimately. Beyond that poor are always in disadvantageous position in Indian society, governance and administration. But the poor are the real saviours of Indian democracy.

Growth to Development

Enough attention was paid on economic growth by using the new opportunities arose out of globalization, liberalization and privatization. Equal attention was paid on taking our economy from recession. These two achievements are not smaller achievements. They are laudable achievements. But the government managers have not received appreciation from the masses for their efforts in building their economy. Because the achieved growth has not benefited the masses, though the government document substantially argue for inclusive growth and inclusive development and in real terms the ground reality at the grassroots depicts the poor performance of the government in achieving development of the poor[15]. Substantial work has to be done on development front at the grassroots especially for the poor and the marginalized. And for which an institutional mechanism has to be created and a development methodology has to be in place at the grassroots. To bring an alternative paradigm for development and deepening of democracy[16] a governance design was introduced in India. It was created constitutionally. But it is not properly shaped to the level of expectation. They are very weak, powerless and resourceless and they are left with inadequate functionary. They are at the mercy of the State government. The bureaucracy is very strong and able to control over the local government. In such a way local governance has been shaped in India with some exceptions. Further, the leader recruited for local bodies have not been properly oriented and sensitized on governance and development issues. Their capacity is also poor[17]. As a result they also follow the path of the other elected representatives of the people to the State Legislature and the National Parliament.

For inclusive growth and inclusive development the institutional mechanism created through the constitution for development and governance has to be strengthened with adequate resource base[18]. Unless governance at the grassroots is made vibrant, there will not be any possibility to achieve equitable development at the grassroots. In a communitarian society constitutional and democratic governance is essential prerequisite to deepen democracy and achieve equitable development. The governments both the Centre and the States have to ensure the people the basic facilities to lead a decent and dignified human life. They should not struggle even for minimum facilities which are basic entitlements of the people. Further the governments have to be humanized to treat the people as citizens with self respect and self dignity. But at present the conditions of the poor are pathetic. Since majority of the people are treated as petitioners and beneficiaries by the Centre and the State governments' people have conveniently abdicated their citizens' responsibilities. When they are not able to get their entitlements people are losing confidence and faith in the existing governance arrangements. When people get to know who gets what and how through the media, the anger of the poor goes up and the intensity of their angry will go further if they are organized and facilitated properly by a conscientised leader in a democratic way for socio-political action. Recently we have seen the public reaction to the initiative of Anna Hazare against corruption. At present people and governments are struggling for development and growth respectively. But the problem is how to achieve equity in development for the poor with the available economic growth. All micro and macro initiatives have not achieved the expected targets. Macro issues could be achieved through micro actions provided grassroots institutions are strengthened and people are made as participants. The problem before us is to restore credibility to the legitimate political and governance institutions both at the national and regional levels.

Pulling out from Scam Politics

Over a period of time, we have seen politics substantially on non-issues rather than on concrete development issues. Totally development issues had been given to government officials and experts. Development issues had not been addressed politically by the political parties. Our political leaders are not having clarity on the issues of development. Hence they are not addressing those issues in public. Substantially our political parties have not focused attention on the basic development issues of the people. They are food security, nutrition security, habitat security, water security, environment security, livelihood security, health security, and so on[19]. Neither people nor the politicians are conscientised on the above development issues. That is why 53 per cent of the women in India are affected by anemia and 43 per cent of the children are affected by malnutrition. The political parties are finding it difficult to touch upon these development issues which are basic and essential for the country. In order to escape from the development issues, non-issues are taken up for politics. As a result political parties often seek sensational non-issues for political activities. Now series of scams become sensational issues which relegate the development issues to the background. Totally people have been drawn towards scam politics. People are tired and soar over it. Totally a negative image has been projected on Indian Political and governance system. An image has been created to the effect that corruption is the only activity that takes place in Indian governance and administration. Substantial evidences have been shown that the money goes out illegally from India and under the table has increased its volume. Further, the volume of money goes out from India is ten times more than the money comes from foreign countries to India as development aid. People are made as mute spectators and they are helpless. Party men take a line on the arguments of their own parties. Citizens who are not affiliated with political parties are watching the whole episodes helplessly. The politics of economic growth has been overtaken by the politics of scams and scandals. Excepting the left parties (substantially they are not linked with enormity of scandals and scams) all political parties are drawn towards the politics of scandals. This is not good for the country and society. In the whole process all the legitimate governance institutions are losing their credibility[20]. All those institutions are shown in the bad light. Previously only leaders have lost credibility and respect but now it has come to institutions. Parliament, executive and judiciary have been slowly losing their reputation and credibility. This is a dangerous trend. The leaders of today are not having such a stature to rebuild the edifice of the institutions by bringing credibility to them. Quickly politics has to be taken out from scams and it is to be drawn towards development. Fastly steps are to be taken to give impression among the people that the institutions meant for tackling corruption will deal with corruption sternly and strongly. At the same time, a new development engagement for people has to be found out. An eminent lawyer has made a public statement that "every Indian will get Rs. 2.5 lakh if the Swiss Bank illegal money meant for Indians is brought back". It has attracted even the middle class to ponder over this new idea. People are attracted towards this issue. In the same way development issue has to be found out to draw the attention of the people. A new kind of engagement is necessary for the people. In the new engagement people will find hope that the current situation will be tackled and in future of the poor and excluded will get what they could not claim in the past. In such a way the new engagement has to raise hope. It is fully a hope raising move.

Issue of Governability

The problem in India is not in achieving material prosperity but it is in its governability. Governance institutions have their own level of capacity and capability. In a given context to the level of requirement at the dawn of independence capacity was built up for institutions. The nature and quantum of work in governance at present have substantially changed and increased respectively after the initiatives of globalization[21]. In governance aspect Indian institutions have miserably failed in delivering distributive justice. Hence, pressure has been continuously exerted on the governance institutions for proper distributive justice. Further, the development aspiration has also been increased unfathomably even among poor and this has also added pressure to the governance institutions. The new context has increased the volume of work to be transacted in the power corridor but the required capacity and skill for the decision making authorities are more. From the lowest governance Unit – Panchayat to National level— one can easily gauge the required capacity and capability of the governing institutions at present. The gap between the expectation and reality is wider and vast. To bridge the gap, capacity and capability of the institutions of governance have to be enhanced. It requires serious thought and commitment on the part of our national leaders. Unless the governance issues are tackled appropriately, by building up the capacity and skill, the politics will continue to be in the domain of scam which ultimately will damage the systems which have been created for good governance and effective administration. What we see today is surplus economy and deficit governance. Primarily the regulatory authorities have to be repositioned and reformed to meet the new requirements. This is the most important requirement to contain corruption and take the politics from scam and corruption. While doing so machinery created for distributive justice has to be strengthened and its capability has to be enhanced. Governance leaders are using old instruments to tackle new problems arising out of globalization and its impact.

Governance institutions have to learn lessons from the market. Innovation and working on demands are the key principles of the market and it follows constantly. This is to be followed in governance also. The new context requires a different set of skills for governance institutions and hence the needed skills have to be built up. Now governance requires constant learning and fast adoption of innovative practices[22]. The effect of changes in governance could be felt by the people in the shortest period. In such a way government has to perform. Otherwise people mostly the deprived and marginalized section will lose hope in the present system of governance and administration. Since major segment of population belong to that category, the discontent of the people may erupt at any time which ultimately weaken the democratic base of the governance institutions and it is not good for India.

Reforming Parliamentary Practices

The present day Parliament and Legislative Institutions have not evolved and developed to the level of the expectations of the people. Demands of the people are on the increase. Aspirations to achieve development and to enjoy democracy are on the increase. Science and technology have reached their peak. To harness the benefit of science and technology, newer policies and decisions are needed. Suitable policies and decisions have to be evolved. To perform the above task our Parliamentary Institutions have to be equipped. Legislative institutions are the key for the development of political institutions and hence they are to be reformed. When we talk about political reforms, electoral reforms, governance reforms and administrative reforms, why we are not taking initiatives for reforming parliamentary and legislative institutions. In the west periodically parliamentary institutions are evaluated and according to the contextual requirement they are repositioned and reformed. Even while reforming parliamentary practices constantly in the west, they are not able to meet the expectations of the people. People in the west continuously expressed their displeasure to the governing authorities. They are also in search of alternative instrument but it is not readily available. In the same way, policy making and decision making institutions have to be reformed and Members of Parliament and Provincial Legislative Assemblies have to be rigorously oriented and trained as they have to participate in the legislative process of the Parliament and State Legislatures in the new context. The task before the Members of Parliament and State Legislatures is highly technical and volume wise it is heavy and to perform the above they are to be properly equipped. But in reality there is no worthwhile training institution barring a few symbolic institutions to train the Members of Parliament and State Legislatures. In the same way for legislative research, a highly sophisticated institute has to be created to do research in legislative behaviour and legislative performance of the parliamentary and legislative institutions. In such a way our parliamentary institutions have to be reformed and innovated[23].

Mobilization for Development

People belonged to different sections of the society with unified goal were mobilized and rigorously organized during the freedom struggle. Subsequently there was no such wider mobilization of people with a focused goal. All mobilizations of public subsequently were sporadic, regional, lingual and more of sectarian in nature and not in the whole country for a unified cause. Further such mobilization had been done for narrow political and social purposes. These movements could not go beyond certain levels. People are continuously engaged politically but they are not properly and continuously engaged for development. Of course, political parties by presenting divisive development aspiration mobilize people with narrow considerations. Beyond that they could not make larger and broader mobilization of people to focus the well-being of all segments of the Indian society as it was evolved during the freedom struggle under the leadership of M.K. Gandhi in the name of a *Sarvodaya*. That is the reason why even after 63 years of democratic governance we could not see a sanitation culture in the country. There are volume of issues to reach people and people are to be sensitized on those issues. Because people are the main stakeholders of the process of development. Unless the prime stakeholders participate in the process, there will not be any remedy for all the issues and problems of development. They are waste management, water conservation and water management, increasing productivity in agriculture, soil conservation and enrichment of health of children and women, biodiversity, climate change, global warming, earth warming, livelihood and others. Never these issues are taken to the people for dissemination and sensitization. People are not properly oriented and sensitized on development and related issues. Serious thinking is needed for political engagement of people. Political parties are engaging people not on development issues but on sensational political issues which are non-developmental in nature. At present our politics and governance should be made development oriented. How to engage the people all over the country for development as a movement? An appropriate development mechanism has to be found out for mass mobilization. At present we have Panchayati Raj Institutions and they are appropriate instruments to engage people politically and administratively to achieve development. The grassroots institutions can engage people on development but they require strength and capacity to do the above job[24]. But unfortunately the present local body institutions do not have such strength and capability to engage people. Of course, there are institutions, processes and procedures at the grassroots but they are weak systemically. Panchayat institutions were created only for development engagement. But now the Panchayati institutions are not strong enough to engage people for development. A development engagement of people is an imperative need and it can be done by the local bodies and in such a way local bodies have to be strengthened and to be made them as development institutions. Time and again it is being lamented that the Panchayat institutions have got potentials but no systematic effort on the part of the State governments barring a few to activate the Panchayat institutions.

Outcome and Outlay

Our spending on poor is not a small amount. On an average government departments of both Centre and State through schemes and programmes directly and indirectly spend at least seven crores of rupees for a period of five years in Gram Panchayat areas. If the entire amount is spent in the villages, the villages would have become a self sufficient republic. But unfortunately it is not so. Even the basic needs of the people in the rural areas are not met even though 369 schemes are in operation through 48 Departments of the Government working in the villages in Tamil Nadu. How the earmarked money is being spent, through whom it is spent, when it is spent, for whom it is spent and who knows it are the real questions and myths and they are to be answered. It is a serious issue to be investigated but it is not done. When Rajiv Gandhi was the Prime Minister of India, he made a statement based on a study conducted by an institute in Mumbai that when Delhi gives one rupee the village receives only 12 paise. Now it is calculated as per another study that village gets only 16 paise out of one rupee allocated. Where the rest of the money goes is a myth still unanswered. Someone says it is being taken by the development brokers who act as link between poor and government and some others argue that it is the management cost. Realistically development activist argue that both explanations are wrong. Something is wrong in the systems, functions and process of development at grassroots and it is to be found out. Tracking of development finance is the difficult task in the whole process of governance in India. Because the whole process of governance is much complicated in India. Equally administration is also mystified and complicated. As a result one will find brokers for mediation between poor and the government in development engagement[25]. They act as a link between the people and the system. The mystified and complicated governance and administrative system really enables development brokers to thrive. The whole corrupt practices start only from here. It is to be noted here that the expanding corruption in public institutions is due to the faulty system of evaluation of performance of governments in our country. In our evaluation, we focus on output and not on outcome.

Further, the whole evaluation of performance of government should be not on outlay but on outcome. So far over a period of time we have carried out around 2,000 development schemes in India and yet, our improvement in human development indicators is below the level of some of the African countries. Hence, the whole evaluation has to be changed from outlay to outcome. Responsibilities have to be fixed on the individuals and institutions for achieving the target outcome and not outlay.

Ensuring Responsive, Responsible and Accountable Governance

Our laws, policies, programmes and schemes are with lofty ideals and goals. Commensurate with the above, resources are allocated and they are being spent. Yet what we wanted to achieve have not been achieved. Despite constitutional provisions, laws, good policies, excellent programmes and schemes with reasonable allocation of resources why we could not achieve what we wanted to achieve is the major question. There were two answers given by all to Rajiv Gandhi for the above question. One is that there is no responsible office or a representative legitimately created at the community level to look after the needs of the people and as a result one will find development brokers everywhere between the people and the government machinery. Mostly they are party men. In collusion with the bureaucracy they have been acting and making the system corrupt. As a result the benefits have reached somebody but not the target groups. Further, there is a heavy cost involved in reaching out the people to deliver benefits.

Further, there is no scientific evaluations mechanism to assess thoroughly the impact created by the schemes and programmes. All our assessments are output assessments and not outcome assessment. Further, the accountability mechanism which is in vogue is upward accountability and not downward. Government is accountable to the people and in the same logic government machinery is accountable to the people. So the officials instead of responding to the higher level officials they have to look towards the people. For every programme intended for the poor, social audit has to be conducted. In order to achieve the above new

Panchayati Raj System was created. But it has not developed a mechanism to conduct social audit very scientifically. By using the Right to information people have to get the information and conduct social audit.

Ground Heavy and Top Light

At present our governance system is designed top heavy and bottom light fashion. As a result the federal government keeps more responsibilities and powers and State and local governments are having lesser responsibilities and powers to manage the affairs of the society. For a country with wider differences, disparities and variations of needs based on the social, economic, cultural and religious conditions, people need context and location specific decisions with much flexibility for operation at the ground to meet the local requirements. But in reality one fit model for the whole country is being designed to achieve development and hence we could not see the expected outcome from our schemes and programmes. Unless it is changed and altered, the country will have to face more fundamental problems in governance and administration as more number of people joins in the anti-state group to work against the state by stating that they are deprived all along and that is the reality also. Further, people are losing hope and faith in the present democratic system as governance has not delivered the deliverables to the poor. As a result the fury of the poor against the system is also increasing. Day by day the territories which are effectively under the control of Indian Administrative system have started decreasing. But out of 600 districts, nearly 200 districts are disturbed districts. It means one-third of our territory is not effectively under our administrative control. In the absence of engagement of the people in the process of development, people are engaged in divisive politics. This resulted in increasing of conflict and violence in politics and society. Hence, the need of the hour is development engagement of the people through the process of decentralized governance. In our country we have a system to perform the above task but it is not strengthened. Local governance system created through the 73rd and 74th Amendments to the Constitution of India has to perform the task of engaging the people for development. The local governance system will enable the people of all the sections of the society to participate in the process of governance and development and thereby inclusive governance and inclusive development could be achieved. In the whole process people will be empowered. To make the people to participate in governance and administration both have to be simplified. Local administration has to be task oriented. By doing so, the burden of the Central and State governments will be reduced. So also corruption, social tension and social conflict will be reduced. At present the Federal government has assumed major responsibilities of governance and as a result both State and Local governments are made as subservient to the Central government as they look for resources and guidelines for development. As long as this arrangement continues the micro issues will be accumulated and they will not be solved. In the alternative paradigm of decentralized governance macro issues will be solved through grassroots institutions. By doing so, India will be up in development indicators. For development what grassroots institutions require is generic policies and decisions and needed resources. Further the development schemes and programmes will have more flexibility at the ground as variations are wider in India among regions.

Capacity Building

In the era of globalization, knowledge economy, high scientific and technological advancement, policy and programme requirements are totally different from the earlier eras. Issues are highly technical and complex in nature. In two fronts governments face problems. On the one hand, governance has to tackle poverty; and on the other hand, it has to manage the crises in development. To tackle the both, governance mechanism has to be fine tuned, repositioned and activated with much of vigour and innovation. At every level fine turning and contextualization are needed. What all we see in governance in the form of scam, stealing, corruption and mismanagement are due to the poor capability of the managers of governance. It is not only the officials who do not have the requisite capacity but also the elected representatives and party leaders. Since market and technology triggered the new opportunities, capacity building is needed for all those who are in governance as we see in market managers. People who are in business and companies are more capable than our leaders of governance. Our Members of Parliament, Members of Legislature and our Members of Local Governance do not have needed capacity. In India we do not have institutions to build their capacity. At least for the local body elected representatives we have some institutions to build their capacity. But, for the MPs, MLAs and Ministers we do not have such professional institutions to build their skill, capacity and capability in governance and administration. Governments have to think of a training mechanism to build their capacity. Rajiv Gandhi took initiatives in this regard but it was not continued. For this kind of exercise the training institutions should be highly professional and more research oriented. More number of policy related, legislation oriented journals in vernacular have be published. These institutions have to be fully technologically equipped to have live interaction with institutions of this nature of various leading democratic countries in the world. The above institutions should be autonomous but they have to be funded by the governments both at the Centre and the States. These institutions are really the new leadership schools. Now we find only business leaders but not governance leaders. The governance leaders are being managed by the business leaders and as a result the governance leaders are made as dealers for business groups. In such a way perception has been developed. Now we need 'L' schools (Leadership Schools).

Reducing the Cost of Politics

There is yet another major issue namely the cost of politics is to be tackled. At present the cost of Indian politics and elections is high which led to scams and corruptions in governance and administration at different levels from the Centre to local governance. Election being the target, mobilization of people for politics becomes a constant and imperative exercise, and for which political parties and their managers need huge amount of resources. Because of the technological advancement and communication development newer nuances are needed for political mobilization of people. As long as political activities were carried out at a lesser cost and in simplistic way, parties have mobilized resources from the people and cadres in the past. Now the whole processes of political activities have taken the methodologies of the corporates and whereby an impression is being given to everyone that a formula "invest and get reward" in politics works very well as business. If any one works for the party, the party will reward in the form of position when it comes to power. Position can be used to make private profit. Politics was a space for service once and now it has been converted into a business option. Thus it becomes a political business. Thus present day politics has oriented the party men and women to invest in politics and get the reward in the form of spoils when their party comes to power. A new concept is being developed to explain this phenomenon. It is called political capital. Making profit by using power without doing any business. This term was used by Max Weber long back and now it is being operationalised. Very few exceptions are in Indian Political Parties to this new venture. As a result, politics becomes violent, conflict centric and mutually antagonistic. This kind of political practice has sabotaged the finer values of democracy. At present what we need is reduction of the cost of politics and election and for which state funding for election is an imperative need. To initiate the process credible leaders join together and they should keep away from the mainstream political parties and constantly compel the mainstream political parties to get away from the costly corporate company politics. The mainstream political parties should make a declaration that the political space should not be used for making money and if there is any violation it should be dealt with seriously. The whole process has to be monitored through a strong civil society intervention comprising of strong opinion makers and intellectuals of repute.

Culture of Feudalism

In a democratic country political parties have to conduct themselves in a democratic way. A democratic culture has to be created in organizations and institutions functioning. But in India, even to conduct election, the political parties are to be pressurized by the Election Commission. Even while conducting the party elections, great amount of manipulation takes place within the parties. Further, the political parties have developed huge corpus for them. The new corpus culture has diverted the political parties from political activities based on ideologies to profit oriented business ventures. In order to keep the corpus and business, the family members of the leaders of the parties have entered into the parties, structures and remain strong in the party. As a result political parties are brought under the active control of the family members and consequently business characteristics have crept into the party structures. Over a period of time the political parties have earned unfathomable profits through the business ventures and valuable properties have been acquired. Thus, political parties have emerged as giant companies. Literally people with business interest moved closer to the party leaders by driving out the people with ideological commitment. It is a new phenomenon in Indian politics for worthy examination by adopting management models for investigation. Modern day political parties in the Indian context has to exhibit a new democratic culture but contrary to expectation they exhibit only the feudal characteristics which are antithetical to democracy. Absolutely there is no democratic mechanism to perpetuate democratic culture in the party politics. Unless some structural changes take place in the political parties through some laws, politics will become profession and business. The political parties will be in the hands of the families. Ultimately this syndrome will weaken the very basic foundation of democracy. Though politics becomes profession, politicians have not performed their roles and responsibilities professionally. Like President of the USA, a maximum of two terms can be fixed for an individual in any position in the political system whether be it M.P, MLA, party leader, secretary or any position. One should not hold position in any political organizational structure, more than two terms. By doing so, people will move from positions of the organizations. A person, holding a position for two to three decades has been hailed as an achiever but in reality it is a curse and black mark on the person. Because he /she have not allowed any other to occupy the position on which he is holding. In order to eliminate such a feudal culture from democracy a number of reform measures have to be taken. Cleansing polity will cleanse governance and administration. To do the above discussed reforms a new paradigm of governance is needed for political parties.

The new framework argues powerfully the need of involving people in the process of governance and development. So far over a period of time people have been slowly kept out of the orbit of governance and development. An image has been created that government will alleviate poverty and government will do everything for the poor. By doing so they have been driven to the beneficiary level which is deprived them from participation in the development process.

Further, the continuous sidelining of the grassroots institutions, the people are kept aloof from participation in governance and development engagement. Now a new opportunity has been created. By passing the 73rd and the 74th Amendments, local governance institutions have been created and they are in position. But these institutions have not been strengthened. In the tribal areas PESA has not been implemented in letter and spirit. In order to involve the people in the development process, the existing newly created local bodies have to be strengthened. In the same way the tribal areas PESA has to be effectively implemented. By strengthening the local governance institutions opportunities can be created for the poor and marginalized to participate in local governance and thereby their problems could be solved through the local bodies. By doing so, the governance system can instil confidence in the poor that their voices are heard and respected. Not only their voices are being heard and respected but based on them decisions are to be taken which will build our democracy from the bottom.

People have to be engaged immediately and it should not be a mere discourse engagement as done by the political parties. It should be a development engagement as MRNEGA and for which a constructive programme has to be developed based on the constructive programme evolved by Mahatma Gandhi. What are the relevant aspects to be taken from the constructive programme of M.K. Gandhi have to be taken and we have to add many more works in the new context. Climate change environment degradation, global warming are to be added. For development engagement of the people, 29 subjects in the 11th Schedule and 18 subjects in the 12th Schedule have been added in the Constitution. Many of the critical issues of development can be incorporated in the constructive programme to be developed from M.K. Gandhi's constructive programme. To achieve Millennium Development Goals, many of the basic social development issues have to be incorporated more specifically in the new constructive programme. All macro issues can be achieved by breaking into micro issues to be addressed by the local bodies with the active participation of the people. A massive mass mobilization has to the done for new constructive programme at the grassroots as mass mobilization was done by Mahatma Gandhi during freedom struggle. It is possible to do this exercise through the new local governance machinery established through the two historic constitutional Amendments (73rd and 74th Amendments to the Constitution of India). To do so, adequate powers, professionals and resources should be made available for the lowest unit of local governance in India. It is being reiterated by second Administrative Reforms Commission of India.

Conclusion

Indian polity, governance and administration have come to the lowest ebb in terms of their moral turpitude and managerial ability. The institutional structures have gradually acquired insurmountable weaknesses. Further, the institutions have started losing their credibility in the eyes of the public. The leaders who are in the helm of affairs have lost the confidence of the people. Urgently the above problems are to be attended to. No doubt there is no better institutional mechanism for governance today better than the present representative democracy. So we have no other alternative to the existing Parliamentary Democracy for governance. What we have to do is to find out remedies for all the problems within the framework of representative democracy. The ills what we found in operations of the Parliamentary Democracy are not the outcome of the system itself and they are the outcome of the system operators faulty operation who have operated the system faultily. Needed corrections have to be made in the system immediately. When India got independence, it was believed that as other Nation-States, Indian State will deliver justice and service together to all concerned. But in reality it could not deliver the distributive justice as Indian society got such diversity and disparities. At the dawn of independence state sovereignty was considered essential and paramount. Over the years the state has acquired enormous powers and leaving the people especially the poor as powerless when we analyze the conditions of the people more particularly the poor, the marginalized and the poor women it is equally important to restore sovereignty of the people. Thus, empowerment of the poor is an imperative need. One can easily underline the importance of the political equality. Now in the new context as the poor have got a whip through the adult franchise conferred on them by Jawaharlal Nehru and by which at least opportunity was given to the poor to safeguard and protect their interest at a limited level. Otherwise today the poor will be driven out and they will be left out in the discourse of the mainstream politics and development process easily.

Now it is to be realized that the people's sovereignty is much more important than the state sovereignty. People are sovereign. Hence, a governance arrangement has been created at the grassroots level with an enabling condition for the poor to take part in the governance and development process. The grassroots governing institutions should have a strong resource base to meet the local requirements. At this juncture the present day local governance has got the legal and constitutional sanction and it is to be supported and strengthened. While strengthening the grassroots institutions, people have to be mobilized massively and intensively for the rural reconstruction activities. This exercise has to be done euphorically and consciously and by doing so consciousness of the people will be on development activities. The whole exercise has to be done in a movement mode as the freedom movement. It requires huge resource mobilization and resource pooling along with the changing mindset of the bureaucrats and other stakeholders. At the federal and state levels governance mechanism has to be repositioned and reformed to meet the new challenges of our time because of globalization. Regulatory authorities have to be made independent to regulate governance. The system managers' capacity has to be enhanced and their mindset has to be changed. The whole evaluation process of governance and administration has to be changed to look at from the perspective of outcome rather than on outlay and output. Accountability mechanism has to be made downwards and for which social audit system could be created. Further, the elected representatives have to be oriented and fully capacitated to tackle the crises through their policies otherwise multinational companies will bring policies to our country. Reform initiatives should be made for not only economic globalization but also for alleviating poverty and for which governance and administrative reforms have to be evolved. Above all people have to be mobilized for development engagement.

REFERENCES

1. H.S. Shylendra, (ed.) *New Governance and Development: Challenges of Addressing Poverty and Inequality* New Delhi: Academic Education, 2009.
2. M. Lester Solomon, *The Tools of Government: A Guide to the New Governance,* New York: Oxford University Press, 2012.
3. Atul Koeshi, *Democracy and Discontent: India's Growing Crisis of Governability,* "Cambridge: Cambridge University Press" 1990.
4. Subash C. Kashyap, "Reforming Parliamentary Polity" in Ajit M. Banarjee and K.A. Chandrasekaran, *Reviewing Governance,* New Delhi: Tata McGraw Hill, 1996, pp. 277–304.
5. Subash C. Kashyap, *Basic Constitutional Values* Delhi: Ajanta Publications, 1994, 1–21.
6. Atul Kohli, *Democracy and Development in India,* New Delhi: Oxford University Press, 2009, pp. 1–3.
7. Bhikhu Parekh "The Crisis in Indian Democracy" Jawaharlal Nehru Memorial Lecture 2011 delivered in Trinity College on 21st November, 2011.
8. Second Administrative Reforms Commission has submitted series of Report correct the maladies in governance and administration.
9. Myron Weiner, *The Indian Paradox,* New Delhi: Sage Publications, 1989.
10. Thomas E. Weisskopf, "Why worry about inequality in the Booming Indian Economy" *Economic and Political Weekly.* Vol. XLV, No. 47, November 19, 2011, pp. 41–51.
11. Anirudh Krishna, " Poverty Knowledge and Poverty Action in the context of the Changing Governance Agenda" in H.S. Shylendra, *New Governance and Development: Challenges of Addressing Poverty and Inequality,* New Delhi: Academic Foundation, 2009, pp. 159–191.
12. Bhikhu Parekh, *op. cit.*
13. Myron Weiner, *The Indian Paradox,* New Delhi: Sage Publications, 1989.
14. B.S. Baviskar and Tulsi Patel (eds.) *Understanding Indian Society: Past and Present,* New Delhi: Orient Blackswan, 2010.
15. Venkatesh Rama Krishnan, "Neoliberal Plan" *Front Line,* 28: No. 21, Oct., 21, 2011 and C.P. Chandrasekar, "Changing Priorities" *Front Line,* Vol. 28: No. 21, Oct. 21, 2011 Prabhat Patnaik, "Things, not people" *Front Line* Vol. 28: No. 21, 2011.
16. Madhu Purnima Kishwar, *Deepening Democracy: Challenges of Governance and Globalisation in India,* New Delhi: Oxford University Press, 2005.

17. Shubham Chaudhouri "What Difference does a Constitutional Amendment make? The 1994 Panchayati Raj Act and the attempt to Revitalize Rural Local Government in India" in Pranab Bhardhan and Dilip Mookherjee (eds.) *Decentralisation and Local Governance in Developing Countries: A Comparative Perspective,* Oxford University Press, New Delhi, 2007, pp. 153–202.
18. B.S. Baviskar and George Mathew (eds.) *Inclusion and Exclusion in Local Governance* New Delhi: Sage Publications, 2009.
19. Kanchan Chopra and C.H. Hanumantha Rao (eds.) *Growth, Equity, Environment and Population,* Sage Publications, New Delhi, 2008.
20. Bhilkhu Pareksh, *Op. cit.*
21. Bidyut Chakrabarty and Mohit Bhattacharya (eds.) The Governance Discourse: A Reader, New Delhi: Oxford University Press, 2008; Bid Yut Chakarabarty and Mohit Bhattacharya (eds.) *Adminstrative Change and Innovation: A Reader,* Oxford University Press, New Delhi, 2005.
22. G. Palanithurai, *Indian Polity: Myth and Reality,* Kanishka Publishers and Distributors, 1993, New Delhi, pp 19–116.
23. G. Palanithurai "Planning for Development at Grassroots in Tamil Nadu" in S. Bhaskaran and B.S. Sumathi (eds.) *Human Development in India Initiatives and Experience,* The Icfai University Press, Hyderabad, 2009, pp 192–225
24. G. Palanithurai (Eds.) *Rajiv Gandhi Vision on Local Governance,* Concept Publishing Company Pvt. Ltd., New Delhi, 2009.
25. G. Palanithurai "Governance and Administration Reform" *The ICFAI University Journal of Public Administration* Vol. 4: No. 4, October, 2008, pp. 38–39.

III

Anti Corruption Movement in India

Anna Hazare's Anti Corruption Movement in India is a significant political development which carries volley of messages for analysis and inferences[1]. People look at this movement from different perspectives. But people who participated in it without political parties' background have got one clear and specific demand that is strong action against corruption and they need a clean government. The whole problem now lies in containing corruption and tackling the anti corruption movement by the Cental government. Normally intelligent political leaders will turn all challenges into opportunities but sometimes even the intellectual political leaders fail to make use of the opportunities and turn the opportunities into challenges. By acting fastly and speaking loudly about their action, the present regime could have turned the movement towards their side. But it did not take place. The government could have handled it very effectively by using it positively for its own advantage and for the benefit of the people. Instead it got a bad name as if it shields corruption and corrupt people despite its action against corruption. Because the whole issue had not been handled effectively and strategically. Many accused in Parliament that the UPA government has bungled without acting promptly and politically. The whole issue was handled through technological perspectives. Though this movement has damaged the image of the UPA government substantially it seems that it has not helped the opposition political parties to enhance their images by using this opportunity. It is natural when spontaneous outbursts are emerging against the ruling regimes from the people, the opposition forces will make use of it. In a democracy it is logical and unavoidable. But the critical fact is that some strong signal should emerge through decision to tackle corruption which is yet to emerge from the government. People's resentment had been outpouring against the corrupt practices in this country and it is coupled with socio-economic problems accumulated because of globalization. But the government has reduced the whole issue into a theoretical debate whether Parliament or the civil society got legitimate authority to make laws without addressing the larger issue of tackling corruption by its strong political will and determination.

Primarily the whole issue stems from a new context and from a new process. Globalization has created such an opportunity to unleash the potentials of the individuals, organizations, institutions, companies and societies to make wealth. In this process the corporate, bureaucrats, new political class and a section of the middle class have made wealth unfathomable. But the wealth making process has marginalized the major segments of the society. Even though a sizeable section of the society has been brought under market as consumers, substantially mass deprivation has increased. The modern media in the competitive process has brought to light both wealth making process and the process of mass deprivation sensationally. People belonging to difficult socio-economic segments have waited for an opportunity to express their anger. Anna Hazare has given this opportunity to people to rise and revolt against the government. Ultimately solution is not on sight for the substantial issue but everyone is blinking what to do with the democratic uprising of the people against corruption. Now it is confined to urban middle class on corruption but if it extends to the rural areas it will become a serious governance issue. Mass deprivation, development displacement, unemployment, poor functioning of the public institutions, denial of basic entitlements of the poor and ill treatment of the poor by the bureaucracy will become a serious governance issue[2]. Neither the ruling coalition nor the opposition coalitions do not have scientific formula based governance solution to the problems and ills but they have full of rhetoric without moving towards conscious scientific, decisive conclusion. But Anna Hazare has given the hope to the people and hence people spontaneously reposing confidence in him. The whole issue needs a scientific analysis.

Anna Hazare is neither a mass leader nor a networked civil

society leader till he took up the issue of corruption as a major issue for the whole of the country. He was a development worker, worked with people at the micro level and got success and thereby he drew the attention of many. Subsequently he moved from micro development action to regional governance action through his tirade against governance corruption at the state level. Even when he was a development worker in his village he had developed a perception that the Sarkari corruption will not allow the people in the rural areas to achieve development. Hence, he took up this issue at the state level and emerged as a crusader to fight against corruption. He got substantial victory in his attempts. Anna Hazare had picked up the nuances to fight against corruption in his own home state where he succeeded in his attempt as Mahatma Gandhi evolved his nuances to fight against the British in South Africa. His Gandhi fashion has added strength to his mission. It cannot be compared with Aruna Roy's campaign for Right to Information Act (RTI). He has gone beyond campaign to build a movement to fight against corruption. It is not only for Lok Pal but also for bringing many changes in the institutions of governance at all levels. One has to understand the larger context of the movement. People's anger has increased substantially not because of corruption alone, the very basic regimes are inhuman and it was highlighted many times by the late Prime Minister Rajiv Gandhi[3]. That is why he wanted to create responsive, responsible and representative governance by the participation of people at the grassroots through the establishment of constitutional local governance. But unfortunately it is a biggest challenge in this country to change the behaviour of the ruling regimes whether 'X' rules or 'Y' rules. People have joined with Anna Hazare not to oppose the UPA government but to change the behaviour of the regime.

The utilization of the movement for anti corruption activities in a broader perspective depends on the rest of the civil society as to what extent they are taking forward this movement by giving a concrete structure to the movement. After the expose of massive corruption in the Central government and some of the State governments by the media somehow or other Anna Hazare has sensed the mood of the people and took up the issue. He tested the mood of the public and more specifically the mood of the middle class. While he observed fast in New Delhi in Jantar Mantar in April 2011 for initiating a strong Lok Pal, Prime Minister, and the UPA leaders have taken note of it and responded positively. Despite the presence of such a kind of mechanism in some of the Scandinavian countries, the Indian political parties have not taken up this issue by citing an instrument to contain corruption as it has been done by Anna Hazare. Indian political parties have not learnt lessons from other countries to update themselves to act proactively. This vacuum created by the political parties has been used very effectively by Anna Hazare. Up to that level the UPA government acted proactively. Subsequently the government managers failed miserably in managing the situations. That is why many argued that Sonia Gandhi's absence has contributed for such confusion in tackling this crisis. There is logic behind this argument. Here one has to understand the silent mobilization of youth against corruption in India by the former President of India A.P.J. Abdul Kalam. When he was the President of India and even after, his tirade against corruption was much vociferous that too among the students' youth. Wherever he went outside for public meeting, while addressing the youths and the student community he made a fervent plea that youths have to fight against corruption. A.P.J. Abdul Kalam was and is the icon for the youths. Many expected that he would give clear cut direction for the youths to fight against corruption. But he has not given any direction organizationally. That is why many criticized A.P.J. Abdul Kalam by asking, what he has done as President of India. He could have strongly acted as K.R. Narayanan, R. Venkataraman and Shankar Dayal Sharma. But instead of using this office, he althrough involved in sensitizing the students against corruption.

The political parties for the past two to three decades had stopped mobilizing the students and educated youths for political activities. Only the dropouts from the schools and colleges have joined politics. Having sensed the reality Rahul Gandhi has started mobilizing the youths for politics and too more of student youths. But the mobilization done by A.P.J. Abdul Kalam helped Anna Hazare to mobilize easily huge support from the student's youth to fight against corruption. There is yet another phenomenon one has to notice in Indian politics, namely the leadership crisis. Though opportunities are plenty to mobilize the Indian masses for cleansing Indian polity, governance and administration, there is no credible political leader from the existing political parties both national and regional as somehow or other all political parties have been carrying the corruption tag. Even the left political parties could not emerge as the West Bengal story has created added disadvantage to them to take up the corruption issue. Further, the failure of the left parties in contextualizing the party has not attracted the youths towards them. Virtually that vacuum has been filled up by Anna Hazare. In this regard one has to accept the fact that Indian political parties are honest in admitting the truth that corruption has deeply entrenched into every walk of life. They have admitted the massive corruption in governance, administration and political processes[4]. But the political parties have lost their moral stature.

There is no dispute over the issue between political parties and the civil society. Both Prime Minister and the Finance Minister have admitted in unequivocal terms that corruption has taken massive shape in public sphere. Equally the opposition parties have also admitted the fact. But the confusion prevails only in finding solution. Since corruption has been hitting every individual, when a single point agenda has been chalked out by Anna Hazare, everyone affected by corruption jumped into the movement and extended support to Anna Hazare[5]. Corruption has many dimensions[6] and of them only two aspects emerged obviously in the present discourse. The new wealth created by political class for their own advantage by using globalization and the same created by bureaucracy by using development schemes. It is to be recognized that people who indulged in corrupt practices by using power had a perception that people could be managed and systems could be manipulated through money power. These corrupt politicians have underestimated the potentials of democracy. They forgot to realize the power and sovereignty of the people. Had they visualized such a scenario what we are seeing today against corruption, they would not have indulged in this much of corruption. Politicians have indulged in corruption systematically by making alliance with all the institutions. Something went wrong in the functioning of Indian political parties. It is to be noted here that in each and every political party one can see the presence of honest leaders and representatives but they are mostly marginalized. Over a period of time a strong oligarchic alliance had been developed among political parties, bureaucracy and market[7]. To break this nuanced alliance people expected a mighty power. Everyone expected the emergence of another Mahatma Gandhi. Anna Hazare has given the needed leadership.

Having tested the water in the first fast undertaken by Anna Hazare in Jantar Mantar in New Delhi the Government should not have underestimated Anna Hazare's power of attracting the masses towards this cause. Unfortunately the government managers have thoroughly underestimated him and as a result, he and his team had been made members of the committee constituted by the Government to draft the bill. While it was criticized by the opposition parties it was argued by the government that it was a new exercise. RTI also came as Jan Lokpal but it came through a different route and processes. The draft submitted by Aruna Roy underwent substantial change through a process of consultation and discussion. Everyone expected that this will take the same route to reach the destination. But innovatively the government has adopted a different path. Nothing wrong in adopting an innovative path as parliamentary democracy needs always innovation. But unfortunately it could not achieve the desired results.

While constituting the committee, the government should have made it a broad based committee by putting more numbers of members from civil societies and political parties. By making the committee broader and inclusive the views of the members could have been reconciled within the committee itself. Since it was a narrowed down committee the government managers are unable to manage Anna Hazare and it was one to one between the government's team and Anna Hazare's team. The concept of team was the creation of media. Everyone in the committee is a member. No one is superior or inferior. There is no team in the committee. The fault line started in the functioning of the committee itself. Fundamentally it was only the UPA Government made that it was a fight between civil society and the Government by projecting an argument that Anna Hazare undermines the power of Parliament by insisting his version of the bill has to be adopted in the Parliament. Instead of going through this route which the ruling UPA government claims an innovative route, the government should have gone through the routine route of preparing the bill as adopted for enacting the Right to Information Act. It was also based on the pressure exerted by the civil society. Once the bill was prepared, it should have been put in the public domain for people's perusal and comments. By doing so the government could have tackled it easily. Here one has to notice the failure of the deliberative aspects of our democracy[8].

Further one has to understand that Anna Hazare never gave an impression to the public that the UPA government is alone corrupt and all other parties are honest. He made it clear that public life becomes so corrupt, and governance becomes corrupt and hence he wanted to cleanse the public life and for which he made cleansing governance is an imperative needed. He never argued that the UPA government is corrupt and hence he is fighting against UPA government. It is only the managers of UPA government by taking anti Anna Hazare's position projected a picture that as if Anna Hazare is fighting against UPA government. For the vituperative verbal attack on Anna Hazare by a few in UPA government made the Prime Minister Job more difficult and cumbersome. At this point of time politics become violent and parochial[9]. The Government having constituted the committee for that purpose, somehow or other it should have found it a way to pilot a bill formulated by the committee, instead of piloting the government team's bill. Otherwise the government instead of constituting a committee, it should have given a promise to Anna Hazare that government will act immediately and based on that it should have piloted a bill. If the government is able to pilot a bill, naturally it should have obtained the views of all segments of the society and based on the views of the wider segments the bill could have been passed. But instead of doing the above, the government has further made a mistake by keeping Anna Hazare's team in the committee and after Anna Hazare's team refused to accept the official version of the bill the Congress spokespersons unleashed verbal and abusive attack on Anna Hazare which made the government's position further weak in the eyes of the sensible and sensitive citizens. Anna Hazare's teams could have been tackled very effectively by putting a brave face by steadfastly making a declaration that Government of India will spare none if they found corrupt. It has power and authority and it will act firmly. The tone and tenor which the government managers have used to attack Anna Hazare could have been used very effectively to tackle corruption. It is an irony that despite its actions against corruption the government has given an impression to the public that it acted against corruption as per court's direction and not on its own. Public memory is short normally but now the media is always bringing debates with comments passed by the leaders in the past reminding the memory of the public. On this case also consistently brought to light the slackening of the government in dealing with corruption. Somehow or other the government has given an impression that it is not acting sincerely and on its own. It started acting on all the cases only after it was directed by the Supreme Court.

Because the Government has given an impression that it does not own responsibility to combat corruption and it is shielding the corrupt politicians and it is always acting not proactively but acting reactively that too after getting direction from the Supreme Court. While explaining the stand and position of the Government on combating corruption the used phrases such as "Prime Minister does not have magic wand, coalition *dharma,* and political compulsions" should have been avoided. Because these phrases used by the Prime Minister have been interpreted by the media differently and the media have given a negative connotation that it has no energy to fight against corruption. This message has reached the masses and more particularly the educated middle class. People have started believing that somebody has been acting behind and Prime Minister is only the mask. His honesty is a shield and he is not able to use the authority vested in him. When he is able to achieve the economic growth, he is not able to distribute the same for the benefit of the poor. It is not able to control over the prices of essential commodities. Moreover, he is not able to curb the activities of the corrupt Ministers. He is efficient in economy and ineffective in governance. In such a way perception has been gained by the people.

When Anna Hazare has determined to undertake fast to exert pressure on the government to pass the bill prepared by his team, it had to be dealt with politically instead of giving it to police. This was also a weak management strategy. Unless clear cut governance direction police action might work against the government. It is not a small petty issue. It is a larger political issue and people's involvement on this issue is larger. Hence, the government managers should have handled it sensibly sensitively and seriously. Unfortunately the government managers have taken shelter under the police which has given a poor image of the government.

The police look at the issue from its own perspective and it has no political perspective. Hence, it handled the issue very badly by putting up unusual conditions for the protest fast. In a democracy why people organize agitations? It is for registering their protest to change the course of action of the government regimes. It can be done only by showing the strength and its intensity. Government should have known the simmering discontent against the government for its poor handling of corruption. It has been coming out to the surface through this protest. It had to be tackled seriously. In this context the police stipulation to protest fast is construed as stifling of democratic voice. By handling of this case by the police wrongly the police added more crises to the UPA government. Moreover, the media managers of the government have given a sense to the public that it is a law and order problem and hence it was handled by the Delhi Police. By doing such a kind of service by the media managers of the party, they have added more problems to the government.

It is to be noted here that Anna Hazare has demanded one month permission for his fast. He had a clear design of heating the climate to get what he wanted. In a given context one month political mobilization will change the mood of Indian public against the government. A few States are going to face general elections to their Legislative Assemblies in the coming year. In this context how the UPA is going to face the election with this damaged image in all these States is a big question. This corruption issue can be used effectively by the opposition parties. At this juncture one has to carefully evaluate the political performance of Rahul Gandhi. He had started the "peoples' politics" long back and started mobilizing youths and the poor in the rural areas. In this process he started building the party from the grassroots. It is a single handled work of Rahul Gandhi. The party is not in robust health and hence he has to deal with that also. No one from the Nehru family has done this much of grassroots mobilization as Rahul Gandhi has done. Obviously the party managers have not added strength to his grassroots activities. He tried his level best to consolidate the strength of the Indian National Congress by mobilizing the poorest segments in the heart land of India. No Congress Party leader has faced such challenges as Rahul Gandhi is facing. In this process he has enhanced his political capacity enormously. Secondly, he has an open mind to get views, ideas and perceptions on issues from all quarters. He is moving beyond the party to build a movement. On many of the occasions he demonstrated to the cadre how a cadre has to struggle in the field for taking up the cause of the poor and build party and solve the problem of the poor. Unfortunately he has not gained success as expected. The party managers have added more weaknesses by mishandling issues by their ineffective and inefficient management strategies. Ultimately for the poor handling of the issues by the managers the leadership is held responsible. The issue of Anna Hazare's Anti Corruption Movement has posited a biggest challenge to the Indian National Congress because of the poor handling of the same.

The UPA government's managers have raised a question which is supreme whether the Parliament or the civil society in enacting law with the thinking that this political discourse could be diverted easily without knowing the mood of the middle class and more particularly the educated youths. No one has disputed over the supremacy and prerogative of the Parliament in enacting the law. When a proposal of the ruling party is weak it is natural that civil society will give pressure to change it. Anna's team has got readymade proposal and the team was exerting pressure on the government to consider the same. Anna's team is questioning the content of the bill and not the authority of the Parliament. There is yet another question in a democracy. If Parliament is not acting or it acts wrongly who will correct it. It is only the people. People's sovereignty cannot be questioned. There is no supreme power over people's sovereignty. In a democracy people are sovereign. The argument of UPA managers on the procedural issues is redundant and uncalled for. It is to be remembered here that many times Indian Parliament has enacted legislations based on the pressure given by the civil society. Even the Right to Information Act is one such classic example. Many times National Advisory Council has engaged the civil society for seeking opinion, views and clarification on critical issues which affected the Indian society. Here one has to recognize the role of National Advisory Council in the governing process of the country. Of course, there is a strong criticism against its formation and its functioning. Sometimes it is considered as a tool to weaken the office of the Prime Minister or the power of the Ministers. But if a scientific evaluation is made one can easily argue that many of the historic welfare schemes came only through National Advisory Council under the leadership of Sonia Gandhi. Sonia Gandhi has consistently maintained that she has been open to civil society ideas to shape pro-poor policies. Indian National Congress was pro-poor ideologically but in action it was not so far. But the Indian National Congress is pro-poor in action only now. The Indian National Congress is pro-backward class and pro-marginalized only now in action. Substantial civil society input has gone into the government's policy making mill for pro-poor welfare schemes and legal remedies. Further Sonia Gandhi's balanced level playing leadership never gave a room for damaging the power and prestige of the parliamentary institutions. It has been witnessed in the recent past that the recommendations of the NAC have been rejected by the Government. Having done all those things, Sonia Gandhi's absence at this juncture has been felt very much. Anna Hazare's episode has identified the leadership vacuum in the ruling arrangement.

There is yet another issue is being raised that Anna Hazare's team looking at Parliament contemptuously. It is not true that Anna's team is looking at Parliament contemptuously. Parliamentarians are being looked at contemptuously. Our parliamentary behaviour has given such a perception to the people. When a Parliament has got more than 150 members with high criminal records in their background how sensitive citizens will view the Parliament. For all the mistakes committed by the political parties and their leaders, shelter should not be taken in the garb of the institutions. Corrupt and criminal politician by going over to Parliament through political party route made the system and institutions mockery. It is not the people who made the institutions mockery. It is only the political parties which made the institutions mockery.

Yet another issue was also raised by the managers of the UPA government. Sovereignty of the Parliament and governing institutions has to be protected. When this was raised, there is yet another question raised by the civil society. Government is not sacrosanct. When government is abusing its power against the people who will correct it? M.K. Gandhi has given definition to *Swaraj*. It is nothing but the power of the people to defy the government when it is abusing its power against people. In this context the civil society is asking a basic question. Are not the people sovereign? Whose sovereignty is ultimately final and valid? It is only the people. It is people who are sovereign. In such a way arguments have been projected.

The government managers have raised yet another question. Are the Anna Hazare's teams the real citizens of India? Are they really representing Indian masses? For these questions also explanations have been given. In any society active citizens will act and passive citizens will support. One cannot expect all citizens will come to streets and demonstrate. If it happens, government cannot function. Now the argument of Anna's team is that corruption is rampant in governance and administration and they are to be tackled. They are suggesting that through a strong legislation it could be tackled and hence the present government has to take initiative. Opinion makers of the society have come out strongly against corruption and it is being supported by the middle class. If the British raised the same question to the Indian National Congress as to what extent the Indian National Congress represented the Indian masses, Indian society would not have achieved independence under the leadership of Indian National Congress. If the government really wants it, it has to conduct a referendum as Swiss Government is doing on this issue. In fact opinion survey was also conducted in many places and in all the surveys it was demonstrated clearly that a strong Lok Pal bill is needed. When this was the condition in the discourse, the UPA managers have raised unwanted arguments and all the arguments have gone against the UPA government. It is a very difficult and delegate position for the Indian National Congress. At least in the first UPA government the UPA partners were with the Indian National Congress in managing the affairs of the politics and governance. But in UPA II the alliance partners became a problem. The DMK once considered an assert becomes a big liability and it was a source of all troubles to the ruling UPA II at the centre. In this context the government managers have brought unwanted arguments and in no way those arguments have helped the government to tackle it. It was the considered opinion of many that if the issue had been left it to leaders like Pranab Mukherjee things would have been different and it could have been tackled smoothly without much of the complication as we have witnessed.

Since these unwanted questions have been raised by the ruling UPA government managers there is another fundamental question raised in this regard by the civil society and others. In a representative democracy whether ruling party or parties really got the support of majority of the people. Many of the occasions the ruling parties never gained the support of majority of the total population by calculating votes secured by the ruling parties. In two fronts continuously the UPA government has faulted. In handling the issue wrongly and giving opinions against the mood of the people the UPA government has earned a bad name not only among the people of India but even among the International media and institutions.

While looking at the whole issue, Anna Hazare and his team want to exert pressure on the government to modify the bill by incorporating certain vital sections to strengthen the Lok Pal Bill. Parliament has passed many bills and if we really make an evaluation one will find how many are effective. Hence, Anna Hazare's team wants an effective bill and not one more bill. They suggested how it should be. If the Central Government is serious about it, it has to welcome it. But it is opposing it. It means it is not serious in it. In such a way image has been projected and it has reached the people also. Unfortunately the media managers of the government have not understood the ground reality and hence the UPA government has faulted in handling this issue.

The UPA government looks at Anna Hazare's movement as a threat to its government because Anna Hazare's team is getting support from various political groups which work deliberately to destabilize the ruling combine. This perception has also been developed by the UPA managers through their arguments in the media. There is no meaning in this argument. Because when there is a movement and mobilization of mass against the government, it is natural in a democracy the political parties which are in opposition will make use of it to destabilize the government.

The opposition parties in India have tried their level best to tackle the UPA government through parliamentary processes in vain. Hence, they found that it is the fine opportunity to make use of the Anna Hazare's movement to discredit if not destabilize the UPA government but they have a design to work on the State Assembly elections against the Indian National Congress by using this issue.

The Prime Minister made statements that the Government of India is maintaining zero per cent tolerance towards corruption but when ordinary citizens under the leadership of Anna Hazare went for peaceful protest against tolerance of corruption, it was not tolerated by the government. Zero per cent tolerance was maintained towards the protestors of corruption. In all political marches people have witnessed violence in the marches but this protest march was only a peaceful march. People have not been mobilized for this protest as political parties mobilize for political protests. People on their own came out from their houses, offices, businesses and joined in the protest march not only in New Delhi but in all parts of India mostly in the urban areas. Here one has to take note of the new developments. Political parties made hue and cry against corruption but it has not attracted the people. In India the political parties are losing their credibility and they could not mobilize the people. In this regard an alternative to the political parties is emerging which is called people's politics. It has many nuanced products to correct the Indian political parties. It has more strength to cleanse the political parties also. Now the governance crisis is looked at from government and administration domain but now time has come to look at it from the political party domain which in fact really dispels many of the clouds surrounded on government. Thus the movement has to be seen broadly to pluck the loopholes in the system, processes and procedures. Anna Hazare has done people's politics. The marches were peaceful and orderly. It is to be seen differently. People's politics is emerging as party politics fails. People's politics is in the nascent stage. It is time to act to build on as an alternative politics to party politics. It requires lot of thinking and proper conceptualization. The same intellectuals have to involve themselves to perform the above task.

Dissemination of information in the society is so fast at present because of the communication revolution. Further media's role in carrying the messages is very effective as they get day-to-day information from the governance institutions by using the Right to Information Act and they are being discussed and they are being put to public domain for open discussion has created needed awareness among the middle class about what is going on in governance. Large numbers of intellectuals have been engaged by the media but the same amount of intellectuals has not been used by the Government for tackling the issues. Media managers of the ruling UPA government instead of managing the media, by unleashing scathing attack on the protestors and by provoking the media issues have been complicated further. Instead of giving answer to the pointed questions they make political attacks on the opposition parties. This kind of argument clearly provides enough opportunity for the viewers to perceive that government is not serious about corruption and it is interested in defaming the opposition parties also. By doing this vituperative attack on the opposition parties, people whether they are in ruling or in opposition who are against corrupt people have turned against the government which ultimately strengthened the hands of Anna Hazare. Even in the ruling UPA government, many have not agreed to the impulsive actions of the media managers. From their interactions, an impression has been created that there is a division within the government in tackling the Anna Hazare's Anti Corruption Movement. This could be seen from the sensible arguments made by the Finance Minister within the Parliament and outside and observations made by media managers of the ruling UPA government in the process of tackling the Anna Hazare's Anti Corruption Movement.

Further the media managers of the UPA government have given an impression that it is a war between civil society and Parliament. Really it is no so. They have done it wrongly. It was to be perceived as a healthy engagement of civil society by the Parliament and Parliament by the civil society. The total engagement has to be done in a matured way but unfortunately more particularly the media managers of the UPA government have taken to a critical stage by denigrating the civil society. This really shows the poor understanding capacity of the media managers of the UPA government.

The political managers of the Indian National Congress time and again proving the statement of Rahul Gandhi that the old managers of the Congress Party is not allowing the Party to go to the masses and doing people's politics. He made it very clear that one has to face difficulties in democratizing the Indian National Congress. Further made it clear that the party has to be opened for the entry of youth from all segments of the society and by which the Party's course of action could be changed. He started his exercise through the Youth Congress. To some extent he has succeeded with great difficulty. But he found out the potentials from this segment to strengthen the party through democratization. Rahul Gandhi by his speeches and actions he is gaining image and recognition among the poor that he will substantially take up people's issues. He has gone to the grassroots politics. That is the image he has given to the people belonging to the poorest section. Personally I have visited a few places where Rahul Gandhi has visited. Substantially he has got potentials and charisma to influence the perception of the people about the Indian National Congress and that is why many of the regional political parties have developed fear over his style of politics. But the managers of the Indian National Congress by their actions are dragging Rahul Gandhi towards their scam politics and by which they damage the image built up by him by his hard work. When Rahul Gandhi made statements about the behaviour of the government, he argues that he is interfering and taking steps to correct the lapses; the statements are being severely criticized by the opposition as he is running the super government. Rahul Gandhi also picked up the perception of his father late Rajiv Gandhi about governance and administration in India. His language, phrases and actions are pushing politics from party to people. A new line of people politics he wants to develop and for which he wants to engage substantially the youth. But unfortunately the old managers of the party are doing a great harm to the new proposal of Rahul Gandhi. Even in Parliament Rahul Gandhi while making statement on Anti Corruption movement, he went ahead of Anna Hazare saying that constitutionally created Lok Pal is needed to combat corruption along with other institutional measures. He also openly admitted the rampant corruption. But he underlined the fact that for any issue whether small or large it has to be addressed through substantial engagement of democratic institutions. He made it very clear that in the name of addressing the issues urgently the institutions should not be damaged. He got the support of Anna Hazare's team for his new proposal of constitutionally creating Lok Pal.

There is yet another argument projected by Aruna Roy. There is substance in her argument. The three institutions namely Legislature, Executive and Judiciary should not be controlled by one single institution. In this process checks and balances built in the parliamentary democracy through Constitution will be dismantled if the Jan Lokpal bill is accepted. There is no doubt the Lokpal bill introduced will be strengthened. In this process judiciary has to be brought into the Lokpal but through a different mode. The same way all public officials have to be brought under the ambit of Lokpal and Lok Ayukta. There are other segments left out in this process. They are: Multinational companies, business houses, civil society organizations, charitable trusts, educational institutions, religious institutions, media and political parties. These institutions and organizations whether they are public funded or private funded, irrespective of the nature of funding, all the above institutions and organizations have to be brought under the ambit of the Lokpal and Lok Ayukta. All the discretionary powers of the political executives from Prime Minister to Panchayat leaders have to be removed by one order. In the same way the discretionary powers of the officials have to be removed.

Further an argument has been projected as to how an individual by mobilizing the mass can dictate the Parliament to pass a bill that has been drafted by him and his team. In the representative democracy, this kind of pressure will weaken the very basis of the representative democracy. In a representative democracy, the representatives are the ruling elites and they will act as per the judgment which is the best for the country. They are not the reflectors of the people. Further they are not only representing the constituents but also representing the nation as a Member of Parliament and Legislature. On the basis of the above argument one cannot expect the representatives to behave as the constituents wish. For the above argument an explanation is being offered that in the present day context the representative institutions have moved away from the basic framework. For about five decades the representative institutions have not acted on this issue of containing corruption. They have evaded from the basic responsibility and, hence, people have exerted pressure on the legislative institutions. Moreover, popular will is the supreme will and the representatives have to act on a popular will. This cannot be considered as a negative factor working in representative democracy. Moreover, the issue is not for narrower interest. It is a national issue and nobody has expressed any negative opinion about it. All political parties and all political leaders have concurred on this central issue of corruption. But they are not acting substantially on it.

Anna Hazare's movement has been described as a mobocracy since Anna Hazare mobilized the people and through the mob and public support exerted pressure on the Parliament that the Parliament has to pass bill that too the bill drafted by him and further the Parliament has to pass the bill within the stipulated time. It amounts a total expression of disregard for Parliament and it is nothing but denegation of Parliament. In a democracy Parliament has got its own methodological nuances and procedures and they are to be followed and otherwise parliamentary institutions will be weakened. Here it is to be noted that how political parties are keeping the standard of the parliamentary institutions. More than 150 members with high criminal background have been recruited to Parliament and for making parliamentary transactions and saving the government during voting the Members of Parliament received huge bribe. Openly bribes have been given and taken. For all these occurrences, the political parties are responsible and they have brought down the moral stature of the institution. In such a way perception has been formed by the people that the representatives of the people are not really the representatives but they are vote purchasing machines. The modern political parties have started functioning differently and they also involved in mobilization resources. They follow the path of the corporates. The offices of the political parties are appearing as corporate company offices. Previously people used to contribute and support political parties. Now political parties give money to people for votes and mobilize money from the business houses and substantially they owe a lot to the companies and thereby they become part of corruption.

It is to be recognized that over a period of time the political elites and bureaucratic elites by their nexus have given a sense to the people that they act as modern monarchs and never respect the will of the people. People have started a struggle against political and bureaucratic elites to establish the supremacy of the people as people in the West fought for parliamentary democracy against monarchy. In India people are fighting for people's democracy against the representative democracy.

One important criticism levelled against Anna's team is that it argues that it is the only argument everyone has to buy Anna's team proposal on anti corruption. There are many views on it and the team has to allow the flow of thoughts into it and a consensus can be evolved. Everyone argues that government's proposal is only eyewash and it should be strengthened. On that count there is no difference of opinion. Further, handling of Anna's team by the government is outright condemnable and on this also there is no second opinion. The bill prepared by Anna's team has taken a narrower view keeping the corruption in a narrower sense than making it broader and in the background of the theory on representative democracy. Because we have at present no alternative to representative democracy. On this ground people who have concern for representative democracy has suggested the tackling of corruption should not weaken the institutional structure, processes and procedures as the whole reform has to be done only through these institutions. On this count alone some civil society representatives criticized Anna's team. Their argument has its own logical strength.

At this critical juncture the proposal of former Election Commissioner T.N. Sheshan's proposal based on the argument of Rahul Gandhi supported by former speaker of the Lok Sabha Somnath Chatterjee added another dimension. In the current crisis of governance and administration, a few constitutionally created bodies are helping Indian democracy to emerge from the present impasses namely the Election Commission, Supreme Court, Office of the President of India, Comptroller and Auditor General of India. Like this if the Lokpal is created that will serve the purpose. The idea is projected by Rahul Gandhi but it requires two-third majorities in the Parliament to pass the bill and subsequently more than fifty per cent of the States have to accept it. At this hour the Central Government is not in a position to take such a high risk task. It can be taken if the leadership has got moral energy to lead the nation towards the end. But the present government will not take such a huge risk. Beyond idea it cannot move at present. By projecting this idea Rahul Gandhi seemed to gain some advantage but obviously it is being challenged as T.N. Sheshan offered his service and informed that he has a bill and it requires only political will to pass. Now it has not attracted the attention. Yet advice is being given to the political parties that the nation can move towards this end at a later stage.

But on the whole, Anna Hazare has demonstrated to the whole world that Indian democracy is not in the pockets of the Indian political parties. As demonstrated to the world by Mahatma Gandhi, people has got sense, responsibility, energy and they can be used profitably by any individual provided he/she has will, honesty, commitment and leadership. No political party whether it is national or regional, leftist or rightist, they did not have the stature to fight against corruption. People passive attitude cannot be attributed as reason for such poor behaviour of the political parties. People will emerge rise, and revolt provided honest leadership emerges and lead them. Anna Hazare has demonstrated the power of the people and power of people's democracy. He is not an intellectual, he does not have any political background or backing of social or economic class, a truck driver in Army has emerged as a symbol and hope of millions of people in India. It is the real success of people's power and power of democracy. In the whole movement there are lessons to government, political parties and civil society. Every segment has to carefully look into the process and learn lessons for the improvement of their functioning. At this point of time one has to understand that there is no better alternative to representative democracy. If it is on sight, there won't be any doubt the humanity has to move towards the new one. Till then the existing parliamentary institutions have to be strengthened by plucking the loopholes in the existing institutional functioning. At any cost, there should not be any design in the name of cleansing operation to weaken parliamentary institutions.

The surging energy of the people through the movement could be understood properly and it is to be used properly for the benefit of the governance system and the people. The whole energy has come for this movement with an objective of finding out an alternative politics. It is people's politics and development politics. The oligarchic political party system has been perceived that it has failed to deliver the goods as expected. People's surge to support a non-party movement clearly indicate the present dissent of the people towards the politics of the party system. It was perceived that in the globalization process, it was the role of the middle class fast operating and it was believed that middle class acted on a very selfish basis and as a result they act in a way negative to popular uprising. But that perception has been totally dismantled in this process. The middle class who was part and responsible for the corrupt practices have come out openly to fight against corruption through a popular mobilization. It is a welcoming change.

It is to be understood properly that Lokpal is not the be all and end all to curb corruption. There should be a comprehensive reform touching various sectors to combat corruption. While doing so one has to be careful that the reform should not hamper growth and economic development. Large number of reforms has to be done in natural resource management, judicial accountability, election process, political parties, and elimination of criminals from politics and parliamentary institutions. By doing so a new grammar of politics could be developed.

What is coming out from the present Anti Corruption Movement headed by Anna Hazare? Primarily people who are substantially mobilizing the people for development and democracy maintain zero per cent tolerance to corruption. They have not only mobilized the middle class and the youth to fight against corruption but also emotionally sensitized the same collectivities. Secondly, it has been demonstrated that Indians will rise at any point of time to correct the maladies in the society, governance and administration as it is demonstrated during the freedom struggle. No one can force underestimate the people of India. Nobody can manipulate democracy, governance and administration forever. Indian public will rise when they found proper leadership. The above propositions have been demonstrated unequivocally through the Anti Corruption Movement. Indian democracy is maturing and people are maturing more than our political parties as the anti corruption movement goes in a non-violent path unlike the political parties. When parliamentary institutions and governance institutions have gone down in their moral turpitude, some of the institutions have emerged to correct the maladies in the system of governance and administration. They are the Election Commission and Supreme Court and sometimes the Office of the President of India. The rising of the anti corruption movement is yet another phenomenon support and strengthen such initiatives. Thirdly, the Indian National Congress has acted upon the demands of the people. It is demonstrated and proved in the past. Many historic and path breaking legislations have been enacted and welfare programmes have been evolved. In this regard substantially the UPA has engaged the civil society organizations. Making development as right of the people is the historic achievement. Mahatma Gandhi Rural Employment Guarantee Act, Right to Education, Right to Information Act are the monumental contributions of the UPA government. Achieving around 8 per cent economic growth is yet another laudable achievement of the government. Enabling the Indians to make use of the globalization opportunity and thereby expansion of the middle class and participating in knowledge economy are the adding achievements of the UPA. Despite taking credits out of achievements they are taking discredits because of the scams. Even against corruption the Indian National Congress has acted firmly when it is confined to the Indian National Congress. But the coalition partners are hard political bargainers who have to be dealt with cautiously and carefully otherwise the whole exercise would breakdown the government. But the way in which it has acted on corruption given a sense that it acted only because of the direction of the Supreme Court of India not because of its own initiative and will. Because in all the occasions, when corruption charges are levelled against the government instead of openly approaching the issue, the government had taken a stand to defend the Ministers and the people involved in the corrupt practices. This has been highlighted in the media which has created a suspicion among the people that corruptions had been done in collusion with high level leaders. This perception has caused great damage to the image of the political leaders. The soft approach entertained by the Indian National Congress towards the coalition partners on corruption has damaged the image of the Indian National Congress.

It is to be noted here that Dr. Manmohan Singh is not Indira Gandhi or Rajiv Gandhi. He is an academician and an expert nominated by the president of the party with the approval of the party MPs for this position. He is soft, to the point, precise, concise and honest. One cannot expect political rhetoric from him. Further, he is not heading the single party government and he is heading a coalition government. Moreover, he worked previously in the Government as an independent official and a junior Minister under many stalwarts before he became a Prime Minister. But he was appointed and accommodated in all these positions previously not because of the political influence but purely based on his merit, capacity, skill, honesty and commitment. In the same way his impeccable qualities got the attention of the party leader and as a result he was made as the Prime Minister. He is neither a mass leader nor a political party leader; he is only an honest expert in economic matters managing the affairs of the country. He is not the president of the party. Hence, he has compulsions to consult party senior leaders and junior leaders and party managers and he has to consult coalition partners on all crucial decisions of the government. With the view to keep the political forces together for smooth sailing his consultative process has taken much time for every decision. Before coming to decision on all the issues much water has flown under the bridge. Hence, appearance has been given to the people by the media that he is not acting. The office of the Prime Minister has been undermined many times both by the ruling coalition partners themselves and by the opposition parties. Even under critical circumstances he acted patiently. He always maintained dignity and standard in his discussions and actions either inside the Parliament or outside. The managers of the government and the party have created more problems than solving problems. Against this background he is performing his responsibilities as Prime Minister. Neither he was crazy after power nor he enjoys power, he acted honestly in handling the issues. The corrupt Ministers, officials have caused much embarrassment to him. Slowly he has acted and weeding out all smoothly and yet he was branded as a shield of corrupt people and a party to corruption.

The opposition parties could not legitimately take up this issue and mobilize people to oppose the ruling UPA coalition government because they have their own bags and tags. The opposition parties have also lost moral stature. Over a period of time people have been waiting for an opportunity. Even articles have been written on "Waiting for another Mahatma". Now Anna Hazare has taken this gap as an opportunity. Having established his track record in fighting against corruption at regional level he has easily taken up the issue at the national level. Media has given a timely support to his movement. As Prime Minister hide under police as per the argument of the opposition, the opposition hide under Anna Hazare to defame the UPA government. The opposition parties instead of finding a solution and expressing their stand openly on the position of Anna Hazare, they highlighted the lapses of the ruling party in handling the issue. The oppositions have openly admitted that the people have lost their faith the existing political and governance systems and that is why they have gone towards Anna Hazare. The opposition parties could not move beyond their conventional roles of defaming, discrediting and disabling the ruling party. They could not come out clearly that they are not part of corrupt practices of the system as both ruling and opposition levelled charges against each other.

The media managers of the UPA have caused great damage by projecting an argument that Anna Hazare phenomenon is the creation of media and Anna Hazare does not have such a kind of image. Further, the argument that Anna Hazare's movement has foreign hands and their involvement has further damaged the ruling party. There is yet another projection the media managers of the party have given that Anna Hazare does not have any clear cut perception about the details of the Lok Pal bill and he is only a mask and it is being used by the people who are around him. People are not buying this argument also. There is yet another damage done by the police by arresting them and putting them in Tihar prison. It is the damage done by the police. He could have been arrested in his house and he could have been kept in house arrest instead of putting him in prison. This made the government in a very embarrassing position and the government found it difficult to get him out of prison to safeguard the interest of the government. One can see the incredible explosion of popular will against malgovernance and corrupt practices in India. It is also demonstrated that people are ready to come out and join together for a public cause if proper credible leadership emerges. By the explosion of popular will, Parliament has been made to act proactively in responding to the popular sentiments. Youth energy can be channelized constructively for building a vibrant India and it has been demonstrated through this uprisings. By conducting themselves in a more matured way and in a peaceful way the mass has demonstrated that Indian democracy is maturing gradually. In the negotiation process the government's positive response to Anna's demand for peaceful protest indicates the responsiveness of democratic institutions.

The middle class cynicism that corruption cannot be eliminated has been given a positive reply through this protest movement that it can be eliminated through the popular uprisings. It has also demonstrated that the corrupt politicians cannot escape from their wrong doing through their political influence. So far political leaders have conceived an idea that they can manage and manipulate anything by money power and political power. But now they might have realized that there is no escape route in democracy for corrupt people as democracy demonstrates its full potentials. Hitherto people had developed a perception that for any change organizational strength and monetary support are crucial but now through this anti corruption movement it is demonstrated that proper leadership, good cause and truthful means can bring any change in the society[10]. The need of the hour is good leadership and a new path alternative to the political parties. People politics is the need of the hour.

Anna Hazare's "Anti Corruption Movement" becomes a significant phenomenon in Indian politics and governance. It has got two aspects. One is procedural and another one is substantive. The Indian National Congress by its own methodology has faulted and by which it has earned a negative image among the public and more particularly among the opinion making middle class. The Indian National Congress has got an opportunity to turn the movement towards its side by proactively acting on this issue. Procedurally also it faulted by accommodating Anna's team for preparing the bill instead of either taking the sole responsibility of preparing the bill by the government or innovatively creating a committee by broad basing the committee to include representatives from political parties and civil society. Having accommodated Anna Hazare, the Government should have done this exercise collectively instead of projecting its own views in the committee. Even if there are serious differences, all those classes could have been accommodated and the bone of contention could have been resolved in the committee which has been considering the bill now. By doing so, the whole episode could have been avoided. Somehow or other the government has failed to resolve it in the committee itself and as a result Anna Hazare resorted to observe fast. At this point of time also the government has failed to assess the mood of the opinion makers and the middle class. Dialogue process could have been initiated even before Anna Hazare started his fasting. The government could have constructively started engaging Anna's team on this issue and by which it could have avoided the confrontationist approach. Further, the government could have dealt with this issue politically instead of leaving it to Delhi Police and by which it could have avoided the name which it has earned among the public. The Indian National Congress should have controlled the media managers not to resort to personalized verbal attack on Anna Hazare. Since the Government of India has adopted single window approach to deal with this problem, people who are responsible for it should have given instruction to the police not to act pre-emptively and to confine Anna Hazare in his house itself instead of putting him in Tihar prison.

As Anna has been engaged politically now the government should have started this process in the initial stage itself and by which it could have minimized the damage done to the Indian National Congress. Now a situation has been created to deal with procedures rather than a substantial issue by the Indian National Congress. By the poor handling of the issue by the managers of the government it took pain to keep Anna Hazare out of prison. The Central Government has knowingly or unknowingly has faulted in six or seven events in the whole process of tackling the Anna Hazare's team but in all these places when the government has faulted, had opportunities but it failed miserably to turn the opportunity towards the government side and by which the name of the Indian National Congress could have been saved. But broadly looking into the issue and the events associated with the issue there are some positive points emerging which are advantageous to Indian democracy and governance and more specifically to the people.

An uprising has emerged from the society spontaneously to fight against corruption. The middle class, the media and intellectuals have contributed massively for this exercise and gave shape to the thinking of the people to fight against corruption. There may be flaws in the procedures. Secondly, it gave a strong signal that in a democracy opinion cannot be managed and manipulated forever against the ground reality. Thirdly, though it was organized against the corruption, the socio-economic reality has also associated with it and in fact which has complicated the issue. Fourthly, people have demonstrated that they are losing hope in the existing political arrangements. It is not a movement against the Indian National Congress or the UPA government. The sentiments reflected through this event broadly indicate people have lost their faith in the political parties and governance institutions. Incidentally the UPA is in power that is why it faces the problems. Anna Hazare's movement has created an avenue for people's politics and it is the need of the hour. The citizen's voices independent of political parties' voices started influencing governance which is positive and significant. While adopting people's approach the movement has demonstrated without having any structural and organizational backup the peaceful and non-violent course of action would alter the course of action in governance without resorting to political party based activities in the domain of governance. The Indian National Congress has adopted very soft approach to deal with Anna's movement and moving forward in this process of dialogue has demonstrated the maturity of a democratic regime and the civility of people[11]. In the course and process one has to recollect the development achievements made by the UPA regime under the leadership of Dr. Manmohan Singh. It has lot of credits to ponder over but it does not do so as the government faces the scam due to corrupt practices of its own partners.

Though enough opportunities were in the process, the Indian National Congress has not used all its opportunities to change the course towards its advantages. Instead because of its poor management strategies of the government and its haphazard handling of the media managers of the government the Indian National Congress has earned a bad name despite its laudable achievements. Knowingly or unknowingly the government has been driven to crisis management which is not good for a country like India. Secondly, there is no alternative to representative democracy for governance and hence, however, weak in delivery of services it has to be strengthened by plucking out the existing loopholes in governance instead of damaging the institutions[12]. There should not be any room for destablilishing the institutions. The growing people pressure against corruption is positive signal and it has to be handled proactively and positively and by which governance institutions have to be cleansed and strengthened. In this process the unwanted corrupt political elements have to be weeded out and enabling conditions have to be created for the emergence of newer political groups from people centric politics adopted by civil society groups. The civil society has to show its maturity and civility in correcting the governance mechanism without causing much damage to the institutions which ultimately lead to anarchy[13]. In the whole process one could see the traces of maturing Indian democracy and cleaning operation of governance and administration.

REFERENCES

1. Krishna Kumar, "Cleaning the State", *Economic and Political Weekly,* Vol. XLVI, No. 48, Nov., 26, 2011, pp. 14–17.

2. Madhu Purnima Kishwar, *Deepening Democracy: Challenges of Governance and Globalisation in India,* New Delhi: Oxford University Press, 2005.
3. G. Palanithurai, *Rajiv Gandhi's Vision on Local Governance,* New Delhi: Concept Publishing Company Pvt. Ltd., 2009.
4. N. Vittal, *Corruption in India,* New Delhi: Academic Foundation, 2003.
5. Arvind Rajagopal, Visibility as a Trap in the Anna Hazare Campaign, *Economic and Political Weekly,* Vol. XLVI, No. 47, November, 19, 2011, pp. 19–21.
6. Corruption – A Comprehensive Study of its Origin, Growth and Its Solution.
7. Vohra Committee Report, Subash C. Kashyap (ed.) *Eradication of Corruption and Restoration of Values,* New Delhi: Sterling, 2001 Annexure 4.
8. Michael A. Nelbo *et al., Who Wants to Deliberate – And Why?* Faculty Research Working Papers services, Harvard Kennedy School, 2009.
9. Abhijit V. Banerjee and Rohini Pande, *Parochial Politics: Ethnic Preferences and Politician Corruption,* Faculty Research Working Papers Services Harvard Kennedy School, 2007.
10. Matt Andrews, Jesse McConnell and Alison Wescott, *Development as Leadership – Led Change – A Report for the Global Leadership Initiative and the World Bank Institute,* Harvard Kennedy School, 2010.
11. Margit Tavits, "Clarity of Responsibility and Corruption" *American Journal of Political Science,* Vol. 51, No. 1 (Jan. 2007) pp. 218–229.
12. Rohini Pande, *Understanding Political Corruption in Low Income Countries,* Faculty Research Working Paper Series, Harvard Kennady School, 2007.
13. A. Cooper Drug, Jonathan Kricckhans and Michael Lerzting, "Corruption, Democracy and Economic Growth" *International Political Science Review,* 2006, Vol 27, No 2, pp. 121–136.

IV

Governance from the Perspective of Gandhi

Introduction

People's aspiration to democracy and development has increased in geometric proportion all over the world. In order to realize their aspiration, people are organized and mobilized as mass movements both at micro and macro levels to achieve democracy and development in non-democratic and underdeveloped societies in the world. At the same time, people are mobilized and organized in the democratic and developed (including developing) countries to reform democratic governance, to deepen democracy and to manage crises arose out of development initiatives. Thus, both development and backwardness are problems and equally authoritarian and democratic regimes are the problems to the people. The world at large is in deep crisis. It is a crisis of governance and development. Societies are in search of solutions, models and frameworks to solve the problems and to enable the people to lead a decent happy human life with dignity. Nature and intensity of the crisis vary from place to place. If mathematically an index is developed for happiness as developed by Bhutan, no country can get moderate score in happiness index. Problems are complicated as development and democracy have created complexities in the world. Societies which are struggling for development and democracy do not know the path in which they have to move with an objective of achieving development and democracy. Because the societies which have proclaimed that they have achieved development and democracy are also in deep crisis. Even the developed world may not be able to show the way of achieving development to the rest of the countries in the world. Ideologies which had been evolved by the humanity over a period of time for development and governance have disappeared from the world. Countries in isolation cannot meet the challenges and hence they form loose network of governance. Human sufferings have propelled the human collectives to fight against governance arrangements and they also do not know, what is to be done if the existing governance arrangement is destabilized. When there is no alternative paradigm of governance to representative democracy, society has no other option and it has to continue with the same set of governance arrangement by initiating reform measures. In such a way development and governance entangled the human society. In this context, we look at M.K. Gandhi for solution as he had evolved a basic framework for governance. But he did not develop a structure as propounded by the western political and administrative thinkers. The key aspects of the framework are basic promises and principles drawn from civilization aspects and based on the principles governance structure has to be created, modified and contextualized to suit the requirements from time to time.

Framework of Governance of M.K. Gandhi

At present governance framework is structured basically on the relationship among the three major forces namely the state, society, and the market. These three forces are always in intensive interaction. All the human activities in all the domains are the causes and consequences of these three forces and which controls what depends on many factors. These three forces are bringing changes and transformations in the human life which ultimately produces development, crisis and conflict. While achieving development through democratic means, harmony could not be established in the human society. Because the whole perception of development and governance is faultily conceptualized. As if it is conceptualized that market, society and state are interacting with each other in a vacuum. The whole interaction takes place in nature. Nature is the larger system and on which these forces are in interaction. Hence, well-being of human society (not development) depends on the basic relationship between the human society and the nature.

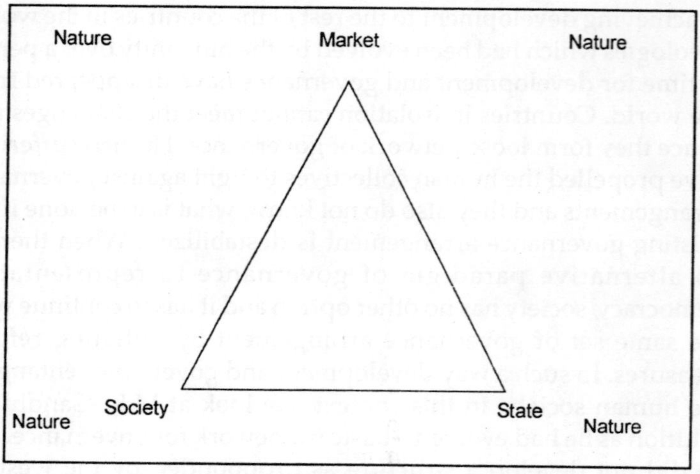

Figure 4.1: Dynamics of State Society Market Relationship

To achieve human well-being, humanity through its action has to use the nature. But nature has to be used to some extent. Now nature is being used to the maximum level as growth being the target of the humanity. Ultimately nature is being exploited. By exploiting the nature humanity has reached the material advancement. While achieving the material prosperity human society has gone to the level of polluting the environment, annihilate the rare species, exploiting the natural resources beyond the limit of recuperation which ultimately caused global warming, earth warming, climate change, natural disasters, and newer diseases. Now humanity has come to a conclusion that in the name of development human society has exploited the nature and this exploitative process cannot continue further in the name of higher growth. It is time to reorganize the development framework to achieve human well-being well within the framework of harmonious relationship between the nature and humanity. In this context the concept of sustainable development is conceptualized. But without using natural resources humanity cannot achieve material prosperity. Hence, society has to use natural resources. Still it is unanswered to what extent humanity can exploit nature. At what level harmony prevails and what level harmony is disturbed in the relationship between nature and human actions which is the core question today to be investigated.

Primarily, there should be harmony in the relationship between the nature and the human society while interacting with each other. Nature should not be used violently and excessively in the name of development and economic growth. Hence, M.K. Gandhi precisely codified and postulated the basic principle of development framework. All human activities in the domain of economy should need centric and not greed centric. To regulate the economic activities he created a basic postulate that it should be need based and not greed based. In this context, he totally disagreed with the present economic activities which are driven by the market. The market centric economic activities are driven by profit. This kind of economic activities will ultimately affect the nature. The world has no such huge quantum of resources to cater to the greed of the people if the whole humanity follow Western model of development. It is a known fact that 20 per cent of the people using 80 per cent of the resources of the world. The West does not have population as the East and, hence, they can use resources. But the East does not have resources to use them for the greed of the people. Growth has its own limit. It cannot go beyond certain levels. For economic activities he stipulated the condition that all the activities are oriented towards meeting the needs of the human society. If you look at development from this perspective nature has abundance to give the human society for its need.

Second, governance is well defined by him. Since he had misgivings about the states capacity and capability in facilitating people especially the poor in the world for achieving development and tackling the crisis he laid an important foundational principle in defining the concept "governance". In this framework he emphasized the sovereignty of the people over sovereignty of state by establishing *swaraj*. His definition of *swaraj* basically relied on the sovereignty of the people. People should have power to resist the state when state abuses its powers. He had estimated the modern state and its functioning. From his perspective modern state will abuse power and it will work mindlessly. Hence, he spoke about the sovereignty of the people. Thus, his conceptualization of state has to be built up from below. It should emerge as pyramid Figure 4.2.

His framework of governance relies on the grassroots organizations. Bottom heavy and top light will be the key feature. While conceptualizing *swaraj* basically M.K. Gandhi unequivocally

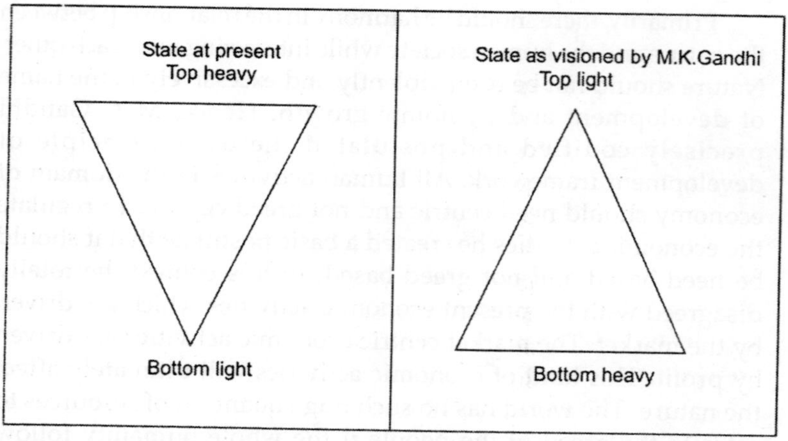

Figure 4.2 : Difference between the existing Framework and Gandhi's Framework of Relations

kept people and their actions in centre. It should be people centric and participation centric. He disregarded the existing bigness of the state and power hungry government and profit hungry market. The poor and the marginalized have to empower themselves by participating in the process of governance and development. It is an empowerment process. By participating in the above process their skill, capacity, and capability to manage government institutions to achieve development will be increased. Further, development becomes their entitlements and not charity. All the above reasons were responsible for creation of strong governance at grassroots.

As per evaluation and analysis of M.K. Gandhi, the existing state system will exclude more number of people in the process of development since the state has no human centric approach. Further, the development and governance process has been complicated as they were drawn from the West which ultimately has driven people more specifically the poor away from governance and development. He visualized and brought forwarded this proposition because of his vast experience in South Africa while dealing with the colonial state system. He had underlined the exploitative character of the state. The existing governance arrangement is so complicated and only a few can understand and operate. People cannot go nearer to the government on their own. They need support structure as

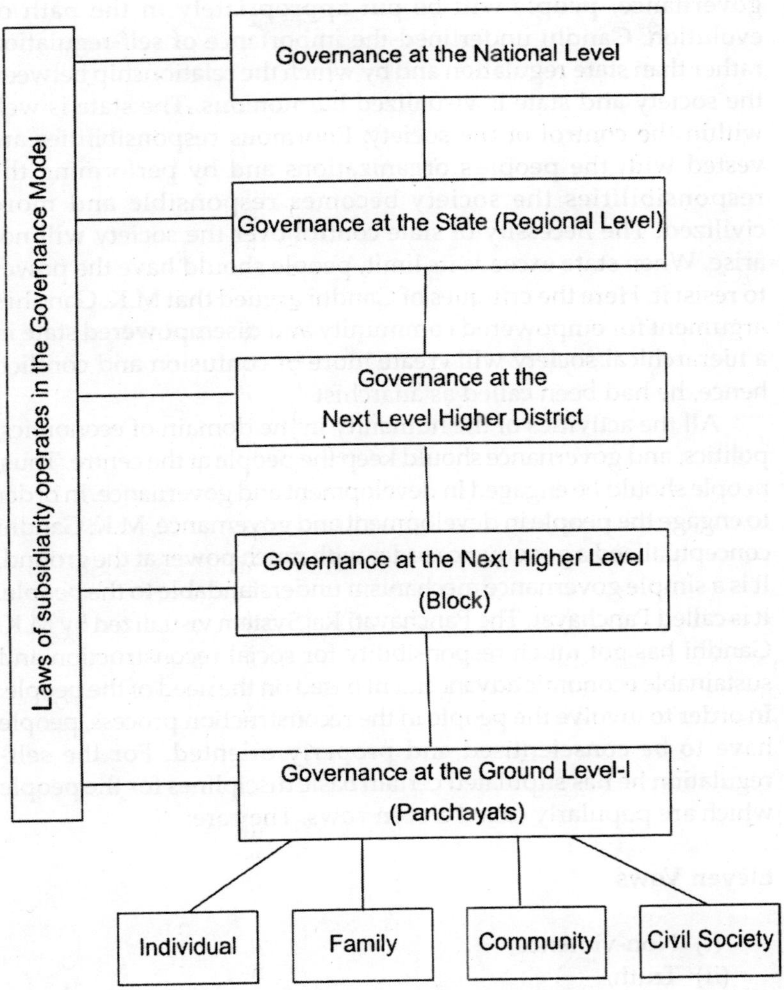

Diagram 4.1: Rational Governance Model

governance and administration are mystified and complicated. Hence, in his scheme of governance more responsibilities will be given to the people and their organizations. In the process of engagement of the people in governance and development, people's capacity and capability will be enhanced. He conceptualized the above process differently. While making the people to participate in the process of development and governance, people will be put appropriately in the path of evolution. Gandhi underlined the importance of self-regulation rather than state regulation and by which the relationship between the society and state is visualized harmonious. The state is well within the control of the society. Enormous responsibilities are vested with the people's organizations and by performing the responsibilities the society becomes responsible and more civilized. The necessity of state control over the society will not arise. When state exceeds its limit, people should have the power to resist it. Here the critiques of Gandhi argued that M.K. Gandhi's argument for empowered community and disempowered state in a hierarchical society will create more of confusion and conflict, hence, he had been called as anarchist.

All the activities of the humanity in the domain of economics, politics, and governance should keep the people at the centre. Thus, people should be engaged in development and governance. In order to engage the people in development and governance, M.K. Gandhi conceptualized a governance order with much power at the ground. It is a simple governance mechanism understandable to the people. It is called Panchayat. The Panchayati Raj System visualized by M.K. Gandhi has got much responsibility for social reconstruction and sustainable economic advancement based on the need of the people. In order to involve the people in the reconstruction process, people have to be conscientised and properly oriented. For the self-regulation he has stipulated certain basic disciplines for the people which are popularly called eleven vows. They are:

Eleven Vows

(i) Non-violence,
(ii) Truth,
(iii) Non-Stealing,
(iv) Self-Discipline,
(v) Non-Possession,
(vi) Bread Labour,
(vii) Controls of the Palate,
(viii) Fearlessness,
(ix) Equality of all Religion,
(x) Use locally made goods, and
(xi) Remove Untouchability.

The above codified disciples will shape the attitude of the people to move in the evolutionary path. Further, in order to bring civility among the people at the community level he advocated constructive works. It is a kind of development engagement of the people. In this regard he formulated a constructive programme. They are:

Constructive Programmes

(i) Communal Unity,
(ii) Removal of Untouchability,
(iii) Prohibition,
(iv) Khadi,
(v) Village Industries,
(vi) Sanitation,
(vii) Basic Education,
(viii) Adult Education,
(ix) Women Development,
(x) Education in Health and Hygiene,
(xi) Provincial Language,
(xii) National Language,
(xiii) Economic Equality,
(xiv) Farmers Development,
(xv) Labour Development,
(xvi) Tribals Development,
(xvii) Lepers,
(xviii) Students,

Having recognized the disparities and differences in the society on the economic conditions, he laid ground rules that a new social order has to be created and this could be done by the trustees of the society. The socio-political conducts are to be regulated through a moral code rather than the rule of laws established by the constitutions. Moral laws are having greater binding on the society than the legal norms. He underlined the importance of self-regulation and self-engagement for achieving development and for which simple activities had been identified by M.K. Gandhi.

Here he clearly brought to light the interconnectedness of the individual family, community and society while they are in action.

He disregarded the individualism and emphasized the communitarian order. The life has got a meaning if it is approached in the backdrop of the interconnectedness. From individual to community, the connectedness explains the sacrifice of the smaller units for the cause of the larger units. In his framework of governance "the Village Republic will be managed by a Panchayat which will be a living political force and entity. Panchayats will be united in a free and voluntary association by an ever widening circle of "Village Republic". "It is not an apex sustained by the bottom but an oceanic circle where the centre will be the individual always ready to perish for the village, the latter ready to perish for the circle of villages and so on, sharing the majesty of the oceanic circle of which they are parts". Hence, individual is seen as an evolving individual working for his/her evolution and in this process a harmonious relationship has to be established in the society. In this dynamic process of the society, individual has to move from consume to conserve, spend to save, and perish to preserve for the sustainability. Thus, he kept the institutions, organizations systems and processes under the basic *dharmic* norms which had been evolved over a period of time. The *dharmic* norms are for the whole society.

In this context, M.K. Gandhi visualized the individual in a different perspective quite contrary to the western perspective of individuals. The individual is being seen in the backdrop of the soul. He is not visualized as economic human being. He is seen not as a consumer or producer or beneficiary. He is seen as a unit of a larger unit with all connectedness always working for the larger units not for the sake of individual benefits. He finds a connection between the inner and outer of the individuals. By connecting the two, the individual becomes transformative individual working consciously for the transformation of the society and for which *swadharma* is the base. An individual has got roles and responsibilities and they are to be discharged. They are not relating towards himself or herself. They are relating to others. An individual may be a son to his father and mother but he is father to his sons and daughters. The same person may be a teacher to his students and member of a community and a citizen of a country. Hence, he has several roles to be performed. But while performing the role, he or she has to follow *swadharma*. By performing the entire role, the individual is purifying, perfecting and transforming his soul. So a transformative individual is a harmonious individual and an evolving individual. Thus, he firmly believed that any transformation in the society could be achieved only by transforming the disconnected individuals into connected individuals, mechanical individuals into organic individuals. For reformation or transformation, the rule of state is very minimal and self rule is the basic. Well-being of the society depends on the well-being of the transformative individuals who are connected with other entities. He firmly believes in good of the individual and good of the society. He never subscribe to a good state. He underlines the premise that good governance is impossible in bad society. The individuals will be made as transformative individuals through a process of continuous conscious action to transform his/ her body, mind and soul. The state has to allow the individuals to take more responsibilities of reconstructing the society and transforming themselves in this process and for which the state has to facilitate the individuals continuously. Thus, for all transformative process and activities we need more transformative leaders at different levels and more particularly at the grassroots level as major development engagement has to be done at that level with the active participation of people. His visualization of development is development activities with the active involvement of the mass. Today's context it is considered that participation is not only to earn the livelihood and empowerment but his vision is to evolve themselves by engagement. When people engage themselves in constructive works their energy is enhanced and released. By doing so, their attitude behaviour and performance will be transformed from one level to the next higher level. His framework of governance and development totally relies on the engagement of people. How to do it is a major question. Because over a period of time state has taken away the responsibilities of the communities and it created government departments. As a result people are kept away from the development initiatives and people's life and their future had been given to the bureaucracy. He wanted to revert the whole process. That is why he suggested a strong, vibrant, moral based Panchayati Raj system. But unfortunately that was not considered at that time. The same opportunity has come to the people now through the new initiative of the Central Government by amending the Constitution of India. When he suggested, it was not taken up by his own colleagues at the dawn of independence but now the whole world moves in this direction by decentralizing powers to people. In this context, in India a new opportunity has been created for engaging people for development and making the people to participate in the process of governance at the grassroots. Taking the key principles of M.K. Gandhi on development and governance and fitting the same into the new system which is being created for governance and development at the grassroots level, the whole governance process can be turned towards the M.K. Gandhi's ideals. We have this unique opportunity to do this exercise at grassroots. Creating local governance constitutionally in India has opened up opportunities to millions of people on to the governance job. What Gandhi formulated basic principles for governance, market and society can be put into practice in every Gram Panchayat. As suggested by M.K. Gandhi for engaging people at grassroots through the constructive programme, Indian Federal Government has evolved a new programme for grassroots by creating Eleventh Schedule of the Constitution of India. Twenty-nine activities have been included. They are :

Eleventh Schedule

1. Agricultural activities including agricultural extension.
2. Land improvement, implementation of land reforms, land consolidation and soil conservation.
3. Minor irrigation, water management and watershed development.
4. Animal husbandry, dairying and poultry.
5. Fisheries.
6. Social forestry.
7. Minor Forest produce.
8. Small scale industries including food processing industries.
9. Khadi, village and cottage industries.
10. Rural Housing.
11. Drinking Water.
12. Fuel and fodder.
13. Roads, culverts, bridges, ferries, waterways and other means of communication.
14. Rural electrification including distribution of electricity.

15. Non-conventional energy sources.
16. Poverty alleviation programme.
17. Education including primary and secondary schools.
18. Technical training and vocation education.
19. Adult and non-formal education.
20. Libraries.
21. Cultural activities.
22. Market and Fairs.
23. Health and Sanitation, including hospitals, primary health centres and dispensaries.
24. Family Welfare.
25. Women and child development.
26. Social welfare including welfare of the handicapped and mentally retarded.
27. Welfare of the weaker sections and in particular of the Scheduled Castes and Scheduled Tribes.
28. Public distribution system.
29. Maintenance of community asserts.

These subjects were included in the Eleventh Schedule of the Constitution with an objective of involving people at the grassroot level in all development activities. These subjects are more or less the same of the constructive programme. Though these subjects are designed in Indian context, they are applicable to all the developing countries. It is suitable for global development. It is worthnoting here the New Millennium development goals of the UN. Annually UN is preparing the development report from the perspective of MDG. No way are the subjects of MDG different from M.K. Gandhi's constructive programme or the subjects included in Eleventh Schedule of the Constitution of India. Even after six decades of development, exponents of development at the UN level chalked out the MDG for action by the states. But M.K. Gandhi advocated the same in his constructive programme for the actions of the community. It is unfortunate that his penetrating analysis of the development problems and futuristic visions on development have been ignored by our leaders by committing the actions of the state. Had our leaders continued mobilization of people for development after Independence as it was done during the freedom struggle, many of the problems the Indian society confronts now would have been solved long back. By doing so,

India would have shown the way to the other developing society for their governance and development. Now the country through its plans is trying to address the problems as it committed to UN to work on MDG.

MDG

1. End poverty and hunger.
2. Universal Education.
3. Gender Equality.
4. Child Health.
5. Maternal Health.
6. Combat HIV / AIDS.
7. Environmental Sustainability.
8. Global Partnership.

To tackle global problem we need only local actions. It was envisaged by M.K. Gandhi through his vision and programme. Now the opportunity has come to people through a new instrument namely Panchayats.

If the leader of every Gram Panchayat is prepared, oriented, trained, conscientised, he and she will become the transformative leader to transform the rustic folk through their involvement in development and governance engagement and that will be done through Gram Sabha and micro plan initiatives at the ground. A new governance culture could be created through the new leadership at Panchayat level. So far we had only the culture of ruling the masses but now a new leadership culture will be in place to lead the society and community. New development paradigm and new governance paradigm could be experimented at the grassroots. In the last fifteen years we have seen an array of transformative leaders in the Panchayat institutions. In this context we have to create training institutions to train Panchayat leaders in transformative process of community and society. Managing Panchayat is one part of it. Transforming the community and society is the major aspect to be incorporated in training programme. The grassroots leaders have to show the way in governance and development to the elected representatives of State Legislature and National Parliament rather than moving in their way of governance. An alternative approach can be evolved locally through the Panchayats. Every Panchayat leader should be a constructive worker. These Panchayat leaders have to be trained in the transformative methodology not in accountancy and income and expenditure. An in-depth training methodology has to be evolved and by which they have to be trained.

There is yet another important aspect included in his framework of governance namely inclusiveness. The last man or woman in terms of their socio-economic condition should feel that they are matter to be reckoned with. They should also feel that they are also part in the process of governance and their voice is also being heard. Such a feeling the poorest of the poor has to entertain in their heart. Now constitutionally people's council has been created at every unit of lowest local government where every segment of the society can express its voice. No more they are noise but now they are becoming voices as they echo it in the constitutionally created council. By doing so a new culture of deepening democracy and respecting the voice of others could be developed at the local level. This is called inclusiveness and deepening of democracy.

Conclusion

M.K. Gandhi has formulated certain basic principles for political and social governance. These principles will explain the relationship between the nature and the human society. Further he visualized the interaction among the three forces namely state, market and society in the larger backdrop of nature. Harmony and connectedness are the linking forces. To harmonize the relationship between the state and the society, state and the market and market and society, Gandhi has stipulated the principles. By adopting these principles people can be engaged in governance and development process. Till the enactment of the 73rd Amendment to the Constitution of India, all those activities were only voluntary. Now a new institutional mechanism was created constitutionally for the engagement of the people for the governance and development. It requires only leaders. They are to be created in large numbers totally different from the present leadership at the state and central level. They are the change makers and path finders. By their work millennium development goals could be achieved. All global targets could be achieved through local actions. For this task transformative leadership training schools have to be created to train local body leaders. By using this principle in the new Panchayati Raj System in India a new transformative culture could be created and a new team of transformative leaders could be prepared. By doing so a new way of governance, a new way of development could be achieved in the new context.

V

Corruption at Grassroots

Introduction

Corruption has taken a demonic form in Indian polity, governance and administration which ultimately affected the society by dismantling the value profile of the society. Though corruption is an unacceptable practice for the society, people have been made to be part of the practice and thereby the whole development process is disturbed and as a result poverty persists at the grassroots. Now it becomes an academic discipline[1] as magnitude of corruption and its implications are huge and complex. Debates and discourses are on to combat corruption with initiative of the middle class[2]. Equally in academic disciplines steps have been taken to conceptualize the corrupt practices in governance and administrative systems. New methodological nuances have been evolved to measure and analyze corruption at all levels from global to local.

But the concern here is to look at corruption at grassroots as it affects the poor very deeply and in turn it affects the very process of poverty reduction and development. Even to claim the basic entitlements, people have been made to be part of the corrupt practices. At the national level to contain corruption initiatives are on because of the intervention of the Judiciary and Election Commission. But at the grassroots what is the step and remedy taken to curb corruption? In India, development schemes and programmes are many and no country in the world has got so much of development schemes as India. But the reach of the above schemes to the targeted groups is always a problematic. How to make the schemes to reach the targeted population? is the critical question.

In Tamil Nadu alone one can find 369 welfare schemes including 99 schemes of the Central Government. As per the statistics provided by the Federal Government and the State governments one Gram Panchayat receives roughly seven crores of rupees for a period of five years through all the schemes. The question here is whether the allocated resources have reached the target groups. When Rajiv Gandhi was the Prime Minister, he lamented that of the allocated resources to the poor in the rural areas only 15 per cent of the amount reaches the targeted groups and the rest goes elsewhere. How do we call the missing 85 per cent of the allocated resources? Can we call it as brokerage or corruption? It is of both. Unless this loophole is plugged from the system, the existing poverty and mass deprivation will continue forever. In order to overcome this problem a new governance mechanism was evolved at the grassroots level by amending the Constitution of India. How this new mechanism – the new local governance – has tackled the crisis is explained in this article. The article has three sections[3]. First section deals with the corrupt practices in rural development schemes based on the field studies. The second section deals with the role of Panchayats in containing corruption in this process. The third section explains how Panchayats can use the new instruments like Right to Information Act and Social Audit effectively to put an end to the corrupt practices. In all the exercises we tried to get some new insights and instruments for effective use in anti-corruption activities at the grassroots[4].

A Word of Clarification

In this exercise the phenomenon of corruption is not visualized from either the World Bank perspective or from the academic discourses developed by economists and social anthropologists[5]. Here the issue is analysed from the perspective of a social worker who has a concern for the poor in a democratic country where the benefits of the poor were shared by the development brokers and the bureaucracy and as a result the problems of the poor are mounting up and the poor continue to lose faith and confidence in the governance and administrative system. The primary concern here is not to develop a theory or typology on corruption but what is the way out to prevent corruption in poverty alleviation activities in the rural areas and by which how to build confidence among the poor that the democratic institutions will deliver goods. This exercise is based on action research conducted at the grassroots. Ideas and options are generated from the experience what we have gained in the field while we were in action.

Background

From our deep observation and analysis of the studies conducted so far it is found out that some of the factors which are at the ground responsible for growing corrupt practices in poverty alleviation rural development programmes. In India the government departments had started perceiving people as beneficiaries from middle of 1960s after the departure of community development programmes. This kind of perception and treatment made the poor away from their main role of participation in the development process as stakeholders. Further, the same poor have been further termed as petitioners if they submit petitions for claiming their entitlement. This treatment has made them to lose their self-confidence, and self-dignity. Thus, the people especially poor are systematically disempowered and made them as powerless and bureaucracy is empowered. Conveniently even the poor had also perceived themselves as beneficiaries and petitioners. As a result they forgot the role of the participants. This syndrome has created a vast gap between the government and the poor. They are always in periphery without having any access to information channel of the government departments. Further, our politics is not development oriented but it is always election oriented which requires huge money to conduct electioneering by the political parties. Since election is costlier and election oriented politics is also costlier, at every level money is needed for politics. Hence, political parties which are in power have to manage money and hence they indulge in brokerage in the process of development at the grassroots by using the gap between the people and the government. Further, over a period of time some kind of spoil system has been developed. Party men entertain an idea that if their party comes to power they can make profit and achieve prosperity. In such a way party politics is perceived by the party men. Office of services has been converted into office of profit. In the recent past we never heard a story that because of he or she joined in politics, he/she has lost huge money by spending it in politics. We have million stories that because he joined in politics he has achieved unfathomable prosperity. In such a way politics becomes a profitable venture. Now we see political capitalism[6] everywhere making huge money by using political offices. Without doing any business, the politicians make profit unfathomably more than industrial class and business class by using power. This is a current discourse everywhere and systematic knowledge is emerging on this subject. In order to evolve a strategy to eliminate political capitalism (corruption) at grassroots a study was conducted in selected villages purely with an objective of understanding it properly and perceptively.

Experiment in Phase I

Through focus group discussion in selected villages in Dindigul district, details have been gathered as to what extent the welfare schemes meant for the poor have reached the target groups. The above focus group discussions were conducted by involving the *dalits*, women and youth of poor families in the rural areas. In fact, we found out from the discussion that around 60 per cent of the people got the benefits from the government schemes. But the same 60 per cent of the beneficiaries have not got the full benefits as they had to part some of the amounts to the middlemen who acted as a link between the beneficiaries and the bureaucracy. In the analysis of the causes for not directly claiming their entitlements, the participants replied that they did not know the details of the schemes, details of the officers who are dealing with the schemes, details of the offices dealing with the schemes, details of eligibility conditions for availing the schemes, details of the process through which they can claim the benefits of the schemes and more specifically when the scheme benefits are distributed. In the absence of the above information necessarily they had to seek the help of the middlemen who are mostly ruling party men. The ruling party men are professionals in dealing with the government officials and the poor. They have information and power connections. They know the procedures and process also.

It is only the ruling party men approach the beneficiaries for two reasons. One they can get some amount from the beneficiaries for the work they are doing for them. From getting application from the relevant offices to getting the benefits, all the procedural formalities have to be completed only by the middlemen and for which they feel it is legitimate to get some amount and it may be considered as a processing charge. The second reason is that by doing such a kind of help to the poor beneficiaries, the poor can be enrolled themselves as party members or at least they can be turned towards the ruling party as sympathizers. So there are two kinds of advantages by doing this brokerage. Personally they are gaining and the party is also gaining the support base of the poor. This becomes a culture, a value, a habit and behaviour in Tamil Nadu for several decades. One can easily calculate when a new scheme is announced how much they have designed for party men and how much will reach the poor. Only a handful of people in every village where we collected data got benefits without the support of the middlemen. But the story is full of struggle with bureaucracy to get the benefits.

The officials who have to reach out to the poor, clear everything based on the instructions of the ruling party men. Even if eligible applications are in the pipeline, they will not be considered if they are not supported by the ruling party men. Sometimes even ineligible application will be considered positively if recommendations come from the ruling party functionaries. It is not rule of law but it is always rule of the ruling party men. It could have been contested by the bureaucracy because rule application is the responsibility of the bureaucracy. By the bureaucracy did not do it for two reasons. One is that they did not want to face the wrath of the ruling party men. By doing so they have to struggle in their career. Secondly, they are not losing anything in this process but gaining something because the ruling party middlemen fix a rate and they pay periodically to the dealing officials who are involved in the process of distribution of benefits. But the percentage of money to be given to middlemen and middlemen to officials vary from period to period. The justification offered to officials taking money is very serious to the very public administration itself. The whole money is not for personal purpose. It includes public purposes also. For many of the government programmes, functions, officers visit, ministers visit, there is no approved budget to the level of the money which they spent for the above. To meet out the unforeseen amount spent, they use this graft money. They have common pool money. In the same way, the ruling party middlemen give reason for getting money from the beneficiaries. From getting application from the office, getting signature from competent authorities to prove he or she is the eligible person to get the benefits, the middlemen have to go and spend money. Middlemen are not getting money from party for many of the party activities. They have to spend money for the party from their packets and for which they have to earn money. Hence, they argue that they are getting this money from the beneficiaries and it is almost a processing charge. Thus, the party men who act as middlemen or brokers have to give money to officials and spend money for party activities only from the money collected from the beneficiaries. Money goes to brokers pocket is only limited as per the arguments of the middlemen. The beneficiaries who have given money to middlemen never argued that it is wrong. They too feel that they are being helped by the brokers in getting the benefits and, hence, there is nothing wrong in taking some amount from the benefits due to them. Their argument is that unless they come to help the poor, how poor will get at least this much. Further, they argue that they take money only when they give the benefits. They are not cheating. If there is any arrangement in the government departments that the officials have to deliver the benefits to the doorsteps of the poor, this will not happen. In the absence of the above the middlemen involved in this process and they are really reaching out to the poor. It is almost a parallel to "everybody loves drought" of Sainath of the Hindu. In the whole process of corruption justification is given by indicating the lapses in Public Administration[7]. The above study was conducted before the creation of New Panchayati Raj System in Tamil Nadu.

Experiment in Phase II

We had a hope that after the implementation of the 73rd Amendment to the Constitution of India, every village will have a governance system in the name of Gram Panchayat. And there will be responsive, responsible and representative set-up in the villages to meet the requirements of the people and bring government departments closer to the people in delivering goods and services to the people. But in reality the village Panchayats is asked to assist, advice and help the government departments to deliver services to the poor. It is almost a voluntary work. How to assist, advice and facilitate is not known either to Panchayat leaders or to the officials. Hence, the officials acted in their own way and the village Panchayat presidents looked after their assigned duties. Further, the officials had not been oriented to work with elected representatives[8]. The government departments which are working in the rural areas, are independent and accountable to their masters in bureaucratic system and not to the real masters "people" Panchayats have not emerged as units of governance but they have been designed to work as implementing agencies. As a result corruption continues as it was even after the establishment of Panchayats in the villages. Here, a point is to be noted. If the Gram Panchayat president belongs to the ruling party, he started acting as middleman. Otherwise he will mind his business and the ruling party representative will do the job of getting the benefits from the government to the poor. In Tamil Nadu Gram Panchayats are freed from party based electoral contest and yet after the election many Gram Panchayat Presidents used to give a picture that they belong to the ruling party. This kind of atitude the Gram Panchayat Presidents have developed because of the fact that the officials have supported only the Presidents who belong to the ruling party in the State by extending help to implement government schemes and programmes. Further, every Panchayat President wants to get such a kind of support from the officials to get the benefits of the government in his/her Panchayats and the beneficiaries of his/her villages. Hence, Panchayat President gives an impression that they belong to the ruling party.

At this juncture, Rajiv Gandhi chair selected a Gram Panchayat Vadugambadi, a Gram Panchayat in Gujiliambarai Block of the Dindigul district for an experiment. It was headed by Mr. Perumal a CPI (M) cadre. He committed himself for a new leadership to the people and through which he wanted to give clean and good governance to the people. He believed in collective leadership for social and economic transformation of the rural society. He wanted that Panchayat should be people centric and not leader centric. Hence, we brought the entire Panchayat functionaries to Gandhigram Rural Institute and they were fully trained and oriented in new local governance processes. They were provided with all necessary information packages for effective corruption free local governance in the villages. As a result the village Panchayat had made a declaration that it is going to mobilize people for corruption free governance in Vadugambadi Panchayat. The Panchayat put up a board in the main road that it is corruption free Panchayat. Panchayat or people will not give money and get money for any development work at their village. Further, it is mentioned that it is a people centric Panchayat and not leader centric Panchayat. It is only a collective leadership that works in this Panchayat. In such a way messages have been written on the board. A wide publicity was given. All the newspapers have carried stories of this Panchayat in this regard. It drew the attention of all the officials and social workers.

First, the Panchayat President convened the Gram Sabha meeting and briefed the members of the Gram Sabha about the benefits to be distributed to the beneficiaries by various government departments based on the information package provided by the Rajiv Gandhi Chair through its book[9]. Later he finalized the beneficiary list in the Gram Sabha for all the welfare schemes of various departments. While preparing the list priority was given in the list based on the severity of their poverty. It was a list prepared by Gram Sabha and submitted to all the government departments. The Panchayat President visited all the government departments along with the ward members. He met the District Collector and informed the decision of the Panchayats and the Gram Sabha. An interesting point has to be mentioned here. While preparing the beneficiary list Panchayat President only facilitated and the whole list was prepared by the people. In that process many names in the list prepared by the officials have been removed and a large number of new names have been included. Finally, while analyzing the list prepared by the people in Gram Sabha and the officials, total number of poor has been reduced. Many real poor were not found in the list prepared by the officials. While ordering the list poorest of the poor will be placed first and accordingly the list was prepared. Since the District Collector was very proactive, he asked the officials to go by the procedures. He has given clear direction to the officials that the officials have to go by the list prepared by the Gram Sabha. It was a good support extended to the Panchayat by the District Collector. In this process of eliminating corruption, the first test came when the students applying for higher studies after school final examination. Normally, they have to get the community certificate before applying for higher studies. In Tamil Nadu it is a known fact that one has to give minimum of Rs. 300 to get a community certificate. In this context, the village Panchayat President went to the village administrative officer and informed him about the resolution of the Gram Sabha. He requested him not to collect money for community certificate. If anyone requests for fraudulent certificate he can make criminal complaint in the police station. That was the plea he made before the village administrative officer. Really it was a moral and legal threat to the village administrative officer. Since the village Panchayat President was honest, the village administrative officer could not do anything. As a result he saw to it that all community certificates were delivered without paying a single rupee. It was a tremendous success. In the same way some of the departments have proactively distributed the benefits to the beneficiary without asking any amount from the beneficiaries. This has helped the Panchayats to move further in this direction. People of this Panchayat started believing the collective leadership and its strength.

Panchayat took another decision of conducting social audit for the infrastructure development works carried out in the Panchayat areas by the contractors who have involved in laying road and other construction works. The contractors have been approached by the Panchayat functionaries for agreement deeds for all the works they have taken for implementation in this Panchayat areas. Initially they were reluctant and subsequently they have given the documents. Based on the document all the works have been examined and the drawbacks were indicated. The same was brought to the notice of the District Collector. In response to the request of the Panchayat the contractors had been instructed by the officials to carry out the works as per the agreement. As a result quality of work was ensured. In such a way corruption was eliminated. It is not a simple task. It was a struggle for the President. The vested interest in the same village and other places created problems to Perumal and his family. Because many had lost income. The contractors refuse to come to this village for any work. No contractor was willing to take work in this village. Officials though extended support they created problem for the President. He had to be vigilant in maintaining accounts and records of Panchayat properly otherwise he will be booked by the officials. Once he completed the full term of five years, he refused to contest in the next election. When he was asked he replied that he was in struggle for the whole five years. He was unable to take care of his family. Her wife, a government employee, was disturbed. He had not spent money in the election when he contested for Panchayat President post. Later he went to party work as a worker. In the subsequent election another person won the election and removed the resolution and the board erected by the previous President. When he was asked about the reason he made it very clear that when the whole politics, governance and administration are in corruption systematically how can a Panchayat be corruption free. Mr. Perumal waged a struggle against bureaucracy and vested interest. It is very difficult to eliminate corruption in this country. This was the reply given by him. It was also captured in the newspapers. But one thing was demonstrated in the whole process of administration for a period of five years from 1996 to 2001 that the leadership is critical and leadership style and behaviour are all the more important for the success of governance and administration[10]. For about five years it was corruption free Panchayat. But it was full of struggle. Adequate support structure was not found in the system or in the society to protect and support the honest Panchayat leaders. The whole exercise was fully documented for process analysis.

Experiment in Phase III

Third experiment was through micro plan initiated in select Panchayats with the support of select district administration. This was with the financial support of the Hunger Project. Through this micro plan all government schemes are brought in the plan document itself and thereby plan was prepared through a participatory process whereby all the marginalized sections have been integrated in the development and governance actions. Seventy-four Gram Panchayats in four districts namely Dindigul, Pudukkottai, Sivagangai and Tuticorin have implemented the micro plan. The Panchayat leaders who have involved in evolving micro plan had formed a Federation among themselves and they approached the respective District Collector and persuaded them to give direction to the officials to implement the planned activities as mentioned in the plan document. Since the District Collectors have signed the plan document as inspector of Panchayat the District Collectors have promptly instructed the officials to implement the plan document. Thus, the beneficiaries identified and approved by the respective Gram Sabhas were given the individual benefits without asking for any bribe. The Panchayat Presidents federation worked to some extent effectively get the plan document implemented. The whole success is due to the support extended by the District Collector, initiative taken by the Rajiv Gandhi Chair for Panchayati Raj Studies, financially supported by the Hunger Project and the honest and committed efforts of the Gram Panchayat Presidents. In this experiment we found out that micro plan is an instrument through which we can make the government departments to work in the people's plan and reduce corruption[11].

There is yet another experiment conducted in many of the Gram Panchayats using Right to Information Act to try to get the details of the schemes available in the government departments and how they are spent. For this exercise also the Panchayat Presidents formed a federation and submit application in almost all the departments which are working in the rural areas. This exercise achieved limited success and could not bring expected results. Many of the Panchayats have to incur the displeasure of the officials of the line department while asking for information by using Right to Information Act which ultimately affected the routine Panchayat activities. Further, the Panchayat Presidents who seek such information from the offices by using the RTI are considered as problematic creating problem in public offices. They were viewed negatively by the District Administration. For this exercise also the Rajiv Gandhi Chair for Panchayati Raj Studies extended assistance. But a few Panchayats necessarily to wage a war against the government office have used it effectively. They also faced a volley of problems in Panchayat administration due to filing of RTI application in the government offices. Yet they succeeded in getting information. But they could not move beyond. A new perception has been developed among the officials to view the RTI applicants as problematic and anti-bureaucrats. By developing this perception the officials have started non-cooperation with the Panchayat leaders who seek information through RTI. Hence, this experiment met with limited success. To operate this provision, Panchayat leaders have to mobilize support from the people or at least the elected representatives have to join together and file such a kind of application to get the needed information from the government departments. Otherwise Panchayat Presidents will be threatened by the officials[12].

Integrated Analysis

From the given context, it is inferred that the middle men role is inevitable and it is to be eliminated only by strengthening the Panchayati Raj System. Panchayats should be given the role and responsibility of tracking development finance and schemes and to be used for the beneficiaries. To perform the above task officials have to be oriented to give needed information to the Panchayats proactively. Panchayats have to develop micro plan and in which the schemes have to be matched with needs of the people. These kinds of exercises have to be done collectively in all the Panchayats. It should become part of the Panchayat responsibility. Every Panchayat should be made an information centre and it should provide needed information to the public. All development programmes carried out by the government departments have to be examined and evaluated by the public through social audit process. By doing so the government departments will be made to work with the Panchayats. Here civil society support to Panchayats is critical. It is necessary that more number of Panchayat friendly civil society groups have to be formed to support Panchayats for their activities. In Tamil Nadu more than four hundred such civil society groups have been formed to help Panchayats and people by providing information. It was initiated by Catalyst Trust in Chennai with the support of the Ford Foundation on all the places information centres have been created in the name of "people centre". They helped the Panchayats to get such vital information from the governments by using RTI. Though the process is difficult, many Gram Panchayat Presidents emerged successfully by waging relentless war against the bureaucracy. It was possible because of the training they had undergone and the commitments they had developed[13].

Conclusion

From the micro studies it is found out that the development

schemes which are meant for poverty eradication and enhancing livelihood opportunities could not achieve the intended results as the development brokers mostly ruling party men (not women) involved in getting the schemes to the needy. In the process of getting the schemes to the needy forty to fifty per cent of the scheme benefits are taken away for them. This process is getting concretized because of the information gap between the government and the needy targeted groups. Further, the link between the ruling party men and the bureaucracy is strong for their mutual benefits. The beneficiaries are not having the feeling that they are losing their benefits in the process as in the absence of such a help they feel that they could get at least even the minimum what they get through the political brokers.

Even after the Panchayat came to power, the Panchayat leaders have neither vision nor commitment to break the link between the development brokers and the bureaucracy as they are more powerful than the Panchayat Presidents. It is only a few Panchayat Presidents have emerged successfully by breaking the link between the development brokers and the bureaucracy. It requires vision and strategy and for which a professional training programme is needed for the Panchayat leaders. There is no such transformative professional training programme for Panchayat leaders. For this kind of transformative work at the Panchayats poor have to be mobilized and the Panchayat leader should enjoy the confidence of the people by conducting himself free from corruption and transparently in all Panchayat activities. Panchayat Presidents should wage a relentless war against this development brokerage and for which they have to be prepared. This kind of leadership we find rarely as the whole system of governance and administration is corrupt. Yet by federating such honest, transformative leaders with the support of civil society and media corruption can be tackled at the grassroots. There is yet another instrument available for Panchayat Presidents now. The Right to Information Act is the timely remedy for the ills what we found out in rural development schemes. It is known that nearly forty-eight departments are working with people by delivering goods and services to the people at the grassroots. Every Panchayat by using the Right to Information Act can get details regarding the amount they are going to spend this current year for the Panchayat areas both for the individuals and the groups. After collecting the details from all the forty-eight departments the details can be shared with Gram Sabha members. After the month of March of every year, a social audit can be conducted for each and every department activities at the grassroots. By doing social audit repeatedly for a few years, people who are involved in such brokerage activities will be exposed and the government departments will be made answerable to the public. Further, all the government departments have to be compelled to disclose their activities and allocation proactively to the Panchayats where they are going to work every year for easy follow-up. By doing the above corruption can be eliminated or at least it can be reduced at the grassroots level.

REFERENCES

1. It is not only an Indian phenomenon but also a world phenomenon. Studies have been conducted extensively for details. *See* Elixabeth Harrison, "Corruption", *Development in Practice,* Vol. 17, Nos. 4 & 5, Aug. 2007, pp. 672–678.
2. The pervasive corruption in the development activities of the developing countries was highlighted by the donor agencies like World Bank; DFID of the UK and subsequently institutional mechanism was created by Transparency International (TI) with the support of such donor agencies to conduct studies across the world. For more details *see* S. Sampson "Integrity Warriors: Global Morality and the Anti Corruption Movement in the Balkans" in C. Shore and D. Haller (eds.) *Corruption: Anthropological Perspectives,* London: Pluto Press, 2005. Several websites and portals have been created.
3. This is based on my presentation in Senegal. "Containing Corruption at Grassroots" in international policy dialogue organized by CODESRIA from 1st to 3rd October, 2009 in (Dakkar) Senegal.
4. For the experiments and studies the Hunger Project New Delhi and the Ford Foundation have helped through the projects sanctioned to us. I profusely thank both the Hunger Project and the Ford Foundation.
5. Margit Tavits, "Clarity of Responsibility and Corruption" *American Journal of Political Science,* Vol. 51, No. 1 (January, 2007), pp. 218–229; A. Cooper Drury, Jonathan Krieckhaus and Michael Lusztig, "Corruption, Democracy and Economic Growth", *International Political Science Review* (2006), Vol. 27, No. 2, pp. 121–136.

6. This concept "Political Capitalism" was introduced by Max Weber but now it has been elaborated and explained through systematic studies. The concept political capitalism refers to make illegal money by using power. Without doing any business. For more details see Ganev, V, "Preying on the state: Political Capitalism after Communism" Ph.D Dissertation, Department of Political Science, University of Chicago, 1999.
7. G. Palanithurai, "Corruption at micro level and ways to contain it" in *Corruption at the Grassroots: The Shades and Shadows*" (Eds) N. Narayanasamy, M.P. Boraiyan and M.A Jeyaraju, New Delhi: Concept Publishing Company Pvt. Ltd., 2000.
8. G. Palanithurai, *Panchayati Raj System in Tamil Nadu* (Monograph) Gandhigram: Rajiv Gandhi Chair for Panchayati Raj Studies, 2002.
9. The book given to all the trainees is a Panchayat Manual or Hand Book which contains, 73rd Amendment, Tamil Nadu Panchayat Act, Panchayat Rules, Government Orders, Welfare Schemes and Programme in simple language with commentaries. Later it was published as a Panchayat Manual for Panchayat Leaders. G. Planithurai, *Panchayati Raj System, Act, Rules, Government Orders and Schemes and Programmes* (in Tamil), Chennai: South Vision, 2009. 5th edition
10. Palanithurai, *Containing Corruption: A Micro Experiment*, Gandhigram: Rajiv Gandhi Chair for Panchayati Raj Studies, 1998.
11. Palanithurai, "Development Roles Reversed: Peoples initiative and governments participation" in L.C. Jain (ed.) *Decentralization and Local Governance*, New Delhi: Orient Longman, 2005.
12. G. Palanithurai, *How Some Panchayats Becomes A Model? Actionable Agenda to Become A Model* Gandhigram: Rajiv Gandhi Chair for Panchayati Raj Studies, 2009.
13. G. Palanithurai, *Report on the Study of Market and Democracy in Tamil Nadu*, Gandhigram: Rajiv Gandhi Chair for Panchayati Raj Studies, 2009.

VI

Visionary Framework for Managing Crisis in Governance

In the era of coalition governments we witness large scale corruption in governance and administration and the prevailing corruption has been justified that we have to pay a heavy price in the form of corruption in order to maintain stability in governance in India. It is argued vehemently that political stability is the basic requirement for achieving prosperity. More precisely many argue that political stability is essential for economic growth and development. There is yet another argument posited by another group of scholars that corruption is a global phenomenon and India in no way an exception. It is argued that it is part of the globalization process. These are some of the arguments projected by opinion makers in the recent years. The prevailing "Political Capitalism"[1] which emerges out of globalization and coalition has made the institutions of governance to lose credibility and stature. So also the leaders who are in the helm of affairs are losing credibility and stature[2]. Will democracy find solution for it or will it continue without check and control is the basic question. All over the world initiatives are on to check corruption. In India also initiatives are on to control corruption. In this regard, there are three institutions which are very vibrant in managing this crisis in India in the recent years. They are the Office of the President, Election Commission and the Judiciary Supreme Court including some of the High Courts[3]. Now the above mentioned institutions have emerged visibly in the eyes of the public in tackling the crisis in governance and given hope that the political and government systems will be regulated and thereby stability and accountability of the above systems will be ensured. The above mentioned institutions have suddenly plunged into action because of the leadership of these institutions at a point of time. For the emergence of the Election Commission to function as an independent agency clear road map was given by T.N. Sheshan when he became the Election Commissioner of India. In the same way for judicial activism Justice V.R. Krishna Iyyar and Justice B.N. Bhagwati had given road map. The Office of the President of India rose to the occasion and transformed itself from a ceremonial office to regulatory office in shaping governance by using the powers conferred on it by the Constitution of India. After Rajendra Prasad, it was Ramasamy Venkataraman who gave the leadership and framework for formation of government in the context of crisis in government due to indecisive elected outcome. The guidance and the framework given by the guidance and the framework given by R. Venkataraman are being hailed by many. There were criticisms against R. Venkataraman on political grounds from the perspective of political parties but his handling of issues at a point of crisis in the nation has clearly demonstrated his vision, and commitment towards the nation and its future. As a student of Political Science I try to look at his leadership in the Office of the President and analyse his intervention strategies in bringing stability and accountability to governance.

He developed a framework for presidential intervention during the time of crisis and he made it in such a way that the framework has to be followed by his successors in the best interest of the Nation. Since the middle of 1980s the Prime Minister, the Chief Ministers, the legislators, executives and the civil servants who serve their above masters have discredited themselves before the opinion makers of the society mostly they are from the middle class.[4] This disappointment set in Indian Politics in the middle of 1980s as Rajiv Gandhi could not fulfi! his own tall promises in politics and governance due to scandals in governance and administration which were brought to the notice of the public and in turn they were blown out of proportion by the media and the political parties. More specifically the middle class played a significant role in creating such an opinion among the public against Rajiv Gandhi and the Indian National Congress. It is to be noted here that the amount involved in those years compared to the amounts involved in corruption in governance and administration is very negligible. Moreover, it was also argued that the corruption highlighted at the point of time was interpreted as the involvement of external forces to destabilize Indian economy and polity. Because Rajiv Gandhi's emergence as Prime Minister in India had given a signal that India's enduring role in this region as leader was visible. Rajiv Gandhi, when took up responsibility as Prime Minister, he made a tall promise of giving good and clean governance as the prime objective of his government. As a result he gained an image of "Mr Clean" from the middle class and the media. When scandals emerged one after another when he was the Prime Minister his image had gone down and as a result the opinion making middle class was disappointed. The disappointed middle class extended their disappointment to the poor also. Consequently, the next general election witnessed unprecedented outcome and thereby no political party emerged victoriously in the election to stake the claim to form a government at the Centre. At this point of time the media and the middle class through their opinion tried to shape the opinion of the then President of India. The then President of India, Ramasamy Venkataraman with his foresightedness had evolved a framework for guiding the country. The framework was formed in such a way that his successors can follow in future easily to guide the country in formation of government. He had emerged beyond politics and party consideration by following the spirit of the Constitution of India. He considered himself as copybook[5] of the Constitution of India. In this sense he invoked the basic spirit of the Constitution. Being a lawyer himself and a statesman he visualized the events in the years to come and accordingly he evolved the framework.

In his framework he unequivocally kept accountability and stability of government as essential for this country and accordingly action has to be taken while forming the governments. It is a major question in the context of coalition government and coalition politics, whether stability can be seen above accountability or it has to be seen along with accountability or stability at the cost of accountability.[6] He clearly indicated that stability is not at the cost of accountability but accountability and stability should be the essential principles of governance and from that perspective alone decisions have to be taken in the Office of the President of India while forming governments. While looking at both principles, accountability is non-negotiable from the perspective of good governance. Secondly, the credibility of the institutions has to be maintained and in such a way decision making has to be done in the Office of the President of India. Otherwise the Office of the President has to lose its credibility and stature. In the context of no one political party is able to get majority, what will be the decision of the President of India with regard to formation of the government is the key question. He made it clear that the party which has secured more number of seats has to be invited to form the government. Further opportunity has to be given to the party to prove its majority in the House itself. The test has to be conducted only in the floor of the House and not outside. The whole process has to be conducted in a transparent manner without giving any room for speculation.[7] To overcome the crises arising out of coalition he has developed a constitutional design which kept the constitutional spirit and principles intact. Till he assumed such responsibility as President of India, there was no such crisis in government formation. Mandate was given by the people clearly in the earlier general elections and hence it was only ceremonial function of government formation and that was to be done by the President of India. When R. Venkataraman was in office as President of India, he faced such a situation and he ably tackled the crisis and carved out a design to tackle such a crisis in future also. Moreover, the whole exercise has to be done very transparently and by following the constitutional norms. By creating such a design he made it a point that no one can speculate what will be the decision of the President in the event of split verdict. In 1989, the Ninth Parliamentary Election witnessed a hung Parliament. R. Venkataraman made the basic rule that the President has to ask the party which has secured more number of seats in the election to form the government and within two or three weeks the Government has to test its majority in the floor of the Parliament. If the party which has got more number of seats declines or fails to get majority, the President of India would ask the next largest party in terms of the number of seats secured in the election to form the government. He also made another basic rule that the test has to be done only in Parliament and not in the Presidents chamber to count the heads. He made the decision consciously because the supremacy and value of the House should be kept in fact. He made it as a convention and he implemented this design when V.P. Singh staked his claim under the banner

"National Front". He unequivocally informed V.P. Singh that "as the Indian National Congress had not staked a claim to form the government, I invite you to form the government as the leader of the second largest party to form the government and take a vote of confidence of the House within thirty days"[8]. After the fall of the V.P. Singh government he asked the main opposition party, the Indian National Congress to form the government. The Indian National Congress has not exhibited its willingness to form the government. But, it extended its support to Shri Chandrasekhar to form the government. Subsequently, in 1991 when P.V. Narasimha Rao was elected as leader of the Congress Party, he was invited to form the government as the Indian National Congress was the largest party in Parliament but it could not secure majority. R. Venkataraman invoked the same rule and asked him to form the government and test his majority in the floor of the house within four weeks time. Since he formulated this design with a futuristic vision, his successors have followed the design in letter and spirit when they faced such a crisis in 1996, 1998 and 1999. His successors Shankar Dayal Sharma and K.R. Narayanan with high reputation and impartiality operationalised this design very effectively.

Shankar Dayal Sharma had faced such a political crisis in 1996 when Eleventh Parliamentary Election witnessed the hung Parliament. During this period, the BJP has secured large number of seats but it had no majority as the Indian National Congress in the previous period under the leadership of P.V. Narasimha Rao. The United Front and the Indian National Congress had secured seats second and third respectively in terms of number of seats in the election. S.D. Sharma adopted the design of R. Venkataraman and thereby he invited A.B. Vajpayee to form the government and asked him to test the majority within two weeks time in Parliament. But A.B. Vajpayee could not succeed in getting majority in the floor of the House and subsequently the President turned towards the second largest grouping, the United Front a fourteen party coalition to form the government. The United Front formed the government and with the support of the Indian National Congress, it won the vote of confidence. The Indian National Congress extended support from outside. It was not the part of the government. K.R. Narayanan followed the design of R.V. Venkataraman in March 1998 after the twelfth Parliamentary

Election by asking the BJP to form the government as it is the largest party in a hung Parliament and to test its majority in the floor of the House. The BJP has proved its majority this time.

R. Venkataraman's framework has been expanded by his successors both S.D. Sharma and K.R. Narayanan by asking the State Governors to act constitutionally in an impartial way and transparently in dealing with State government. Both Presidents S.D. Sharma and K.R. Narayanan instructed the governors through organizing a conference for the governors. Both Presidents had instructed the Governors to take serious note when they make recommendation for dissolution of the government and imposition of President's rule by invoking article 356. The instruction was very clear that the Governors should act constitutionally and not politically. Both of them have kept out of controversies when governors involved in controversial decisions. This was the good tradition created by R. Venkataraman when he was the President of India. When R. Venkataraman was in office, some of the Governors got involved in Political controversies by their actions. But he kept himself away from all those controversies. He wanted to keep the image and reputation of the Office of the President of India very high.

R. Venkataraman has invoked the provision of the 44th Amendment to the Constitution of India judiciously. By this amendment the President of India has been given some discretionary powers to send back the decisions of the Parliament for reconsideration. This provision was created by Morarji Desai as Prime Minister by amending the Constitution. It is a process through which the Parliament has to be made vigilant on some important matters which are being returned by the President of India. He returned the Postal Bill passed by the Parliament. Subsequently S.D. Sharma returned two bills to Parliament and in the same way K.R. Narayanan returned two bills. Subsequently A.P.J. Abdul Kalam also returned a bill. While returning the bill the message is not rejection. But the President wants reconsideration of the issue in the Parliament for the decision. If Parliament passes again, the President has no option; he or she has to sign and accept the same. But while returning the bill to Parliament by the President for reconsideration the President anticipated a debate nationwide which ultimately compel the government to think over the decision again either for modification or giving it up. Here the President takes a judicious decision to make the Parliament to think again on the same matter. This exercise was initiated by R. Venkataraman.

By the actions of the President of India under the leadership of R. Venkataraman, it has been demonstrated that the Office of the President of India is not a rubber stamp and it established itself as a powerful think tank equally capable of examining options of decisions like Parliament. Through the scholastic approach of approving decisions of the government, scrutinizing the decisions of the government R. Venkataraman made the Office of President is crucial in upholding the constitutional values, principles, ethics and proprieties. The high tradition set-up by him was followed by his successors during the period of crisis. Both S.D. Sharma and K.R. Narayanan were not his followers but they were with their own standing. They followed R. Venkataraman as he evolved the framework in such a way that nobody can deviate from the basic principles.

His actions and his successor's actions during the period of crises demonstrated to the country and the world that leaders with impeccable character with intelligence will manage any kind of crisis in democracy. When we face such a moral crisis in governance we need people with upright character and intelligence as demonstrated by Ramasamy Venkataraman. His tract record from pre-independence period to the period of crisis proved strait, prudent, impact making value orientation with paramount national interest and he rose above party, region, caste and colour. He was always keeping high moral and intellectual tradition in his approach and action. Whichever position he held and occupied, he left an intelligible mark in that office to be followed by others. He is to be remembered forever not in a ritualistic way but by taking clue from his actions for our daily life to make our life meaningful and enriching.

REFERENCES

1. "Political Capitalism" was used by Max Weber and now it has been used and elaborated by the scholars by giving operational definition. It is a process of making wealth by using power fraudulently for the family, party and trust by the political leaders

and elected representatives. It happens in authoritarian form governments and now in third world democratic governments. It happens more so in globalised economy very fastly and massively. For more details see Ganev, V. "Preying on the state: Political Capitalism after Communism" Ph.D. Dissertation, Department of Political Science, University of Chicago, 1999.

2. In the Lok Pal drafting committee meeting the whole discussion is on to include the Prime Minister and Judges of the highest courts in the Lok Pal. In such a way people have lost faith in highest offices which have earned global reputation once during the Gandhi-Nehru era.
3. Rudolph and Rudolph, "Redoing the constitutional design: From an interventionist to a regulatory state" in Atul Kohli (ed.) *The Success of India's Democracy*, Cambridge: Cambridge University Press, 2001.
4. Middle class which I am referring here had sensitized the people through their opinion about politics, governance and administration over a period of time. Now the same middle class is working for a different cause and enjoying the fruit of the globalization initiatives without discharging their roles and responsibilities. Only a fraction of the expanding middle class is still working for sensitizing people and working with poor and for poor.
5. Venkataraman R., *My Presidential Years*, New Delhi: Harper Collins, 1995. p. 405.
6. When BJP was in power, there was an initiative to review the Constitution of India and thereby there was a design to shift the mode of governance from Parliamentary form of governance to Presidential form of governance. This idea was mooted with an objective of bringing stability to government in the context of hung Parliament. But K.R. Narayanan by following the tradition of R. Venkataraman assertively with foresightedness made it very clear that accountability is foremost credential for any government than stability. This statement in the Golden Jubilee Celebration of India's Independence created a lengthy debate among the public. *Mainstream*, Feb., 12, 2000, p. 10.
7. The concept "transparency" was evolved and it has been made as an indicator of good governance according to the definition given by World Bank and UNDP. But R. Venkataraman made it a point to emphasise that it should be kept as an indicator in governance in the crisis hours.
8. R. Venkataraman, *My Presidential Years*, New Delhi: Harper Collins, 1995, p. 275.

VII

Accountability and Transparency in Development Activities at Grassroots

Introduction

In the complex and mystified governance and administrative process in India, poor and other marginalized groups cannot gain benefits but the rich, the educated elites and the middle class can gain much and make profit. In a democracy both the rich and the poor have to be protected. If any one segment is deprived, they would not allow democracy to function smoothly. The delivery of services and goods by the departments of government to the poor and the marginalized is ineffective and not to the satisfaction of the stakeholders. As a result large scale corruption is involved in development activities. Even in the case of corruption the poor are the victims. Hence, the talk on transparency and accountability on the part of government and administration is gaining currency with an objective of serving the people better and more particularly serving the poor effectively. Accountability is the basic requirement of governance and it cannot be ensured without transparency. Accountability and transparency go hand in hand. Good governance is being talked of in the context of bad governance due to corruption[1]. No administration can survive without accountability. It appears to be simple and achievable but in reality it is not so as it is a complex phenomenon. Normally, in Public Administration parlance it is an internal mechanism and internal organizational issue. The whole concentration is on internal matters rather than on external ones and more particularly on the impact of administration and governance. It is normally construed as consonance between policy options of the top and implementation of the bottom[2]. In many countries people faced problems in getting their goods and services from the government and as a result the World Bank came out with prescriptions and it evolved a formula for micro accountability and macro accountability from the external perspective namely the implications of the governance on the people. By building the capacity of the institutions a sound development management principle has been evolved. Removing the possibility of capturing the benefits by the socially powerful is an yet another principle incorporated in the framework of governance. Almost all the Third World countries had inherited the colonial administrative model which enabled the dominant class and caste to exploit the people and the accountability enforcing institutions namely Legislative and Judiciary are distant and complex and as a result fail to create a conducive climate for ensuring accountability. Hence, accountability to people is being discussed as an imperative for good governance. But the accountability which we argue about is not the accountability which is in practice now in Governance and Administration in the traditional sense of Public Administration. Accountability which is in practice today is upward accountability. It means accountable and responsible to the superior officers and authorities. The Colonial Administration developed a mechanism which was responsive and responsible to the masters. The masters were not people during the British Rule. Hence, accountability is built up towards the higher ups. But after Independence the masters are the citizens of India. So the accountability has to be reversed. It was not done so far. Hence, the delivery of services is poor and there is large scale corruption in the development sector. Upward accountability is in tact and yet the administration cannot deliver the goods to the level of expectation of the poor and the same is susceptible to corruption. In a democratic government administration is accountable to the people. They should be responsible and responsive to the people. At present such a kind of downward accountability is not in vogue. Therefore, everyone talks about an alternative paradigm of governance and administration whereby downward accountability is to be ensured and thereby government and administration is made accountable to the people. It is to be ensured through a process of audit done by the people. To bring about such a kind of micro accountability, decentralisation is initiated formally through the Constitution[3]. But it is yet to emerge as an institution of governance with autonomy in decision making and resource spending. It is still in the hostile surrounding of centralized administration and inequitable resource allocation and distribution[4]. Whatever may be the difficulties, the new dispensation has to be used profitably for the people and more particularly for the poor. Thus social audit is the tool and mechanism by which downward accountability can be ensured and maintained.

The transparency and the downward accountability in administration depends on a number of factors of which the physical distance between the people and the government departments and the availability of information to the people to the level of understanding of the stakeholders from the departments are primary. Further, the proactive disclosure of information about the roles and responsibilities of the departments is yet another basic factor to make the stakeholder have an eye and hold over the departments. Further, citizens should have legitimate space to do the audit collectively in the realm of governance and administration. This chapter tries to analyse the above issue from the experience of the functioning of the Gram Panchayats with regard to the services rendered to the people by the departments of Government of Tamil Nadu. In this regard a study was conducted in twenty-seven districts in Tamil Nadu to assess the response of the stakeholders about the five important services done by the Panchayats and the departments of the State government by contacting 685 respondents in Tamil Nadu[5].

From the study conducted on the role of the Panchayats and the departments in ensuring delivery of goods and services, it is inferred that apart from the role Panchayats have to fulfil, the Panchayats could not establish their hold over the departments of government for ensuring effective and efficient delivery of services[6]. People are sensitive on certain services which are ensured effectively to the people[7]. The question here is why Panchayats could not establish their hold over the government departments even though the Panchayats have legitimate powers to ensure service delivery by the government departments to the people. To analyse the issue we can take a case of administration from Tamil Nadu. Accountability is primarily a question of distance between the people and the government. The distance is of two types. One is physical and the other one is informational.

Physical Distance

The Government of Tamil Nadu has forty-two (42) departments spreading their wings to serve the people from the State Secretariat to their field office through a layer of hierarchy. From the State Secretariat to the field office there are four layered arrangements. First comes the Secretary in the Secretariat for each and every department heading the same for designing policies and held responsible for implementing the decisions and policies once approved in authoritative bodies. Next to the Secretary, the Director is yet another State level officer for each and every department carrying out activities. Down below there is the State, a district level officer for each department functioning and directing the field offices to carry out the activities. Further down, an intermediate office between the district and the field office is functioning. Finally, there is the field office covering certain geographical areas to carry out the activities. The structure is not uniform in all the departments. Coverage of areas varies from department to department. It is to be noted here that offices and officials are functioning at four levels above the field office to carry out the activities on the ground. Level of qualification, functional efficiency and professionalism is higher in the State level and regional level intermediate level offices. At the field level one will find poor capacity, capability and professionalism.

But the Panchayati Raj System in Tamil Nadu provides opportunity for the people to participate in the process of governance by which the stakeholders can inspect, supervise the activities of the departments of government and advise suitably for effective implementation of schemes and efficient delivery of services[8]. The statutory committees can perform the function of supervising the activities of the Government Departments and make a report about it and place it before the Gram Sabha for examination and recommendation for remedial action. The new Panchayati Raj System has got rich potential to transform the rural society in terms of their social, economic and political dynamics[9]. In Gram Sabha meetings all the schemes of the departments have to be disseminated for which proactively the departments have to give details of their schemes and programmes. More particularly how much of resources are available with the departments and who is handling the schemes are to be disclosed. The Gram Panchayat Presidents and the committee members have to get the details from the departments and they are to be disseminated to the people[10]. But in reality the schemes implemented directly by the Panchayats are known to the people but the schemes and programmes implemented by the departments of both governments are not known to the people. It is because the Gram Panchayats are far away from the governments' departments. While assessing the physical distance one can easily gauge the distance between the departments of Central Government and the community which is long. Next to the Central Government, the State Government departments are far away from the communities. The distance varies from department to department. One department in the field will cover the geographical area of four Gram Panchayats or five revenue villages but the other departments' coverage areas may vary. It depends on the volume of work to be carried out by the departments. Physical distance prevents the communities from establishing hold over the departments. Moreover, from the colonial days the departments of the government have created the impression that the departments are controlling masters and the people have to obey the order of the departments. This perception continues even today. Establishing the hold over the departments by the stakeholders is unacceptable to the officials working in the departments. To overcome this barrier the Panchayat needs information about the activities, responsibilities and the volume of resources with which they are functioning in a given geographical area to have its hold over the departments. The barrier of distance could be overcome by transferring the information about the activities of the departments to the communities through Panchayats either by electronic mode or by mailing the details through post as peoples' charter. By proactive disclosure of information about the activities of the departments the community will get the details and claim their entitlements. Table 7.1 gives the picture of the official arrangements in hierarchy for functioning and delivery of services of all the departments. The Panchayati Raj and the Rural Development is the only department that maintains close link with the communities. The distance between the communities and the Panchayati Raj is close. All other departments

Table 7.1: Organization Structure of Various Departments

S. No.	*Name of the Department*	*State Level Officer*	*District Level Officer*	*Intermediate Level Officer*	*Field Level Officer*	*Coverage of the Areas*
1	2	3	4	5	6	7
1.	Agriculture	Secretary Director	Joint Director	Agri. Development Officer	Asst. Agriculture Officer	S/He represents more than one Panchayat
2.	Animal Husbandry	Secretary Director	Joint Director	Asst. Director (AH)	Veterinary Asst. Surgeon	S/He represents more than one Panchayat
3.	Health	Secretary Director	Joint Director	Block Level Medical Officer	Medical Officer	S/He represents more than one Panchayat
4.	Rural Development	Secretary Commissioner	Collector / Project Officer	Block Development Officer	Panchayat Assistant	At every Gram Panchayat
5.	Revenue	Secretary Commissioner	Collector / District Revenue Officer	Tahsildar	Village Administrative Officer	S/He represents more than one Panchayat
6.	Social Welfare	Secretary Director	District Social Welfare Officer	Executive Officer (SW)	Rural Welfare Officer (W)	S/He represents more than one Panchayat
7.	Co–operative	Secretary Registrar	Joint Registrar	Deputy Registrar / CSR	Secretary (PACB)	S/He represents more than one Panchayat
8.	Education	Secretary Director	Chief Educational Officer / District Elementary Educational Officer, Regional Director	Asst. Elementary, Educational Officer, Joint Director	Teachers in the schools and colleges	Covering the area of small village to a region
9.	Police	Secretary Director General of Police	Superintendent of Police	Circle Inspector	Sub-Inspector	S/He represents more than one Panchayat

Table 7.1 (*Contd.*)

S. No.	Name of the Department	State Level Officer	District Level Officer	Intermediate Level Officer	Field Level Officer	Coverage of the Areas
1	2	3	4	5	6	7
10.	Adi Dravidar Welfare	Secretary Director	Collector / District Adi Dravidar Welfare Officer	Tahsildar	Deputy Block Development Officer (ADW) /VAO	S/He represents more than one Panchayat
11.	District Backward Class Welfare	Secretary Director	Collector / District Backward Class Welfare Officer	Tahsildar	Deputy Block Development Officer (ADW) /VAO	S/He represents more than one Panchayat
12.	Fisheries	Secretary Director	Asst. Director	Inspector	—	S/He represents more than one Panchayat
13.	Forest	Secretary Principle Conservator of Forest	District Forest Officer	Ranger	Forest Officer	S/He represents more than one Panchayat
14.	Registration	Secretary Inspector General of Registration	District Registrar	Sub-Registrar	—	S/He represents more than one Panchayat
15.	Highways	Secretary Chief Engineer	Superintendent Engineer	Divisional Engineer	Asst. Engineer	S/He represents more than one Panchayat
16.	Transport	Secretary Commissioner of Transport	Regional Transport Officer	Break Inspector	—	S/He represents more than one Panchayat
17.	Treasury	Secretary Director	Treasury Officer	Sub Treasury Officer	—	S/He represents more than one Panchayat
18.	Rehabilitation	Secretary Commissioner	DRRO	—	—	S/He represents more than one Panchayat

Table 7.1 *(Contd.)*

S. No.	Name of the Department	State Level Officer	District Level Officer	Intermediate Level Officer	Field Level Officer	Coverage of the Areas
1	2	3	4	5	6	7
19.	Statistics	Secretary Director	Regional Director / Asst. Director	Statistical Inspector	Asst. Statistical Investigator	S/He represents more than one Panchayat
20.	Tourism	Secretary Director	Tourism Officer	—	—	S/He represents more than one Panchayat
21.	Employment	Secretary Director	District Employment Officer	—	—	S/He represents more than one Panchayat
22.	Public Library	Secretary Director	District Public Librarian	Inspector of Librarian	Village Librarian	S/He represents more than one Panchayat
23.	Labour	Secretary Chief Inspector of Labour	Asst. Director	Labour Inspector	—	S/He represents more than one Panchayat
24.	Local Fund Auditor	Secretary Director	Regional Director / Asst. Director	Inspector	Auditor	S/He represents more than one Panchayat
25.	Fire Service	Secretary Director	District Fire Service	Station Fire Officer	—	S/He represents more than one Panchayat
26.	Small Savings	Secretary Director	Collector / PA (SS)	Block Development Officer	Deputy Block Development Officer (SS)	S/He represents more than one Panchayat
27.	Hindu Religious and Charitable Endowment	Secretary Commissioner	Joint Commissioner	—	Executive Officer (Temple)	S/He represents more than one Panchayat
28.	Civil Supplies	Secretary Commissioner	Collector/District Supply Officer	Taluk Supply Officer	Revenue Inspector / Village Administrative Officer	S/He represents more than one Panchayat

Table 7.1 (*Contd.*)

S. No.	*Name of the Department*	*State Level Officer*	*District Level Officer*	*Intermediate Level Officer*	*Field Level Officer*	*Coverage of the Areas*
1	2	3	4	5	6	7
29.	Environment and Pollution Control Board	Secretary Director	Executive Engineer	Inspector	—	S/He represents more than one Panchayat
30.	Sports	Secretary Director	District Sports Officer	—	—	S/He represents more than one Panchayat
31.	Energy	Secretary Managing Director	Deputy General Manager	Block Development Officer	Deputy Block Development Officer (ADW)	S/He represents more than one Panchayat
32.	Housing and Urban Development	Secretary Director	Executive Engineer	—	—	S/He represents more than one Panchayat
33.	Commercial Taxes	Secretary Commissioner	Commercial Tax Officer	Dist. Commercial Tax Officer / Asst. Commercial Tax Officer	—	S/He represents more than one Panchayat
34.	PWD	Secretary Chief Engineer	Superintendent Engineer	Divisional Engineer	Asst. Engineer	S/He represents more than one Panchayat
35.	Handlooms	Secretary Director	Asst. Director	Inspector	Manager	S/He represents more than one Panchayat
36.	Khadi & Village Industry	Secretary Director	Asst. Director	Khadi Inspector	Manager	S/He represents more than one Panchayat
37.	Public & Information	Secretary Director	Public Relations Officer	Block Development Officer	Deputy Block Development Officer (SS)	S/He represents more than one Panchayat

Table 7.1 (*Contd.*)

S. No.	*Name of the Department*	*State Level Officer*	*District Level Officer*	*Intermediate Level Officer*	*Field Level Officer*	*Coverage of the Areas*
1	2	3	4	5	6	7
38.	Mines	Secretary Director	Asst. Director	Tahsildar	Revenue Inspector / Village Administrative Officer	S/He represents more than one Panchayat
39.	Tamilnadu Women Development Corporation	Secretary Managing Director	Collector / Project Officer	Block Development Officer	Deputy Block Development Officer (SS)	S/He represents more than one Panchayat
40.	Social Security Department	Secretary Commissioner	Collector / Special Deputy Collector	Tahsildar	Revenue Inspector / Village Administrative Officer	S/He represents more than one Panchayat
41.	Tamil Development	Secretary Director	Asst. Director	—	—	—
42.	Survey	Secretary Director	Asst. Director	Thasildar	Firka Surveyor	—

Source: Computed from the website of Government of Tamil Nadu

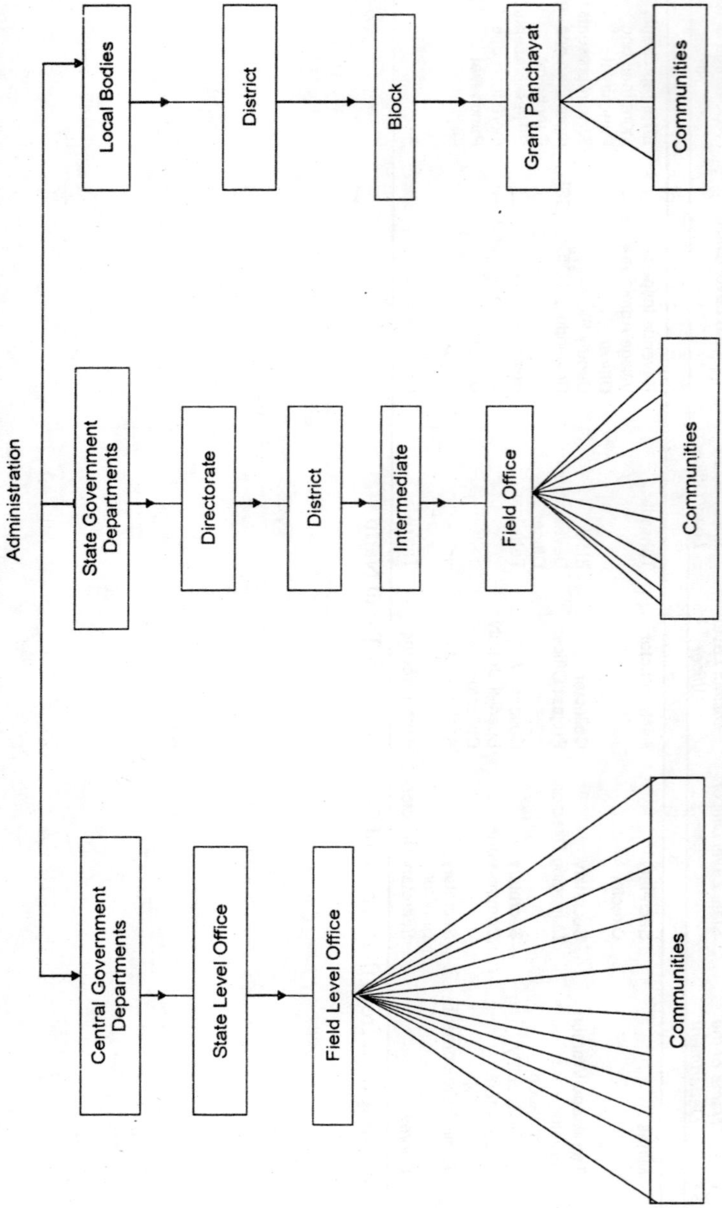

Fig. 7.1 Administration

are far away from the communities. The distance varies from department to department.

Table 7.2: Governance Structure

<table>
<tr><th>S. No.</th><th>Governments</th><th>Coverage</th><th>Governing Body</th><th>Strength</th><th colspan="2">Powers</th></tr>
<tr><td>1.</td><td>Federal Government (or) Central Government</td><td>Whole Country</td><td>Lok Sabha
Rajya Sabha</td><td>543
242</td><td>97 subjects under Central list in the Constitution</td><td rowspan="2">(47 subjects in concurrent list for both Centre and State)</td></tr>
<tr><td>2.</td><td>State Government or Provincial Government</td><td>Entire province</td><td>Legislative Assembly
Legislative Council</td><td>4160 (covering all the states)</td><td>66 subjects in the State list of the Constitution</td></tr>
<tr><td>3.</td><td>Local Government or Local Body</td><td>Entire District</td><td>Three tiers</td><td>30 million</td><td colspan="2">29 subjects (Rural Local Bodies)
18 subjects (Urban Local Bodies)
Under 11th and 12th Schedule respectively</td></tr>
</table>

Source: Computed.

Panchayats live in each and every village. The other departments do not have such a kind of structure close to the people or community. The distance between the people and the departments is so wide. Further, the departments are having 430 development schemes meant for the people. But these scheme details and the eligibility conditions are not known to the people. Some of the departments are not having any office down below the district. To avail of the government schemes people have to locate the office first and to get the details of the schemes and to apply for it and to avail of the same. Unless the stakeholder is an informed person, it is always a difficult job. Further, it involves a cost also. Further, the stakeholder should have resources to spend. It is proved beyond doubt that it is not possible for the poor to do so. Their middle men enter and work as development brokers. Thus, the government departments are far away from the stakeholders. One cannot expect territorial uniformity among the departments but the departments can proactively reach out to the communities by providing needed information. But it is not happening. Getting information is the difficult task. If any department is proactively discharging information to the public about its activities, one can assume that there is no large scale corruption in the department.

Information Distance

For ensuring accountability, proactive disclosure of information is an imperative need. Further, the information about the roles and responsibilities of each and every department has to be provided in the language of the people instead of the language of the clerks and officials for easy understanding and claim. While giving the details of the services and goods delivered by the departments, the point at which they are delivered, and the officer responsible to deliver the same should also be disclosed. More particularly to whom the services are to be delivered and to whom the services should not be delivered should be spelt out[11]. While giving information relating to the services the details of the costs in terms of administration and costs of programmes and schemes have to be clearly mentioned so that the beneficiaries understand the cost of delivery. The information should be always online and they could be drawn upon at any point of time. Since changes are dynamic, the information which is online should be updated. Information, both generic and specific, should be available for reference. In the same way, information conversion has to take place contextually. Thus, the flow of information should be ensured from the Federal Government's highest decision making units namely the Ministries to the lowest decision making units the Gram Sabhas. The computing systems of the two ends one at the Ministry and the other at the Gram Panchayats have to be connected. In the flow process needed conversions have to be done at every point or unit of governance and administration. For example, if the Health Ministry is giving information relating to allocation of resources to schemes, it is necessary that when information comes to a State along with the allocation made to the particular State, information about the whole allocation to all the States should be given. In the same way, when it comes to the district from the State, the allocation to the specific district along with the break-up details of the allocation made to all the districts should be given. Information relating to the allocation of resources up to Gram

Panchayat should be given. If all informations reach the community, the citizens will be in a position to claim it. Otherwise they will be at the mercy of the officials. In the absence of information, citizens cannot claim their entitlements but they can submit only petitions. On many occasions an information gap persists between the community and the departments[12]. Information has to be regarded as power. The information gap has to be bridged and the government departments have to be activated to disclose information proactively. For information disclosure and dissemination, incentives and disincentives have to be introduced. Disclosing information in Government and administration is always complex. Private enterprise thrives on information disclosure and supply while government fails in disclosing information. People need packaged information for their use. General information will be of no use to them. For their claims they need information pertinent to them. Thus, packaging information is the need of the hour. Information packaging has to be done at every level for which enabling conditions have to be created. At every point of governance and administration from the Central Government to the Gram Panchayat, information storage facility has to be created. At every unit information about the services and goods has to be stored. For precise decision making, decision execution, impact evaluation information precision is essential.

The departments at present are not disclosing proactively the details of the services they are rendering to the people. After the passing of the Right to Information Act, the Government Departments are giving information on demand by collecting money. How many of the poor will pay money to get information? There is no information flow to the stakeholders relating to the resource allocation for programme activities. There is yet another area where one has to clearly get to know the cost of programmes delivered by offices and cost of administration. Precise information about the programmes, resources available for the programmes, who executes the programme and where it is being delivered are to be made known to the stakeholders. In the absence of the above, people cannot claim and demand their entitlements. As a result people submit petitions submissively to the officials. While submitting petitions people are treated as beneficiaries and petitioners thereby are disempowered. Now to reverse the trend a new governance arrangement has been created. In the new dispensation all the departments which are working at the grassroots have to work with the Gram Panchayats. By giving the full details about the schemes and programmes the departments are implementing in the given Gram Panchayat area and the Gram Panchayat has to disseminate the information to the people through the Gram Sabha. But there is a provision in the Gram Sabha to conduct social audit and it can be facilitated by the committees created in Gram Panchayats[13]. Legitimately the Panchayats can perform those audits. In the absence of information how can the committees in Gram Panchayat perform the social audit? The Government of Tamil Nadu has published a document containing the schemes and programmes of the forty-two departments. Totally there are about 430 welfare schemes[14]. But these informations are generic. Even these documents have not reached the Panchayats. They are all with officials of the departments. There is no packaged information to meet the need of the community. Packaged information refers here to the allocation of resources for implementation of schemes and programmes for a given geographical area. When information comes to the district, district-wise allocation should be given. If it comes to the Block, block-wise allocation has to be given. All development related informations has to be given proactively to the citizens for their understanding and claim. There is no uniform structure in all the departments from the State Headquarters to the field office as the Panchayat administrative structure. In order to achieve better delivery of services the structure has to be defined and linked with Gram Panchayats to ensure accountability. Information has to be supplied by the government to the Gram Panchayat needed to the Gram Panchayat area for dissemination in the Gram Sabha. By doing so the government departments can move further towards the people. By getting the details from the Departments people can claim their entitlemtns. To claim their entitlements people will participate in Gram Sabha meeting. Even while supplying peoples' charter[15] people have not participated in the Gram Sabha meeting. One cannot expect that all the poor can participate in the process of governance through the Gram Sabha. Further, when the poor are concentrating much of their time on their livelihood where will they find time to discharge the responsibilities of citizenship[16]? The struggle of the poor for their basic minimum needs will defray from the mainstream role of the citizens. To narrow down the gap in distance both physical and informational distance between the departments of the government and the people, providing precise and needed information to the people about the schemes and programmes proactively by the departments of Governments is the need of the hour. Information has to be packaged at every level of governance. To perform the above task reform has to be initiated in administration at the grassroots.

On three aspects reform initiatives have to be taken in administration at the grassroots. They are structural, procedural and behavioural and these aspects have to be considered seriously. At the bottom all service delivery agencies, whether the departments of government or autonomous agencies, have to work together or a synergy has to be created through the Gram Panchayats for effective service delivery. Procedural reforms have to be introduced at the lowest level of administration. The cumbersome administrative procedures have to be simplified to enable ordinary citizens to participate in the process of governance and administration. In the same way, behavioural changes have to be brought about in the staff of the grassroots institutions. The bureaucracy at the bottom are not professionally equipped, yet their behaviour trait is dominant, which prevents the people from participation in governance and administration. The culture of ruling which has been perpetuated has to be changed. They should feel that they are the employees of the people. They never feel that they are responsive and responsible to the stakeholders. Rather they feel that they are responsible to their superiors. The culture of treating the people as beneficiaries and petitioners has to change. People should feel that the rule of law is in practice and it can be enforced. In such a way behavioural trait of the functionaries working at grassroots has to be created.

The administrative arrangement at the grassroots at present has a volley of problems which demotivates the officials to perform their duties and responsibilities as professionals. The Departments of the government have their own in-built weakness and they are not in a position to act proactively as they have the following problems:

Problems in Administration

- Top heavy Bottom slim.

- Top professionalism Bottom *ad hoc* and non-professionals.
- Top periodic skill upgradation bottom no training in service.
- No management of Human Resource Information System.
- No Manpower planning.
- No motivation on the part of the people in service.
- Corruption demotivates.
- Role Ambiguity.
- Inadequate job description.
- Over centralization.
- No synergy among the departments.
- No impact assessment only action assessment.
- Complicated Administrative procedures.
- No Model Code of Conduct for Elected Representatives of the people[17].

Fund Flow

Tracking fund flow is a major task for every development worker. Wherefrom money comes, how much resource comes, through what channel it comes, when it comes, who handles it, how s/he handles it, where it is being spent, of them how much is programme cost and how much is administrative cost are the needed information for the public to ensure accountability and transparency. The following diagram is self-explanatory.

By tracking the financial flow one can easily locate where money flows and where money is stuck up, wherefrom leakage takes place, how it takes place. By getting those informations, one can assess whether the departments are worthy of their spending. One can easily trace whether the departments are spending more on delivery or on administration. By doing so irrelevant structures can be removed and alternatives can be found out. There are many departments eating huge cost as administrative which deliver poor services. They can be easily located and a remedy could be found out. It is possible only by getting information on programme and administrative costs. Tracking development finance at grassroots is not an easy task. It needs a complex and cumbersome exercise as the system itself is complex and cumbersome. There are certain agencies working in this domain over a period of two decades[18]. At present there is no such information flow either at the Central level or at the State level.

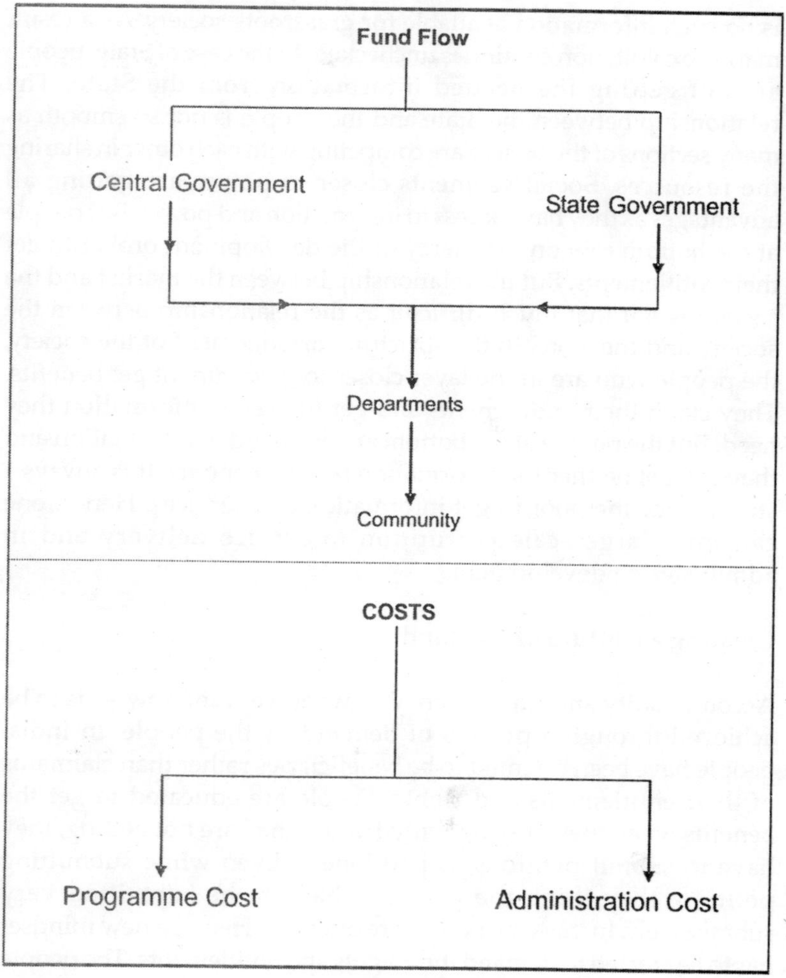

Figure 7.2: Flow of Fund

In a market driven society, the community has to manage both the State and the market for which they need information. Market provides information to the consumers and so the whole information system works for the advantage of the market. The citizens are in need of more information about the other side of the market which is not available. Who will provide such information to the people? It is the civil society and the State that should give the information about he potentials and threats of the market. But in practice, there is no such information available for grassroots society. As a result market exploitation continues unchecked. In the case of State, people are not getting the needed information from the State. The relationship between the State and the people is not so smooth as many sections of the society are competing with each other in sharing the resources. Social segments closer to power are getting all advantages as they have access to information and power. But people at the bottom rely on the mercy of the development broker to get their entitlements. But the relationship between the market and the society is not that much difficult as the relationship between the society and the State. In the structural arrangement of the society, the people who are in the layer closer to government get benefits. They claim their entitlements and get whatever information they need. But the people at the bottom are deprived of information and they can get neither the information nor the benefits. It is always a struggle for the poor to get information and services. Hence, one can infer large scale corruption in service delivery and in administering development.

Creating a Culture of Demand

Accountability and transparency — what we want now — is to be achieved through a process of demand by the people. In India, people have been oriented to be beneficiaries rather than claimants of their entitlements and rights. People are educated to get the benefits when they are distributed and if they are not getting, they have to submit petitions as petitioners. Even while submitting petition, they think the petitions have to be submitted very submissively. In this way people are oriented. Hence, a new mindset has to be created to demand their rights and entitlements. The people are to be oriented as honourable citizens with self-respect and pride and they should claim and demand their rights and entitlements. Totally a new orientation has to be given to the people.

The task is not so easy as people who are on the periphery are always in a disadvantaged position as their social, economic and cultural conditions have made them submissive. As a result, people who are marginalized have started celebrating poverty, enjoying poverty and adoring poverty. In such a way the poor have developed a mindset. People are happy to be beneficiaries as against citizens as citizenship carries responsibilities also. In our country we have Her Excellency the President of India, Honourable Prime Minister, Honourable Chief Minister, Honourable Members of Parliament and Legislatures and respected officials but the most humiliated and dishonoured citizens. We are in search of the Honourable citizen. This syndrome drives the people away from the government. To reverse this trend an alternative paradigm of governance, administration and development has to be evolved and they should be put into practice.

Accountability and People's Participation

The new demand for accountability and transparency is in the broader agenda of good governance. Accountability can be ensured only by the participation of the citizens in the decision making process. Participation as right and citizenship is the responsibility for collective benefits under communitarian thought. In this framework, development is a right. It is to be claimed. To make such a claim the claimant people should have certain prerequisite. People should have the needed time and perspective to participate in governance. On most occasions the poor cannot find time to participate in the process of governance. They are totally involved in their livelihood activities. Their struggle with poverty prevents them from performing their duty as citizens. That is why a school of thought considered citizenship a status[19]. This status cannot be enjoyed by all. In the same way the new dispensation "liberalization' brings an argument that the citizens have to behave as consumers and as a result citizen right has no place. Moreover, it is expected that services are provided as commodities are sold in the market by fixing prices. What we look at as services here is the rights of the citizens[20]. There are certain services to be provided by the government not on payment. The question we face here is that which of the services are to be delivered to the people free of cost? To deliver such services and to claim such services by the people as rights accountability is talked about. To perform the above tasks, people have to be mobilized for political and developmental tasks. By doing so the beneficiaries and petitioners can be made into social citizens.

Conclusion

Accountability, transparency, proactive disclosure of information about services and goods delivered by the agencies, participation of people in the process of governance and administration, empowerment of the poor and the marginalized, democratization and decentralisation are the factors repeatedly discussed in the new paradigm of good governance in the context of globalisation of economy. It is obvious from the arguments of the scholars and administrators that the existing structure of administration, procedures and practices of the same and behaviour of the grassroots bureaucracy are the barriers for the effective and efficient delivery of services. More particularly the denial of information and the information gap between the community and the service agencies, especially the service departments, cause poor delivery of services. Information denial is to be considered denial of rights. But proactive disclosure of information is not happening in our administrative and governance system. Hence, the existing exploitative, dominant corruption ridden administrative system continues to prevail. To reform the administrative system steps are suggested in three dimensions, namely reforming the structure, procedures and behaviours of the whole system. To enable the community to participate in the process of governance as a right and to claim their entitlement as rights reforms have to be initiated. To move further in this direction the administrative system has to be looked at from the perspective of distance between the people and the administrative system. It is found out that the physical distance between the community and the government departments vary from department to department. There is no synergy between and among the departments in delivering the services to the community. The Rural Development and the Panchayati Raj are the only departments maintaining close linkage with the community and the other sectoral departments are not having such a relationship. The departments never maintain their linkages with the Panchayat institutions to connect themselves with communities. There is no sign of proactive disclosure. Even while information is sought under the RTI they are not provided as the officials know the loopholes in the RTI Act of Tamil Nadu. But the Panchayat Act provides an opportunity for the people to command the departments of government to provide information about their roles and responsibilities. The community has got powers to supervise and evaluate the performance of the departments. But the community is not empowered and encouraged to do so. The empowered elites have established their connectivity with the departments but the poor do not have such a kind of connectivity. Further, the information system created in the administrative system is complex and vague and is not usable. An information system has to be created and it is to be packaged to the requirement of the community. Administrative procedures have to be simplified and not complicated. The behaviour of the officials has to be changed. They are not doing charity to the people. They are discharging their responsibilities. Further, the channels through which resources flow have to be identified and they are to be disseminated to the stakeholders at the grassroots as institutional structures are created through the Constitution. Thus, actions from above and from below have to be initiated. Building the capacity of the leaders, mobilizing people for participation and proactive disclosure of relevant informations are the need of the hour.

REFERENCES

1. World Bank, *Governance and Development,* Washington DC: World Bank, 1992, p. 9.
2. Bidyut Chakrabarty and Mohit Bhattacharya (eds.), *The Governance Discourse: A Reader* New Delhi: Oxford University Press, 2008, p. 33.
3. World Bank, *The World Development Report 1999 – 2000, Vol. I* Washington DC: World Bank, 2000, p. 19.
4. Bidyut Chakrabarty and Mohit Bhattacharya (eds.) *Ibid.* p. 34.
5. The Catalyst Trust, *Citizens, Audit of Basic Services in Tamil Nadu* Chennai: The Catalyst Trust, 2008.
6. The Catalyst Trust, 2008, *Ibid.*
7. G. Palanithurai and V. Ragupathy, *Functional Efficiency of Gram Sabha in Tamil Nadu* New Delhi: Concept Publishing Company Pvt. Ltd., 2006.
8. G. Palanithurai, K. Vallinayagam, N.S. Chidambaram, K. Subramaniam, *Hand Book of Panchayati Raj Administration (Tamil Nadu),* New Delhi: Concept Publishing Company Pvt. Ltd., 2006.
9. G. Palanithurai, *Role and Responsibilities of Gram Sabha* (in Tamil) Chennai: New Century Book House, 2006.
10. G. Palanithurai, "Panchayats: Relevance Potentials and Demonstrations" in (Ed.) Yatindra Singh Sisodia, *Indians Development Scenario: Challenges and Prospects,* New Delhi: Rauht Publications, 2009.

11. Bidyut Chakrabarty and Mohit Bhattacharya (eds.). *Administrative Change and Innovation: A Reader,* New Delhi: Oxford University Press, 2005, p. 57.
12. G. Palanithurai, "Containing Corruption at Grassroots" Paper presented in International Policy Dialogue from 1st to 3rd October, 2009 at Senegal.
13. G. Palanithurai, *Committee System in Gram Panchayat (in Tamil),* New Century Book House, 2006.
14. Chief Ministers Special Cell, *Welfare Schemes of the Government of Tamil Nadu,* Chennai: Government of Tamil Nadu, 2007.
15. Many Departments have printed people's charter but they are not distributed. Wherever they are distributed, the information available in the people's charter are generic but not specific.
16. A detailed analysis of the linkage between poverty and fulfilling citizenship roles and responsibilities is found in Naila Kabeer with Ariful Hag Kabir "*Citizenship Narratives in the Absence of Good Governance: Voice of the Working Poor in Bangladesh*" IDS working paper, 2009.
17. Rajesh Singh, "Performance Impediments in Government: Some Suggestions for Reform", *The Indian Journal of Public Administration* Vol. LV., No. 2 (April–June, 2009), pp. 269–274.
18. For more details see the website of centre for budget and policy studies www.cbps.in
19. An Oldfield, *Citizenship and Community: Civic Republicanism and the Modern World,* London: Routledge, 1990.
20. D. Prior, J. Stewart and K. Walsh, *Citizenship, Rights and Community Participation* London: Pitman, 1995.

VIII

Role of ICT in Scientific Data Generation and Management at the Grassroots

Introduction

I have been involving myself in doing research at micro level on many of the social development issues and on occasions, I have approached many of the government offices for data collection apart from collecting data from the field. What I found in all offices was that they maintain progress reports which do not reflect the real data. When I ask the question about the difference between the progress report and the field reality, the officials tend to confess that there would not be any match at all. Only a few offices maintain that the progress reports reflect the reality. They also confess that there may be difference but not too much. Further, in many of the reports I found terms such as (more or less, around and approximately) while indicating the trend. It is obvious that, we have lost scientific precision in maintaining data. As a result, what we find is the mismatch between the decision, allocation of resources and the needs of the stakeholders. We spend huge money for which there is no need and by which we end up wasting money.

Further, the planning at micro level, which is for the Gram Panchayat level we sought data from the Panchayats as well as from many government departments. The Panchayats replied that they have not collected data. Government Departments informed us that they have the progress report of the activities carried out by their departments of the schemes given by the government where one can get data if they rely on them, but they cannot be disaggregated to the level of the Gram Panchayats. All Government

Departments have lowest units of their administration. But they are not co-terminus with Panchayat areas. Each department unit has its own geographical jurisdiction. Government Departments are also collecting data on demand from above for proposal preparation to seek funding.

Even these departments are not scientific systems of maintaining data. They generate data as and when they require. They also collect primary data from the field. But they are not validated. As and when they require data, they go to the field and collect the necessary data. The collected data are not reliable. They are with the government departments. Further, they are not updated periodically. At the lowest level there is no sense or sensitivity among the officials on the importance of data. There is yet another set of data available in Census and on many of the occasions they do not reflect the reality at micro level. Even the Census data are not updated. One has to wait for ten years. In the meanwhile one will find enormous reports of various kinds with the data support contradicting each other's observations. This kind of trivialities is due to the absence of sensitivity on data management at grassroots.

Data is fundamental for decision making, policy making, and resource allocation and for that matter anything which we want to do. Irrespective of the level of operation whether it is micro or macro data is essential and imperative. Further, precision of data are more important. In all aspects of the society data have to be generated, validated and maintained scientifically from Gram Panchayat at the bottom to the Federal Government at New Delhi for all kinds of decisions, programmes and resource allocations. In India data generations at the field level is not sound, and they are not maintained scientifically. Moreover, there is no systematic generation of data done at grassroots in an integrated manner. All data generation activities are *ad hoc,* occasional, need based and unscientific. People who are all involved in data generation for government departments at the grassroots are not well trained in data generation as professionals. Hence, the data generated by the agencies mostly by the Departments of government at the grassroots are not scientific and periodical and yet they are the only reliable database for decision making at different levels of government. Faulty decisions are made because of the unscientific data support provided to the decision making process by the grassroots agencies. Further, the data generated by the researchers for specific purposes contradict the database generated by the government departments. It is to be noted that for all vital matters data are compiled from district data pool. The data generated and compiled at the district level are not considered to be the best and scientific. Down below the district level there is no disaggregated scientific database. As a result, for any reliable decision making, data generated at the district level should not be considered as scientific and dynamic. And yet there is no alternative. Hence, for all decision making we rely on the data obtained from the District Administration. There is no such concept of data management of all aspects of economy, society and development for decision making at grassroots. At the village level, and at the Block level there is no break-up of data on any aspect. The District is considered as a unit. Variations within district cannot be captured; variations within Block cannot be explained. Each department has its own way of keeping the data and each department has its own geographical area of coverage. Hence, one cannot get data relating to school-going children in a Gram Panchayat area, anemia affected women in Gram Panchayat area and likewise all data in the geographical area of Block Panchayat. As the departments function as per their own geographical area, desegregating the data is a difficult task. After the establishment of Local Bodies as units of governance after passing of the 73rd and 74th Amendments to the Constitution of India, the decision making takes place down below the district. Without proper data how will they make decisions?. It is a moot question.

Data collection is a science and it is an art also. How precisely data are collected and accordingly decisions can be made. Decision makers fail to arrive at a exact decision and fail to solve the problem as they do not have exact data. Down below the district level in all offices, they are not maintaining data. They keep only progress report and beyond that they do not know the value of scientific data. To illustrate this I can quote an incident. When I was involved in preparing a report for an international agency, I requested the Health Department to supply me the data relating to anemia affected women, adolescent girls and school-going children affected due to malnutrition, hamlet-wise or Gram Panchayat-wise. First they said that they have only progress report whereby what they have done and what they have achieved were provided in this regard. Secondly, there is no break-up for hamlets or Gram

Panchayat area. The lowest unit in the Health Department is functioning on population basis.

Sometimes a village nurse will look after two Gram Panchayat area. In some cases three or four villages depending on the strength of the population. In the same way I got reply from the school education department. If a researcher wants data for each village or hamlet on all aspects to compare the status and position of each village in terms of economy, wealth, income, livelihood, health education, skill, infrastructure, one cannot get such data with such a break-up. At the district level as and when they need data they rely on the units of the Departments functioning at the lowest level. The lowest units supply the data available at that point of time and they are compiled and forwarded to the State level. Ration card is a very big issue today. Everywhere bogus card brings lots of problem and as a consequence, we have to sell out huge quantity of materials for the public distribution system. It is a criminal wastage of the public money. It is because of the non-maintenance of database at Panchayat levels. If there is a database at every Gram Panchayat, family-wise, all bogus ration cards will be eliminated very easily. If anyone wants to know the status of unskilled labourers in the spread of different Panchayat areas in a Block, status and position of the women and adolescent girls affected by anemia, status of children affected by malnutrition, agriculture productivity in villages, etc. It is not for getting details alone. No one was trained in the Department at the lowest unit on how to generate data, and how to update the data scientifically and how they are to be maintained. These are the big questions. Since data are generated by different agencies a lot of confusion, conflict and corruption occur in development management activities. We are in the Eleventh Five Year Plan with regard to data generation and data management, despite the pronouncement of the importance of data from the First Five Year Plan by Mahalanobis. There are statistical institutes and officers and yet data are not precise, up-to-date and scientific. To overcome the problems, Rajiv Gandhi had started a new exercise by creating District National Informatics Centres through ICT. But they could not reach out to the lowest unit of governance and administration for data generation and data management. After the establishment of local bodies, the basic data about the villages are to be in position. It is not so, as it should be even after the computerization. If what should we do now?

Long back, my friend from the management field argued with me that India has got all potential but unfortunately India does not have systems approach to make use of the potential available in India. He told me a formula and asked me to apply it. The formula is India + System = America in terms of wealth and income. India can do and achieve this. For this, we have to create a system.

Relevant data are not generated simultaneously. For example, the Labour Department collects data from the rural areas, at a point of time and it has to collect during the Agricultural season and the non-Agricultural season. Data relating to migration have to be collected only during the off season. In our Departmental Administrative System we never sensitize the officials about the importance of scientific generation and management of data. As a result, they will go to the field as and when they require data. The same data are being recycled continuously till they get direction from their higher officials for upgradation. There is another issue, i.e., data manipulation. If a State government wants to get more funds for poverty alleviation, the State government tends to manipulate data. This is the way, the Data Management System functions in India.

Statement of the Problem

At present there is no scientific data management system at Gram Panchayat level in India barring a few States. Hence, it is necessary to create a database in every Gram Panchayat by evolving software and by using the computers provided by the Government to the Panchayats. How are we going to implement this scheme?.

It is mandatory on the part of Gram Panchayat to develop a plan for each and every Gram Panchayat. In the same way, each and every Block Panchayat should have a plan. Town Panchayat, municipalities, cantonments, corporations, and district Panchayats should have plans. Without having a scientific database how do they develop a plan perspective for the development of the region. Data generation at every level is imperative. This exercise has to be started at least now.

Data have to be generated from the lowest unit of governance and administration to the highest level. Decisions are taken at Gram Panchayat level, at Block level, at district level, regional level, State level and federal level. Data have to be maintained in such a way that they can be used at any level. If data are maintained in disaggregated manner, problems and issues could be identified and they can be solved easily. Periodical updating of the data is yet another needed activity. Data have to be owned and for which responsibilities have to be fixed. All government departments are doing the exercise but they are not integrated. Hence, the exercise has to be started from Gram Panchayat level.

At every Gram Panchayat there is a computer. The computer can be used productively for the purpose of administration and providing services. For this, the clerk working in Panchayat, or even Gram Panchayat President or a woman from the Self Help Group can be trained in computer operation. Before data collection, a right mind set has to be created for the individuals who are going to carry out the activities relating to data generation. Computers have got potential capacity and they are to be used fully by increasing the capacity of the individual who are operating the computer.

Software has to be developed to prepare a database which should be so comprehensive as to accommodate a variety of data from the villages. In the same way another set of software has to be developed for towns and cities. And they are to be linked and integrated at district level and State level. At a click of a computer mouse, data can be obtained from every village up to the level of the nation. At every level decisions can be taken precisely.

Data have to be generated for each and every hamlet and pooled at Gram Panchayat level. Town Panchayat has to generate data from each Ward and they are to be pooled. Municipalities and cantonments have to generate data for each and every administrative unit. In the same way Municipal Corporation has to maintain the database for each region of the Municipal Corporation area. From a Gram Panchayat Ward to national level Data flow can be ensured. Periodically the data have to be updated (Figure 8.1).

Basically all kinds of data have to be generated starting from the availability of natural resources, human resources, available human skills, and infrastructure and so on. A comprehensive data sheet has to be prepared. The data generated have to be validated. They are to be updated. There should be comprehensive software to accommodate all kinds of data. The data confirmed and uploaded in the systems of all the institutions can be taken as validated data.

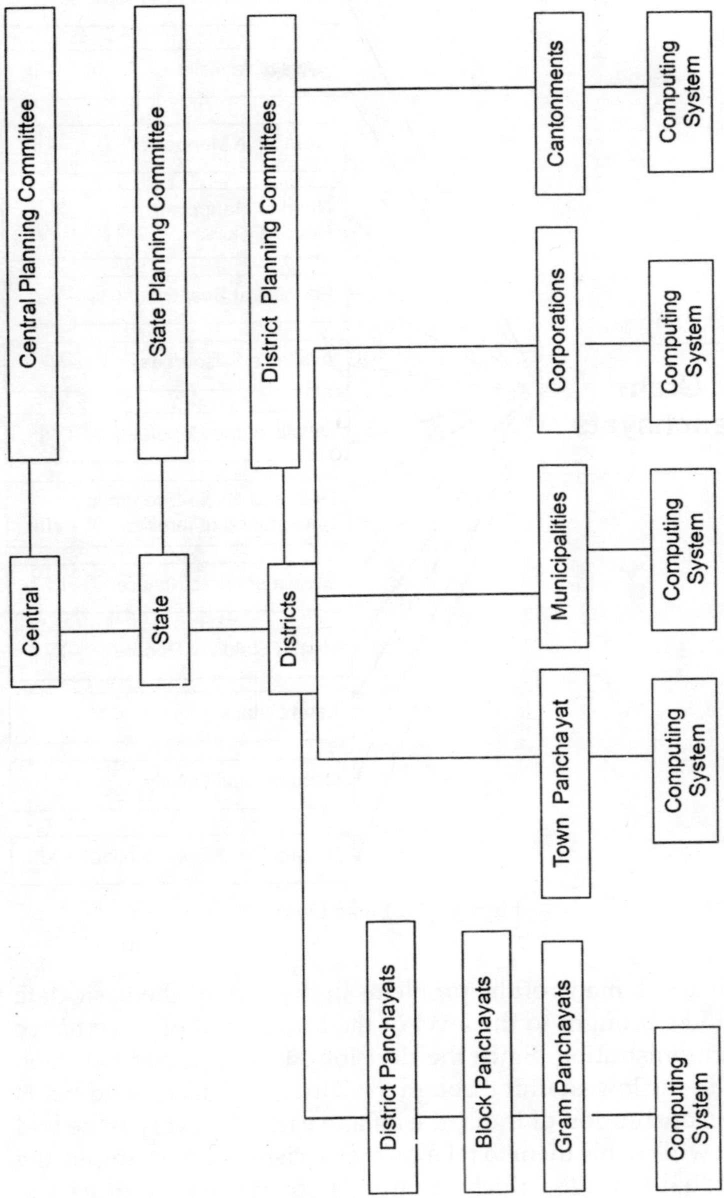

Figure 8.1: Data Generation Mechanism

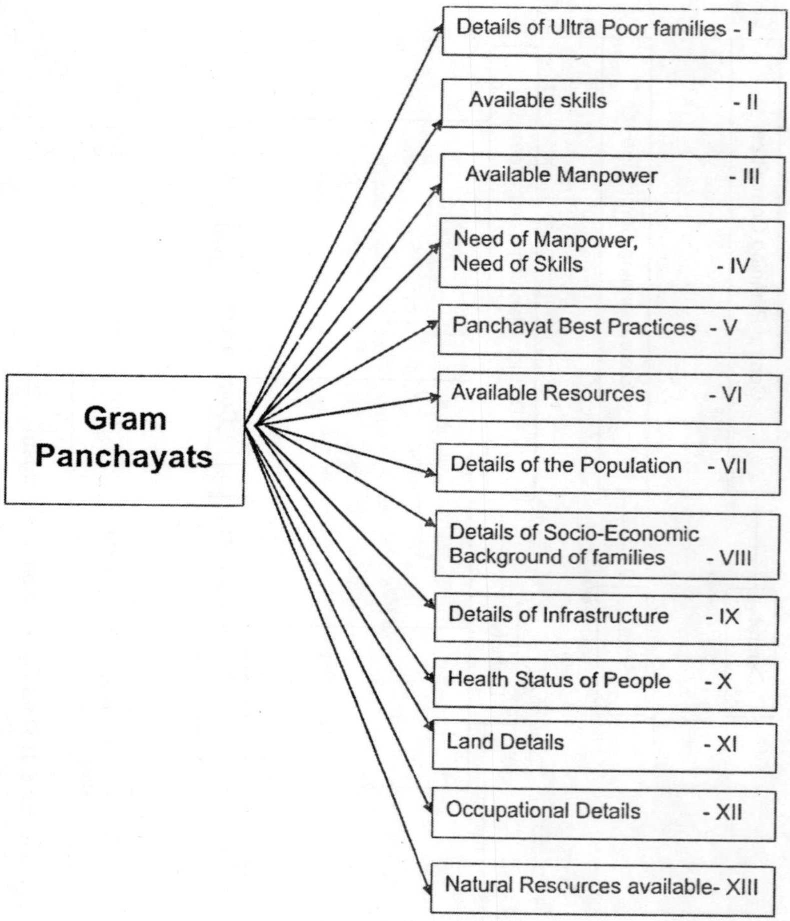

Figure 8.2 : Basic Data

To attack many of the problems in the society, the basic data have to be brought to the level of the lowest unit of governance and administration. Since the decision making power has been given in the lowest unit through the 73rd and 74th Amendments to the Constitution of India, the data to each and every issue and aspect will enable them to take correct decisions. For example, the individual families which are ultra poor can be monitored at Panchayat level by keeping the family profiles in the Panchayat. Panchayats can intervene. In the same way the Bio-Diversity Act

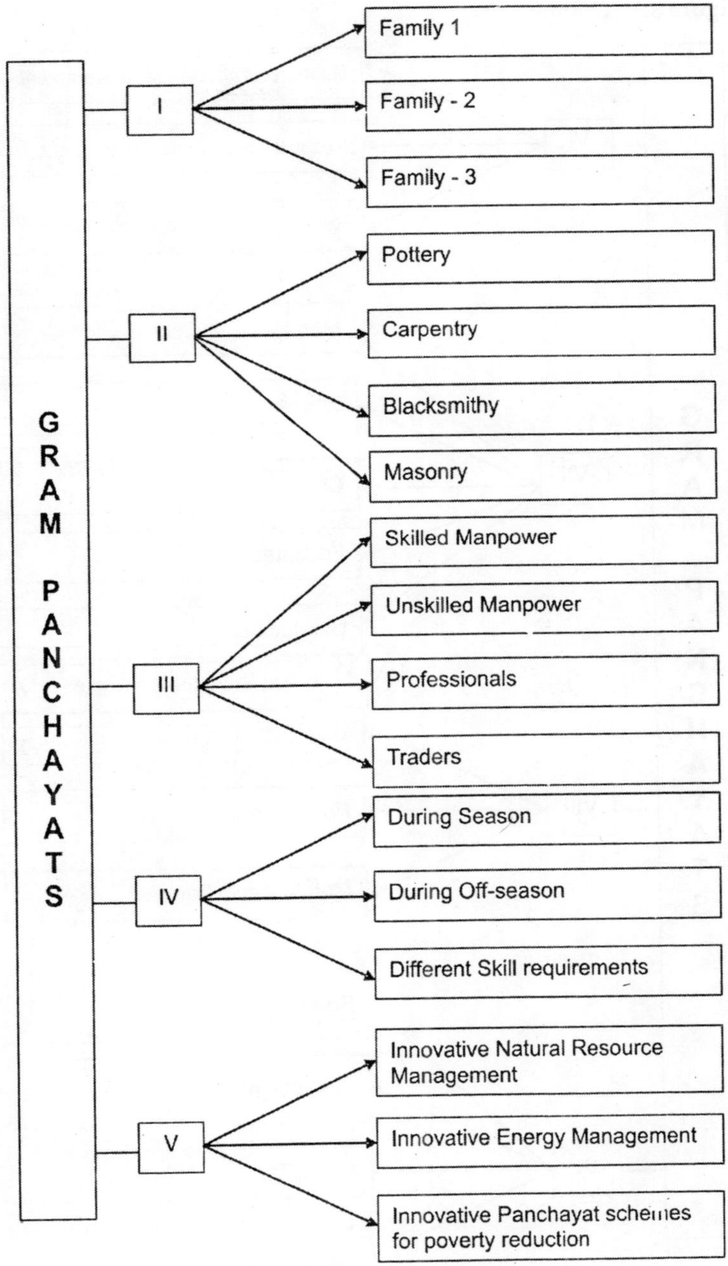

Figure 8.3: Data Details

Figure 8.3: (*Contd.*)

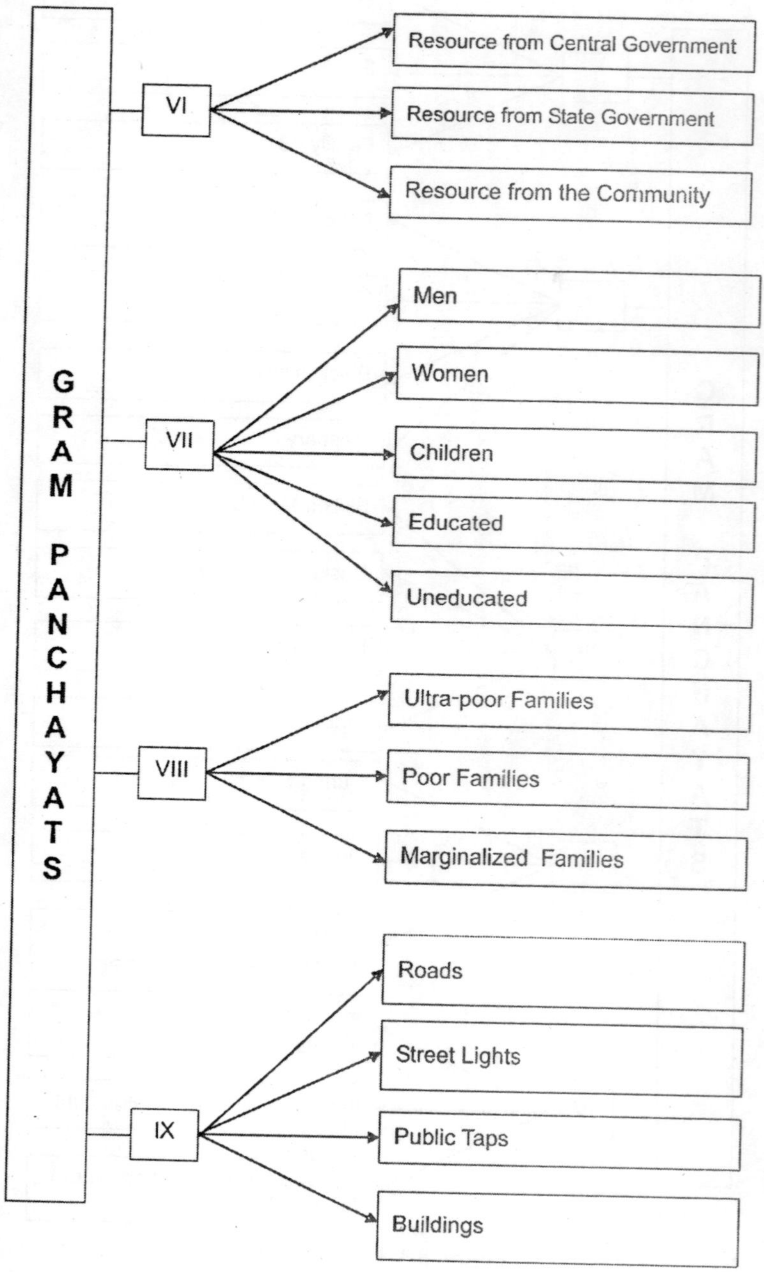

Figure 8.3: (*Contd.*)

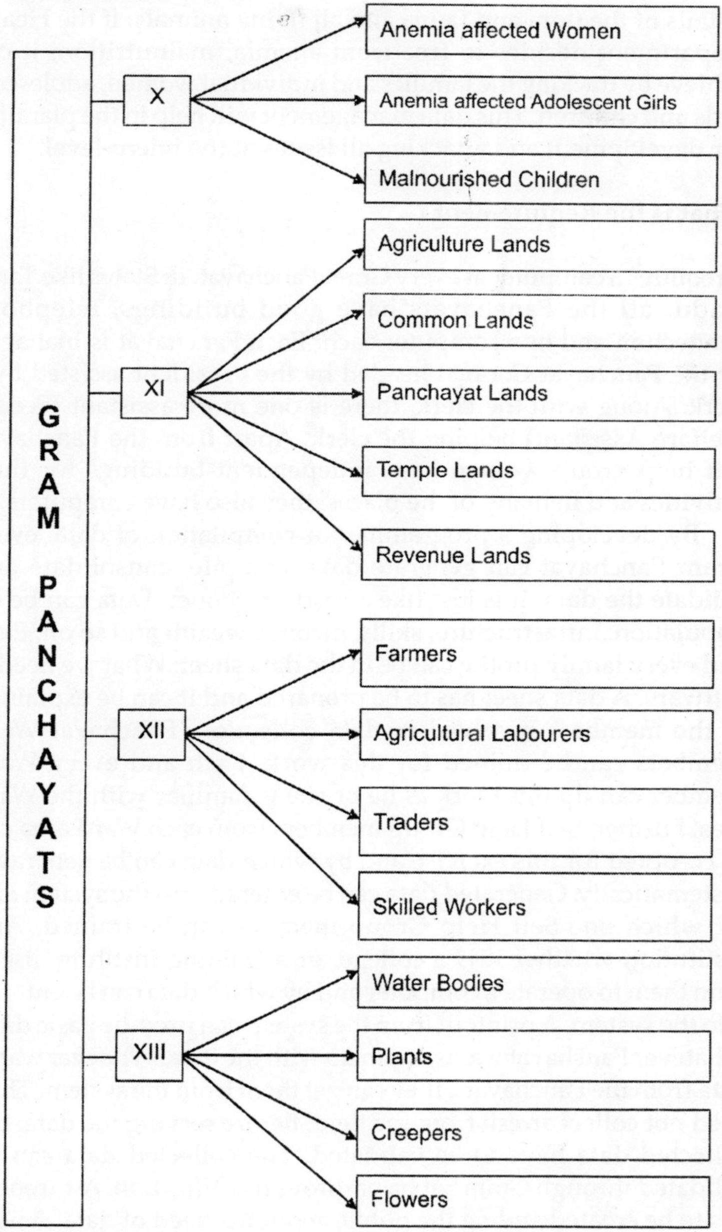

Note: These are only indicative, illustrative and not exhaustive.

insists that the Panchayats should have a register to keep all the details of the flora and fauna and all living animals. If the Health Department decides to free from anemia, malnutrition, it can achieve by tracking the families and individual women, adolescent girls and children. This data management will help in the planning for development and attacking all issues at the micro-level.

What is the Requirement ?

It requires a computer at every Gram Panchayat. In States like Tamil Nadu, all the Panchayats have good buildings, telephone connection and one computer each. Each Panchayat is managed by the Panchayat Council headed by the President assisted by a clerk. Along with the clerk, there is one more assistant (People Welfare Assistant) helping the clerk. Apart from the Panchayat, self help group women have independent buildings for their activities and in many of the places, they also have computers.

By developing a programme for compilation of data, every Gram Panchayat can generate data, compile, consolidate and validate the data. It is just like a ready reckoner. Data can be on population, infrastructure, skills, income, wealth and so on. Each and every family profile can be in the data sheet. What we need is software. A data sheet has to be prepared and it can be explained to the members involved in data collection. Panchayat Ward members can be trained for this work. Each and every Ward member can do this work as he or she is familiar with the Ward area. Further, Self Help Group members from each Ward area can be co-opted for this exercise and by which data can be generated systematically. Generated data can be entered into the system and for which one Self Help Group member can be trained. Any institution whether it is a college, or a training institute, it can train them to operate a computer and by which data can be entered into the system. A printout from the system can provide basic data. Whatever Panchayat wants, it can do with the data. Whoever wants data from the Panchayats, they can get them from the system. They need not collect afresh from the field. Before serving the data; the collected data have to be validated. The collected data can be validated through Gram Sabha or through notification. Awareness has to be created among the public about the need of data. A new culture has to be created among everyone that issues should be projected with accurate data and facts. Today's problems of bogus ration cards can be eliminated easily, ultra poor can be identified easily, and the benefits for the poor cannot be grabbed by the rich. Panchayat financial details, expenditure details, scheme details can be obtained from the system. Hence, a scientific data management system will be in place. From the Gram Panchayat office to the President of India's office, data linkage can be given and further it can be tapped at any unit level.

Conclusion

The present *ad hoc*, unscientific, unprofessionalistic way of decision making and implementation of programmes will be given a go by through placing a system of scientific data generation, data management, data validation at different levels of administration and governance starting from the lowest unit by using the ICT. ICT is an enabler, an instrument and a powerful tool to perform all the activities. By doing so, it can create a new culture of looking at things scientifically. Data available in every Gram Panchayat, town Panchayats, Municipalities, Municipal Corporations, Block Panchayats, and District Panchayats will improve decision making and they will help better policy planning and will enable better management of resources. Wastages can be curtailed. It will reduce corruption considerably. Everyone is looking for a scientific database at grassroots for action. And for which data generation is essential. Data available in all the lower level units will help both grassroots institutions and higher level institutions for micro as well as macro level planning. Many of the micro issues could be tackled scientifically by generating data. This kind of exercise at grassroots in data generation will change the attitudes of the people and the officials. It will also reduce corruption and enhance scientific action. It requires only the political and administrative will. It requires a computer and a programme along with computer operators. The computer operator can be had the youth of the village or a woman from the Local Self Help Group. Once they are trained and oriented, they will perform the task. Thus, data generation, validation and data preservation or maintenance will become an indispensable routine work of the grassroot institutions.

IX

Problems and Scope in Handling RTI : A Grassroot Perspective

Introduction

Of the many historic decisions in independent India, enacting a legislation to ensure right to information, popularly called "RTI", is a path breaking event in the process of empowering the citizens of India and making the government accountable to the citizens. Looking at the existing complicated and complex governance and administrative process, this RTI is a powerful tool to empower the people to claim their entitlement rightfully and reduce corruption[1]. However, crude it is in its present form, it will deliver enormous results to the people, provided it is used and handled very effectively by the citizens[2]. This process is not so easy as it breaks the existing order and questions secrecy and authority. The whole edifice of our administration is built on secrecy and accountability to the higher ups but not to the people who are ultimately the beneficiaries and for which governance and administrative systems are created. There will be enormous barriers and stumbling blocks to make the whole process accountable to the people[3] because of the negative attitude of the officials. So far officials have not been oriented and trained to respond to the people in a responsible and responsive way. They have been oriented to rule the people, which is a colonial characteristics. Moreover, RTI is a milestone in the democratic process as the enactment of the above law came in response to the demand of the people and the civil society. It is not a centralized drive like other decisions and laws. It was enacted basically because of the demand from the people through civil societies. It is to be recognized that in Rajasthan, when the Muzdoor Kisan Shakti Sangathan (MKSS) conducted public hearings where details of schemes and projects were released, false bills, vouchers, muster rolls and non-existent construction companies got exposed and many corrupt public officials were humiliated by the public. This experience generated a demand for enactment of Right to Information Bill[4]. In 1997 itself, in the meeting of Chief Ministers, it was decided to enact such legislation in the States also. There is no death of laws in India. Good laws and schemes are enacted by the Centre and the State governments but when they go to the society, they all will be diluted. Because the constitutional provisions and community practices are interacting with each other. As long as community practices are not disturbed, the practices of constitutional provisions are allowed. Constitution always grants but community only rejects as it is hierarchical, caste oriented and patriarchal. If any response comes from the Government based on the demands of the community it will work effectively. All supply driven activities will not bring such results. Take the case of the New Panchayati Raj System in India. It is a centralized drive. Even after sixteen years of the enactment of amendment to the Constitution of India, the new Panchayati Raj System is in struggle to establish itself as a system of governance at the grassroots. The very spirit of the enactment has not been realized. No doubt every one knows that the New Panchayati Raj System breaks the existing social order and paves way for creating an equitable and inclusive society. Hence, enormous barriers[5]. Normally the theoretical assumption is that if any decision is the outcome of people's demands, the rate of success is very high. Against this background the RTI is being looked at from the experience of Tamil Nadu. It is a proactive state for all progressive policies and legislations and more particularly it is one of the few States which have got plenty of development schemes and programmes for the benefit of the poor and hence it is taken for analysis.

Background

Information is power. Information will make the people informed and the informed individual become enlightened individual.

Primarily people need information about the functions, activities and resource allocations of the government. By getting this information from the government people can ensure their entitlements. Basically people should know as citizens what their entitlements are, how they are being delivered and how they are to be claimed. The delivery mechanism and the institutional process should be known to the people. It is the most important point at the individual level. Secondly, people collectively need information to check whether public offices and institutions are functioning well. There is an underlying assumption beneath these two demands. Governance and administrative institutions are not transparent and accountable to the people in India today. Further, they are not delivering services as stipulated. Moreover, they are authoritarian in nature, not proactive and they are non-responsive to people[6]. People are not aware which institution is performing what function. In this way our governing and administrative mechanism is mystified and complicated. It is a well known fact that large scale corruption takes place in public offices[7] but people cannot unearth all those practices. Ultimately they are the victims of the corrupt practices. More particularly the poor are the worst affected. Moreover, downward accountability, i.e., accountability to the people, is not ensured in our system. In order to ensure a responsible and responsive administration people need information about the functioning of the governing and administrative machinery. To overcome all the above difficulties and to ensure better governance and administration, people put up a demand for such a decision. Based on the demand of the people, an act was enacted. It has broken the myth of secrecy. It is not only breaking the secrecy but also provides an instrument to question authority if it is abused. By doing so the people are empowered.

In India, people's experience with governance is somewhat strange. It is a kind of master-servant relationship. Enacting legislation is so easy and implementing the same is very difficult. Our Constitution is the best example. For many of the ills in the society and polity, non-implementation of many of the provisions of the Constitution of India is the reason. Not only the Constitution but also the laws, politics and decisions. Law implementation is as important as law making. Law making is easier. Law implementation is difficult as it interacts with the society. Many of the occasions Indian State exhibits its powerlessness in tackling many of the socio-economic issues[8]. Further, our government machinery is not evolved suitable to our needs and it is the continuation of the colonial governance and administration which has got the trait of ruling the people and treating the people as subjects and not citizens. As a result, governance and administration are kept away from the people. There is a gap between the people and the government. People are under an aggressive totalitarian state. The development and the prosperity of the people are to be decided by the state. The state is the owner of development. The new expectation is that the state has to withdraw from many areas and leave the space to the people. People will participate in the process of governance and development. But, instead, the state has expanded to all levels and domains and ultimately the weight of the state is unbearable to the people. In the new context of globalization the state has to withdraw from many areas. But in reality the state withdraws from higher level activities leaving many responsibilities but increasing the state control over the society[9] enormously through the new Panchayati Raj System. Against this background this tries to analyse to what extent the RTI helps the poor to get entitlements and to restore dignity through participation in the process of governance[10]. The RTI has got a rich potential to ensure good governance, reduce corruption and deliver services effectively and efficiently. Being a worker in an academic institution working with people, that too the poor, I look at the RTI from the perspective of ensuring entitlements to the poor with dignity. This study tries to analyse to what extent the Local Body leaders and other stakeholders are aware of the RTI and how it is being used by PRI leaders and others. In the same way how many of the poor know their entitlements and how they are being claimed are to be investigated. It is to be noted here that Tamil Nadu is known for pro-poor policies and pro-development initiatives. For new initiatives to achieve economic growth Tamil Nadu stands tall and equally for social justice and equity. At present, for the benefit of the rural poor, individually and collectively the Tamil Nadu Government has volley of welfare schemes operated through the departments of the State Government.

RTI in Tamil Nadu

In Tamil Nadu the RTI is in operation and it is being viewed and analysed seriously by the civil society organizations and intellectuals. Tamil Nadu is the only State having the maximum of appeals to the Information Commission. The State Information Commission has received 1,11,000 appeals over a period of four years. In 2008 alone the Commission received 43,000. From the number one can assume that people are interested in using the RTI. At the same time, one can presume that the officials at the lower level are not responding to the claims of the people. As a result, they go in for appeals. It is a fact that in Tamil Nadu poors are not using RTI effectively. Poors are treating the officials respectfully.

It is to be underlined that, as per the RTI Act, every year it is to be reported to the State Legislative Assembly by the State Information Commission to what extent the Act has been implemented. To prepare such a report all the departments of the government have to help the Commission by giving details of their activities in terms of providing information to the people on demand. The report has to be placed in the State Legislative Assembly. For the past four years there is no such report prepared and submitted to the Legislative Assembly as stipulated. It is yet another pathetic fact that even the Legislators have not raised questions about the responsibility of the Commission. As per the Act, the State government has to create the Commission at the State level and it has to be facilitated by providing enough infrastructure and manpower. It has to function independently. In the RTI Act clearly stipulates the time frame to dispose of the demands by the government departments. But there is no mention about the time frame for the Information Commission to dispose of the appeals. Hence, the delay in the State Information Commission in disposing of the appeals. Likewise as per 4(1)(b) each department of the Government has to give the details of its functioning proactively. But it is not being given.

Further, as per the Act when the demanded informations is not given as per the stipulated time, a fine of Rs. 250 per day and even up to Rs. 25,000 can be imposed. Even disciplinary proceedings can be imposed on the officials when they fail to discharge their duties. For all the lapses, punishment has to be imposed and there is no discretion for the Information Commission. In Tamil Nadu after the enquiry of the Commission based on appeal, 1,200 officials have been issued notice. Of the total officials who have not responded only 40 officials have been punished with a fine of Rs. 25,000 each. It is yet another question whether the imposed fine has been collected from the individuals or not. It is the responsibility of the government officials to collect the fines. Till date there is no data available on whether the imposed fines have been collected. For the effective functioning of the Information Commission interface between the Secretaries and the Commissioners is imperative. We can see this kind of exercise in other States like Andhra Pradesh. In Andhra Pradesh the Commission has prepared annual reports regularly and submitting it to the Legislative Assembly.

Every year the Commission has to present an annual report to the Legislative Assembly. It is mandated. In Tamil Nadu, there is no such report submitted by the Information Commission. Another interesting aspect is that even the State Legislative Assembly has not demanded such a report from the Information Commission. This kind of conduct at the official level and the Commission level waters down the whole framework. It is to be remembered that when the Prime Minister piloted the bill, he made it very clear that it will create a new era in our administration, which will be known for efficiency, which will ensure advantages to all sections of the society, which will abolish the demon of corruption, an era of bringing the problems of the people to the heart of the administration and an era of fulfilling the dream of our founding fathers. It is a big question whether the dream of empowerment will be realized in Tamil Nadu through the proactive actions of the government departments and claiming the rights rightfully by using the Right to Information Act by the citizens[11].

RTI at the Grassroots

Tamil Nadu is one of the progressive States in India. It has got a number of welfare schemes for the poor. The Government of Tamil Nadu has been implementing 430 welfare schemes through the 34 Departments[12]. Apart from the schemes and programmes of the State Government there are schemes and programmes of the Central Government which are also carried out at the grassroots through the State Government[13]. Massive resources are being spent for all these schemes. If all the schemes are reaching the needy, Tamil Nadu should be number one in inclusive growth and inclusive development. In the Human Development Index, Tamil Nadu should be the first State in India. Are the people aware of all those schemes and how are they administrated is a question examined in this chapter.

Tracking the functioning of the government is also not so easy. More particularly financial transactions are not transparent. Where decisions are taken, how they are implemented, how much resources are spent, which office handles the decisions and which officer is responsible for decisions and actions are not known to the people. That is why people meet the Collector and submit petitions. It is only the Collector who coordinates the activities of the departments and directs the concerned officials to redress the grievances of the petitioners. It is not only the Collector, whoever comes to villages from Government Departments or from political parties or representatives, people prepare a petition and submit it to them whether the petitions are relevant to the persons coming to the village or not. In this way people are oriented[14]. People are oriented as beneficiaries and petitioners. They are oriented to submit petitions submissively to the officials and pray for intervention. The whole orientation gives the impression that the government does charity to the poor. Never it is informed the citizens that they have the right to claim their entitlements. By doing so they are making the officials and the representatives more empowered and making people disempowered.

There is yet another issue — the resource flow from Central Government to State Government, State Government to District Administration, District Administration to the field office — not known to the people. Wherefrom money flows, how it flows, when it flows, where it reaches are not known to the people. What are the procedures to be followed to claim the entitlements and how resources are spent for the common good by the public offices are not known to the public. These are all due to the mystification of governance and administration. Governance and administrative arrangements have to be understood. The organogram Figures 9.1 and Chart 9.1 explain the linkages from the State Secretariat to the Village Panchayat. Every department has its own structure to the operational desk at the ground. The structure is not uniform to all the departments.

There are thirty-four departments functioning in the Secretariat. All the departments have websites and the schemes which are being operated by the departments are in the websites.

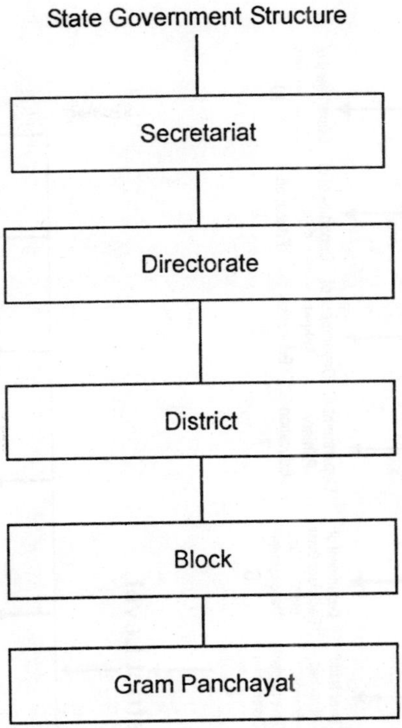

Fig. 9.1: The Structure of State Government

All the district administrations have websites and the details of the schemes and programmes implemented by the district administration through various offices are given in the websites. The Department of Panchayati Raj and Rural Development is the only Department having vertical connection between the Secretariat and the Gram Panchayat. All the other Departments have offices at the District level and, down below, field offices are not established at the village level. Some Departments have field offices at Block level and Some Departments have offices down below the Block but above the village level. Hence, there is no access for the people to Government Departments. Locating offices and identifying the officers who are operating schemes and programmes are very difficult for the people. In this way the administrative set-up has been created[15]. How these Departments are used by the people and how these Departments act proactively for the benefit of the people are to be studied. It is to be understood

Chart 9.1: ORGANOGRAM OF GOVERNMENT DEPARTMENT DELIVERY SYSTEM

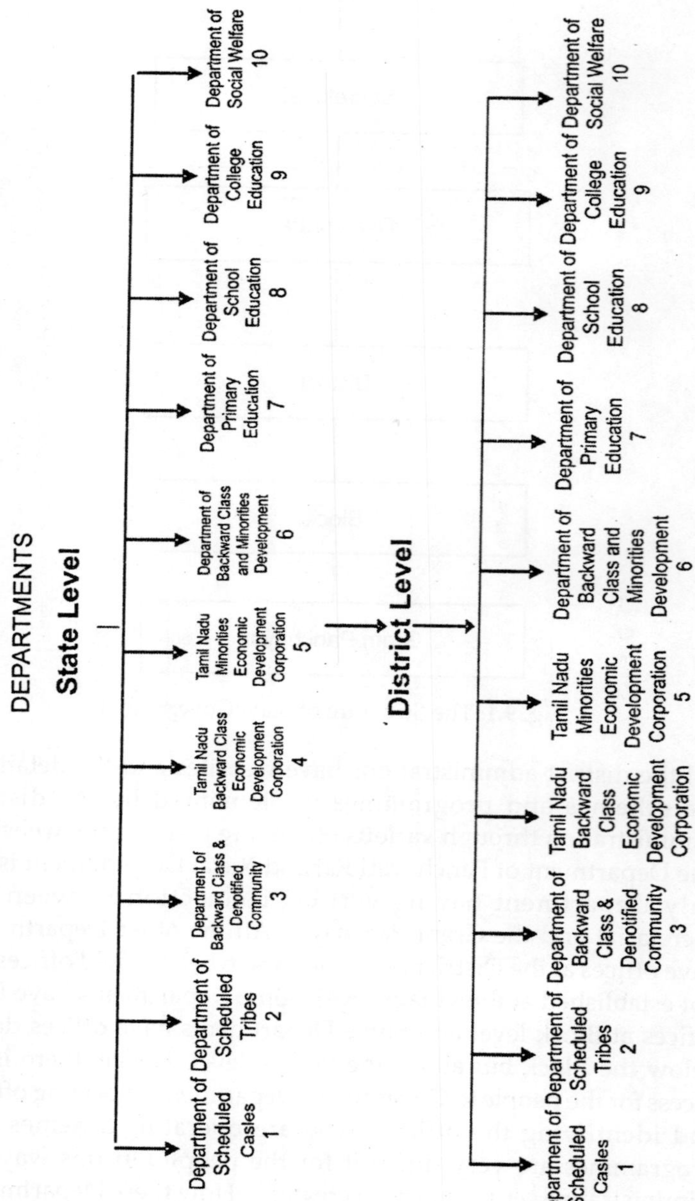

Chart 9.1 (*Contd.*)

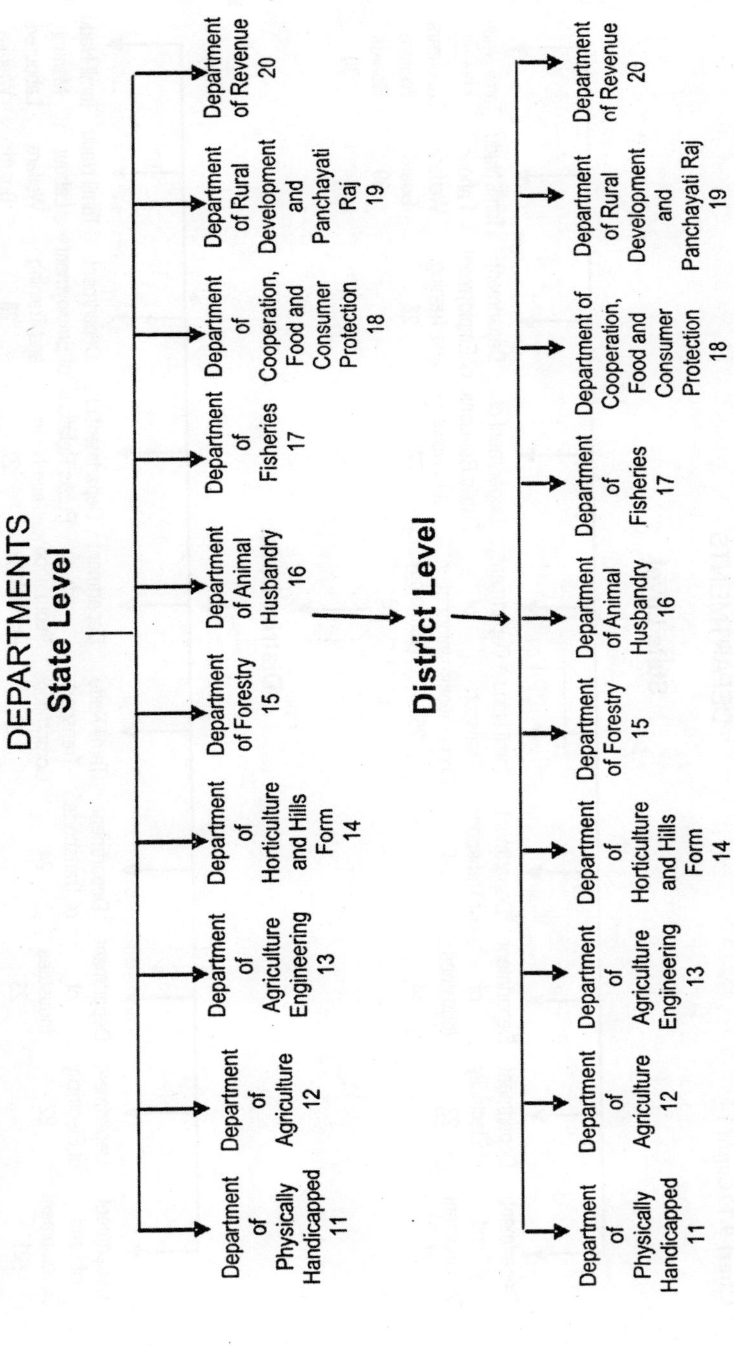

Chart 9.1 (*Contd.*)

DEPARTMENTS

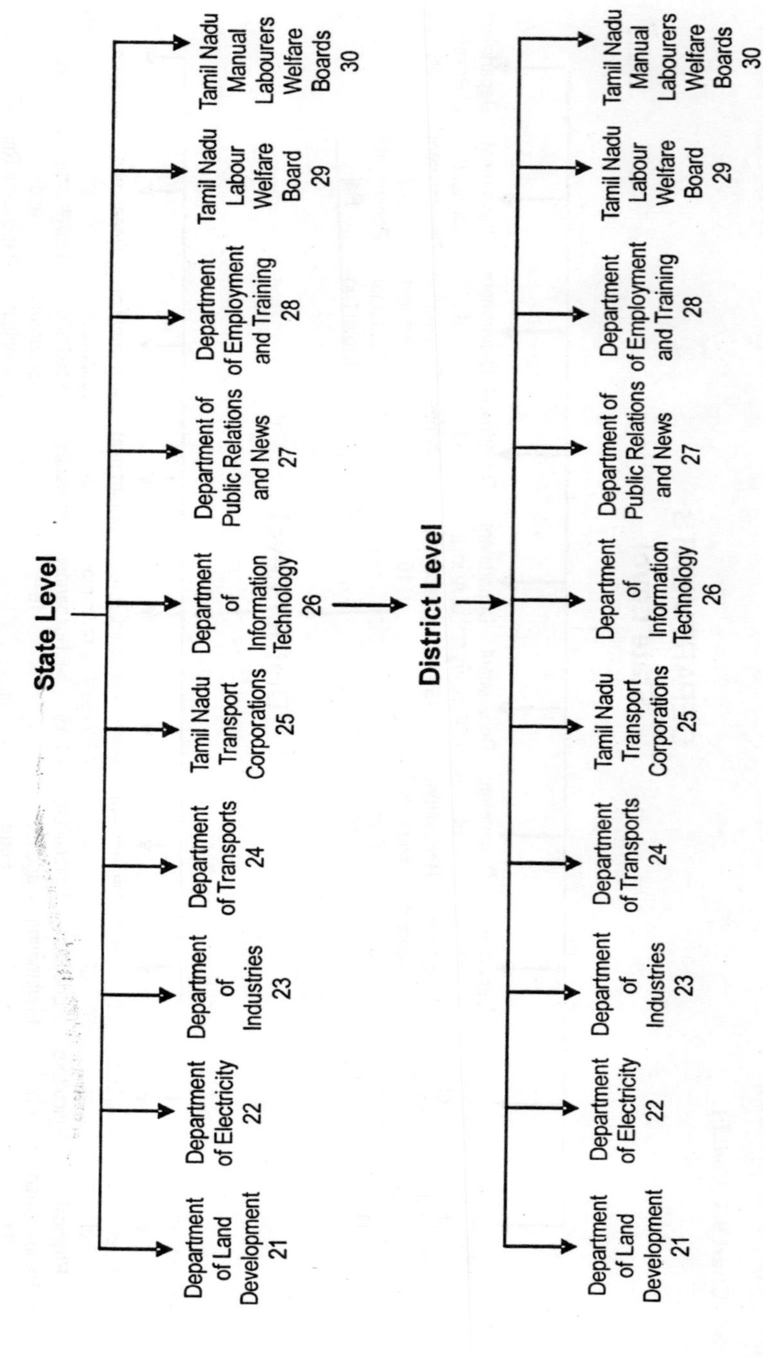

that the feudal mindset of the society has afflicted the administration also and hence questioning is not appreciated and liked by the officials. The officials never have a mindset that they are servants of the people, that it is their responsibility to serve the people and that they are accountable to the people. Against this background the RTI is in operation. The officials feel that it is a design and a tool which will expose them. In this context one cannot expect that officials to act proactively. Against this backdrop this study has been conducted in the rural areas.

Methodology

Primary sources were collected from focus group discussions with Panchayat leaders, farmers, artisans, students of Scheduled Caste, students of Other Backward Classes and poor women. These focus group discussions were conducted by the students of the postgraduate programme while conducting their outreach programmes. The discussions were on the awareness of the people of the schemes and programme for the poor, of the flow of funds to these programmes and of how they are being spent. When they are aware of the Right to Information Act how are they using it? Are they, using the RTI to get the details? If they get information what do they do with the information? Further, questions have been asked pertinent to the RTI and its utility.

Setting

Karisalpatti is a Gram Panchayat in Rediarchatram Block in Dindigul District. It has three hamlets. This Gram Panchayat has got awards for its outstanding performance. It is a multi-caste Gram Panchayat. Agriculture and Animal Husbandry are the main livelihood activities. In this village discussions were held in all the three hamlets.

Results and Analysis

In all the focus group discussions it was found that the people are not aware of the RTI. Only a handful of people are aware of this instrument. Panchayat leaders are aware that there is a provision in the RTI by which they can get the details of the schemes and programmes of the Departments which are meant for the people. But they are not in a position to use it as the officials will treat them as enemies. Such an impression has been created among the Panchayat leaders by the officials. When Panchayat leaders are afraid of the officials one can imagine the predicament of the people. Hence, this instrument was not used by the people to get the details of their entitlement. People generally know the schemes and programmes of the government. They get to know the details only from the media, both print and electronic. Inferring the details from the news will not help the poor unless they know the schemes in detail with all procedures. But they are not able to get the full details to claim their entitlement. Of the 430 programmes only a few programmes are known to them. All popular programmes are known to the people and they are delivered to the people at the doors of the people. But the other schemes and programmes are not known to them.

There are some title schemes which give name to the government which are known to the people. Programmes which have a cash component are known to the poor. But they do not know how to claim them. They do not know which office handles them and which officer deals with them. This is a major problem for the poor. Hence, they rely on middlemen. The middlemen collect money for the service rendered by them. If all the Departments proactively give the details to the people through the Panchayat, the poor can claim their entitlement. But, unfortunately, Departments are not proactive. Only a few Departments are proactive. After the introduction of the RTI, people attempted to use the RTI but the responses were not positive. It is interesting to note that the news items appearing in the newspapers in Tamil Nadu on the use of the RTI are not encouraging the people to apply under the RTI. Newspapers carry news of struggle in using the RTI rather than stories of success. Having seen the struggle people do not opt to use the RTI. A perception has been developed that if the RTI is used by any individual to claim the information, it is construed as anti-social. In this way officials have created an impression. Even the officials who are working in the Rural Development sector treat the individuals who use the RTI as real enemies.

The Panchayat leaders want more information about the amount earmarked for each and every scheme for their villages.

They are unable to track it. Unless the officials call the Presidents and inform them there will not be any chance to get the details. They are not able to use the RTI as it is considered as anti-officer. Many of the leaders who used RTI have been treated enemies of the officials. As such the relationship between the leaders and the officials has been strained. On many occasions the officials respond to the RTI. Complaints against officers are given to Information Commissioners of the State for not responding to demands. Nothing happens in this regard. Originally it was believed that it will help the poor. But now it helps only the educated and the officials to settle their personal scores. Whenever the State Information Commissioner visits the district headquarters, a lot of petitions are submitted against the officials about their non-compliance. Total resistance has been developed by the officials.

Information relating to government schemes and programmes are available to party men as they are with officials as development brokers but not to the citizens. It is interesting that many of the participants in the focus group discussion stated that the people are not able to get details even from the Panchayats. In the beginning the Panchayat leaders were transparent and proactive. But now people are finding it very difficult to get information about the amount spent under the NREGA and other schemes implemented by the Panchayats. A woman who got maternity benefit narrated that she got Rs. 4,500 from the Department after paying Rs. 1,500. Why she had given Rs. 1500 to an individual is the question. Because the poor women is entitled to get Rs. 6000/ But she got Rs. 4500. The woman who got Rs. 4500 was also happy as she got at least Rs. 4500. She openly admitted that she was not aware that she had an entitlement. It was only the development broker (local party men) who brought it to the notice of the beneficiary.

To claim certain entitlements, procedures and formalities have to be compiled with. It is a cumbersome process. This process is taken care of by the development brokers[16]. If the Gram Panchayat President is capable, he will collect all the informations and they will be disseminated in the Gram Sabha. It is taking place in many of the Panchayats[17]. They are well trained and well oriented. As long as corruption is prevailing everywhere, the officials tend to hide facts and in the same way Panchayat leaders also behave. When Panchayat leaders move with officials, they have to do as per the direction of the officials and this has become difficult now. This was the observation of many of the participants. As for what is to be done for information, a lot of suggestions have been given by the participants. They are: (a) it should be made mandatory that while implementing the schemes and programmes in the villages by the Departments of the government, the details of the scheme and the quantum of resources have to be given to the Gram Panchayats; (b) every year the new schemes introduced by the government have to be informed through the Gram Panchayats; (c) the Gram Panchayat should act as a citizen centre where people come and take information; (d) all government schemes have to be explained in the Gram Sabha meeting whenever it is convened; (e) civil society organizations have to play a major role in creating awareness among the people about the RTI; and (f) civil society organizations have to help the poor to use the RTI as a support structure. These were the observations of the participants of the focus group discussions.

Conclusion

It is a well known fact that in the whole country Tamil Nadu is the only State having 430 welfare schemes in 34 Departments of the Government. In the era of globalisation, all opportunities are grabbed for the advantage of the State. To protect the poor, the State government has introduced plenty of schemes. It is quite unique. Except the Rural Development and Panchayati Raj Department no Department has field offices at the Gram Panchayat level. Departments have field office or lower units at different levels depending on their need and convenience. Locating the office and identifying the concerned officer for getting the scheme is difficult. The condition of the poor will not spare time for this exercise and their level of awareness is also very low. Moreover, in a feudal society and an authoritarian bureaucratic set-up respecting the poor and responding to the poor proactively is only a pipe dream. In our system officials are empowered and they will not subject themselves to scrutiny. If someone demands information about an officer, the officer feels that he is being challenged. The existing corrupt practices will not continue if the information reaches the stakeholders. But conditions are not favourable towards giving information proactively.

In the rural areas, especially the poor do not have the needed awareness about the RTI. They are not able to locate the offices on the ground which deliver services to the poor. How will they claim their entitlements? Some of the services are delivered through the Panchayats and many of the services are delivered by the respective Department units on the ground. The public distribution system, water supply and public transport are the essential services delivered to the people. If they are not delivered people will organize and agitate. For all other services they have to get information and track them. Proactively the Departments do not give information about their services and benefits to the people. This information gap is being used by the party men, mostly the ruling party men, who act as development brokers and take steps to get the benefits to the poor and for which they get brokerage.

The New Panchayati Raj System can remove the development brokers from the development domain. All Government Departments have to provide proactively the information pertinent to the services delivered by them to the people. The information has to be disseminated through the Gram Sabha meeting. For claiming their entitlements the poor are to be helped by the civil society organizations. More activities have to be undertaken on the ground. One has to understand that the RTI is the outcome of the activist mobilization of the people. Hence, the role of activists in empowering Panchayats is an imperative one. In every Gram Panchayat there should be at least one activist group to activate and mobilize people and more particularly the poor and the marginalized. Grassroots institutions have to be strengthened structurally and technologically. Every Gram Panchayat should be provided with a computer and they are to be well connected with the websites of the Departments through which all the schemes and programmes can be tracked and disseminated in the Gram Sabha. Every Panchayat should have a building with all facilities. It should be made a citizen centre and citizen information centre. If the Panchayat Secretary and one member from a local SHG are oriented in computer operation, tracking information from the Government is easy and the same can be disseminated. What we need is strengthening of the Panchayat system with all facilities. Awareness has to be created among the people about the RTI and a support structure has to be developed to enable people to use the RTI and claim their entitlements.

REFERENCES

1. Bidynt Chakrabarty and Mohit Bhattacharya (eds.), *The Governance Discourse: A Reader*, Delhi: Oxford University Press, 2008, p. 37.
2. "A Path to Swaraj", *The Hindu*, 7 Oct., 2005.
3. Madhar Godbole, "Unending Struggle for Right to Information" *Economic and Political Weekly*, 12 Aug., 2000, p. 2899.
4. Rob Jenkins and Anne Marie Goetz, "Accounts and Accountability: Theoretical Implications of the Right to Information Movement in India", *Third World Quarterly*, 20:3 pp. 603–22.
5. G. Palanithurai, *Critical Issues in Decentralisation of Powers in India*, New Delhi: Concept Publishing Company Pvt. Ltd., 2009.
6. Rajiv Gandhi, "Responsive and Representative Administration: Panchayati Raj", Inaugural Speech at the Workshops of District Collectors and Magistrates on Responsive Administration, Hyderaba Pvt. Ltd., 13th Feb. 1988, G. Palanithruai (ed.), *Rajiv Gandhi's Vision on Local Governance*, New Delhi: Concept Publishing Company Pvt. Ltd., 2009, pp. 33–79.
7. Eran H. was inferred at the dawn of Independence, for more details, A.D. Gorwala *Report of Public Administration and Efficient Conduct of State Enterprises*, Govt. of India, 1951, Paul Appleby, *Public Administration in India: Report of a Survey*, Delhi: Mangal Publications, 1953.
8. Atul Kohli, "Centralization and Powerlessness: India's Democracy in a Comparative Perspective" in Joel Samuel Migdal, Atul Kohli and Vivienne Shue (Eds), *State Power and Social Forces: Domination and Transformation in the Third World*, New York: Cambridge University Press, 1994, pp. 89–107.
9. Baldev Raj Nayar, *The Myth of the Shrinking State: Globalisation and the State in India*, Delhi: Oxford University Press, 2009.
10. Our Democracy has to be seen in the light of the present crises and people must be made a development participant. More details see Rajnikothari, *Rethinking Democracy*, New Delhi: Orient Longman, 2005.
11. A.K. Venkatasubramaniam, *Kudimakkal Murasu*, Vol. 8, No. 5 (Aug. 2009), pp. 1–5.
12. Chief Minister Special Division, *Welfare Schemes of Tamil Nadu, Vols. I, II* and *III* Chennai: Govt. of Tamil Nadu, 2008.
13. Chief Minister Special Division, *Central Government Schemes*, Chennai: Government of Tamil Nadu, 2008.
14. A.K. Venkatasubramaniam *Participant or Petitioner* (in Tamil), Chennai: Catalyst Trust, 2001.
15. G. Palanithruai, "Reforming Governance and Administration at Grassroots", *The Journal of Public Administration*.

16. G. Palanithurai, "Grassroot Level Corruption: A Cursory Analysis", in G. Palanithruai (Ed), *New Panchayati Raj System: Status and Prospects*, New Delhi: Kanishka Publishers and Distributors, 1996, pp. 57–64.
17. G. Palanithurai, "Corruption at Micro Level and Ways to Contain" in N. Narayanasamy, M.P. Boraian and M.A. Jayaraju (Eds), *Corruption at the Grassroots: The Sheds and Shadows*, New Delhi: Concept Publishing Company, 2000, pp. 169–180.

X

An Analysis of the Status of Dalit Gram Panchayat (Local Governance System) Leaders in Tamil Nadu (India)

Introduction

It is a general expectation after reserving seats for *dalits*[1] in the Panchayati Raj System constitutionally that the condition of the *dalits* will improve and the social discriminatory practices against *dalits* will decrease and thereby the *dalits* will get social acceptance, and thus social cohesion will be created. There is yet another argument that the new social cohesion will be created only through a process of social conflict and that without such a social conflict, social cohesion will not be possible. Getting acceptance and acquiring power from the dominant communities will not happen without an intense social conflict. The *dalit* leaders have to undergo this process of social conflict. Indian States are at different levels of social transformation in terms of abandoning of discriminatory practices perpetuated by the dominant communities against the *dalits*. At present 25 per cent of the total population in India is *dalit*. Eight States, namely, Uttar Pradesh, West Bengal, Bihar, Tamil Nadu, Andhra Pradesh, Madhya Pradesh, Rajasthan and Karnataka account for more than 75 per cent of the total *dalit* population of the country. With such a sizeable population of *dalits* only one per cent of the cultivable land is owned by them. Tamil Nadu is one among the States influenced by *dalit* politics. Tamil Nadu is known for its speed in social transformation because of the Dravidian

Movement which was created to uplift the non-Brahmins including the *dalits*.

The Dravidian Movement in general and the Dravidian political parties in particular (the Dravida Munnetra Kazhagam (DMK) and the All India Anna Dravida Munnetra Kazhagam (AIADMK)) have decisively transformed politics and society in Tamil Nadu quantitatively and qualitatively in the past five decades and in the past three decades very intensively *(N. Palani, 2004)*. The benefits accrued out of the socio-political activities of the Dravidian political parties outside the government and the decisions, the programmes and the resource allocation of the government have helped many non-Brahmin communities economically and politically but they have not enhanced the social and economic conditions of the *dalits* as expected (Sathyavanimuthu, 1981; Gnanaraj Xavier *et al.*, 2002; Hugo Gorringe, 2005). The *dalit* communities have stated that they have not gained much benefit despite the quantum of activities initiated by the State government for the socially and economically deprived over a period of time since the DMK came to power. It has been argued that lack of access to power at the grassroots is one of the reasons for the failure of the *dalit* communities to claim their entitlement even though the benefits were in the pipeline. *Dalits* had developed expectations from the Dravidian political parties as a lot of promises were made for *dalits* in the packages of Dravidian uplift since they were also part of the Dravidian Movement, but they all vanished as the Backward Class got the maximum benefits and even the social discrimination and untouchability were not addressed by the Dravidian political parties very effectively after they came to power. The commitment of the Dravidian political parties to the upliftment of *dalits* is not reflected in action (S. Viswanathan, 2005). Though there have been progressive policies, programmes and resource allocation, while implementing the same, the administration of the governments of the Dravidian political parties failed miserably in reaching out to the *dalits* as expected as they developed the fear that they would lose the Backward Class votes. Issues like social discrimination could have been fought on both political and social fronts. The Dravidian political parties have failed miserably on the social front after they came to power. *Dalits* could not gain gainful economic development and remove untouchability. The Dravidian parties have not even implemented the legislation related to the removal of untouchability (Article 17), control of atrocities [Article 15(2), 29(2), 35, 244 and 371(A)] and they have by and large remained ineffective. *Dalits* have started following two paths to change their conditions in the society. One is to organise and agitate against oppression and discrimination. The second is participation in Parliamentary Democracy through the electoral process and holding offices in various decisions making bodies (Ghanshiyan Shah, 2001). Against this background, the 73rd and 74th Amendments to the Constitution of India opened a new opportunity to solve many of the problems of the *dalits* as seats are reserved for *dalits* proportionate to their population. As a result of the reservation of seats *dalits* have come to power. It is a matter to be seen how *dalit* leaders are being treated in the community and how they perceive themselves in the context of poor skill and non-recognition by the caste Hindus. Moreover, the position of the *dalit* leaders should be seen against the backdrop of the conditions of *dalits*.

As per the report of the Government of Tamil Nadu 2006, discriminatory practices existed in 221 Gram Panchayats and in another 160 Gram Panchayats the same practices were practiced subtly and in 152 Gram Panchayats the practices were very severe and intense. This is the report of the Police Department. While assessing the veracity of the report one will easily say that it is not the real picture. The reality will be much more than the level projected by the police department. The reality is projected by the media instantly. Having realized this condition, *dalits* started moving away from the Dravidian political parties and created their own outfit. When *dalits* and most Backward Class people moved away and started their own outfits, arguments were developed that the Dravidian forces had disintegrated and the so-called Dravidian parties were protecting the interests of the Backward Class alone (T. Parthiban, 1998). When the *dalits* realized their deprivation and marginalization in the process of development and governance, they started organizing themselves more effectively and intensively in the beginning of the 1990s. They also developed a strategy that, instead of a social movement, *dalits* can actively participate as a political force by which they can gain seats in the Legislative Assembly and the National Parliament exclusively as a *dalit* political party, not individually but in alliance with other political parties. Dominant political parties necessarily evinced interest to increase their prospects by getting the *dalit* votes. Further, the *dalits* found a new opportunity to achieve prosperity and social justice through the 73rd Amendment to the Constitution of India. The 73rd Amendment to the Constitution of India has provided them with opportunity to participate in governance at grassroots legitimately by reserving seats for *dalits* proportionate to their population. Positions have been reserved in all the categories from Gram Panchayats to District Panchayats. *Dalits* can form a critical mass in terms of numbers and they can perform critical functions.[2] *Dalit* leaders who are in power have to use this opportunity to gain status, position and facilities for the *dalits*. To claim the opportunity, the *dalit* leaders have to struggle as devices have been found to keep the *dalits* away from power indirectly by the dominant communities. In many places they are allowed to contest in the election but not allowed to come to the offices and handle power (Rajiv Gandhi Chair, 2002). In four Gram Panchayats in Madurai and Virudhunagar Districts communities have declared that they would not allow the *dalits* to head the Panchayat Council. It was an open challenge to the State government by the dominant communities by not allowing the official machinery to conduct the election (G. Palanithurai, 2008). Wherever *Dalits* have tried to keep power with them, the other communities are not cooperating with the Gram Panchayat Presidents to run the administration. In many places the dominant communities are maintaining an indifferent attitude towards the *dalit* leadership in Panchayats. The elected *dalit* Panchayat leaders have to struggle with Traditional Panchayats to uphold the provisions of the Constitution. It is a struggle continuously waged by the *dalit* leaders. How the *dalit* leaders are facing the problems and with whose support are the issues to be studied. It has been reported that in many places *dalits* were forcibly made to keep off from handling power. These kinds of struggles of the *dalits* have removed the myth that Tamil Nadu is free from oppression of *dalits*. In the beginning of the last decade of the twentieth century, *dalits* got awareness and they rose to agitate to claim their due status in the society and their entitlements. Caste violence erupted in the south in the beginning of the 1990s and *dalits* started asserting themselves and claiming their rights. Tamil Nadu witnessed unprecedented violence let loose against *dalits*. In the same period, provision was made in Parts IX and IX-A of the Constitution that the marginalized communities be given representation in governance at the grassroots proportionate to their population. The claim was made that women and marginalized communities have been provided enough space with critical number to perform critical functions in the local bodies. Though the number got increased, they could not perform the function as barriers have been created socially and politically (S.N. Chaudhary, 2004). To overcome the barriers and obstacles the critical mass should have the needed capacity and the *needed support structure* (G. Palanithurai, 2001). In the absence of the above two the critical mass formed out of reservation is of no use and it will not bring about any substantial change in the life of the *dalit* communities. Further, the community will repose confidence in leaders only when they perform and deliver the goods to the people. To perform and deliver the goods, the local bodies should have adequate powers and finance. In the absence of adequate powers and finance what Panchayats can do for people and specifically for *dalits* is yet another problem added to the existing social problems of the *dalit* leaders. It does not mean that the *dalit* leaders have not performed well. There are many leaders from the *dalit* community who have performed well (G. Palanithurai, 2003). For about a decade the problems faced by the *dalit* leaders in the Panchayati Raj system was captured by *Frontline* and later it was edited and published. Mr. Viswanathan covered the stories of the problems faced by the *dalits* in Tamil society and the problems faced by the *dalit* leaders in the Panchayats. As more number of cases of atrocities committed against *dalits* were reported in the press periodically, it was decided to conduct a study in certain districts where the intensity of the issue is very high. Hence, this study is undertaken to analyse the condition and the position of the *dalit* leaders in Panchayats in terms of their performance as Panchayat leaders.

Issues in Perspective

Before looking at the position and status of the *Dalit* Panchayat leaders in the Panchayati Raj System, one has to understand the problems involved in decentralizing powers from the State government to the Panchayati Raj Institutions. The whole scheme is a centralized drive and it has got a potential to transfer power from dominant communities to *dalits*, men to women, and oppressor to oppressed. Before the marginalized and the oppressed realized the potential of the power devolution, the people who were going to lose power realized the potential danger in this system and, hence, they devised a mechanism to keep power with them subtly. The dominant communities have used the communities' law to undermine the constitutional laws (Kripa Anandhpur, 2006).

The issues and problems confronted by the Gram Panchayat Presidents vary from place to place depending on the maturity of the communities. In the same way the intensity of the problem also varies from place to place. Wherever communities are sensitized and oriented to modern democracy, *dalits* are allowed to contest in the election and allowed to work in their respective offices and perform their duties and responsibilities. Wherever the communities are moderate in assimilating the transformation, they allow the *dalits* to contest but do not allow them to take up positions. Devices have been evolved and used by the dominant communities so as to retain power with them. In many places the communities have not been democratized and, as a result, communities strongly resist the operationalisation of the provisions of the Constitution. But, broadly, the *dalit* political parties have emerged as a force to reckon with and, by using this opportunity, *dalit* grassroot leaders can gain power (Raghabendra Chattopadhyay and Esther Dufflo, 2007). Since the Gram Panchayat leaders have to face the problem in the community, they cannot move away from the community practices. To crucial the community practices which are against constitutional laws and social justice, the State government and civil society organizations have to play a major role apart from the will of the Gram Panchayat leaders for committed for social action. It is almost a subtle social struggle the *dalits* have to wage for social justice and rightful claim of their entitlement. Moreover, it is to be seen against the backdrop of an overall framework of devolution of powers in the State as the State government has been made an unwilling partner because of constitutional compulsion. Since many State governments are not keen on strengthening the local governance system the marginalized have to struggle. As a large number of cases have been reported in the newspapers about the struggle of the *Dalit* leaders in the Panchayat administration a study has been designed. Fifteen years are over since the introduction of the new Panchayati Raj System and, hence, it is appropriate to see the implications of the reservation of seats for *dalits*. This study aims at analysing the condition in which the *dalit* leaders work in Panchayats and how *dalits* are in the rural areas despite the presence of *dalits* in Panchayats as leaders.

Methodology

This study has two components, namely the problems faced by the elected *dalit* representatives and the problems faced by the *dalit* families in the respective settlements as per the opinion of the Gram Panchayat leaders. The broad assumption in giving representation to any social group is to make them inclusive in governance and, that, by including them in governance, the *dalits*, hitherto excluded as representatives, will take up the problems faced by the *dalit* community over a period of time for settlement. Hence, it is assumed that by giving representation to *dalits* in the Panchayati Raj System through the 73rd Amendment to the Constitution of India, the community has been included in governance. Secondly, it is assumed that the elected *dalit* representatives know the problems of the *dalits* and, hence, they will act on the problems. After the elections, in many Gram Panchayats, *dalit* leaders were not allowed to perform their duties and responsibilities as Presidents. In many places *dalit* representatives openly came out and lodged complaints against the dominant community leaders. In some places, the whole *dalit* community has been disturbed. Because of this, the new provision of seats to *dalits* has created problems. A series of reports have been published periodically in newspapers as case studies. It is a known fact that many of the districts are known for conflict between the *dalit* community and the dominant communities. So, it was felt that a larger survey has to be undertaken in a scientific way in the districts which are affected by this conflict. In this context a civil society organization, namely, Evidence, at Madurai, has undertaken a study by visiting all the villages and Panchayats which are under the leadership of *dalits* with a well developed interview schedule. Further, a detailed discussion was held with the *dalit* leaders to assess to what extent they are not allowed to function independently to discharge their responsibilities as Gram Panchayat Presidents. The first part addressed the condition of *dalits* in the settlements in the Panchayat area and the second part the problems faced by the *dalit* Panchayat leaders. After getting the written document from the Panchayat leaders about their condition and the condition of the *dalits,* a public hearing was organized. A large number of media representatives were invited to be part of the process. The interview schedule framed to elicit information covered general information relating to Panchayats, total population of *dalits,* housing condition of the *dalits,* location of basic amenities, *dalits* access to basic amenities and police station, types of untouchability and so on.

While interacting with the *dalit* Presidents, data on how they are ill-treated and how they are not allowed to perform their duties were elicited. Totally eight districts have been covered. They are Madurai, Dindigul, Theni, Salem, Sivaganga, Erode, Perambalur and Cuddalore. Totally this study has covered four hundred and thirty-one Gram Panchayats (Madurai-83, Dindigul-60, Theni-20, Salem-27, Sivaganga-80, Erode-30, Perambalur-45 and Cuddalore-86). All the schedules were filled in by the respondents and they have affixed their signatures with their seals in order to ensure the authenticity of the data.

Existing Forms of Discrimination

Based on the existing experience, the forms of discrimination are first identified. There are thirty types of discrimination practiced in the villages in Tamil Nadu. It does not mean that in all the villages where we have conducted the study all the thirty types of discriminations are practiced. In a few villages, only a few type of discriminations are in practice. The same may not be practiced in another set of villages. But a few practices are found in all districts. The intensity of the discrimination may vary from village to village, district to district. The practices are: caste discrimination in using different vessels to serve tea in food stalls; restrictions imposed on *dalits* entering caste Hindu settlements (even if entry is permitted, the *dalits* have to observe certain behavioural codes); restrictions on *dalits* using the public space and government institutions; restrictions imposed on *dalits* using the commons of the villages; discrimination in the use of waterbodies (wells, ponds and tanks); prohibitions on *dalits* entering common temples and participating in temple festivals; discriminatory practices as per the community instructions in schools; restrictions imposed on *dalits* in using jewels and certain types of dress which are being used by caste Hindus; restrictions on *dalits* in contesting in the elections to cooperatives and other democratic bodies (more particularly they are not allowed to participate in electioneering for any party or candidate); restrictions imposed on *dalits* in using the public toilets constructed for the public as they are being used by the caste Hindus; discriminations practiced in the sub-health centres; and primary health centres; restrictions on *dalits* in using the common burial grounds and pathways to burial grounds; forcing the *dalits* to perform scavenging work; prohibiting the *dalits* to cultivate their own lands and forcing them to sell their lands to caste Hindus; forcing the *dalits* to become bonded labourers either within or outside Tamil Nadu; forcing them to perform funeral ceremonies (including burial and burning of the dead body); forcing the *dalits* to work in farm lands as bonded labourers; forcing the *dalits* to follow the decisions of the Traditional Panchayats; inflicting severe punishment on the *dalits* when *dalit* boys or girls indulge in love with caste Hindu boys or girls; discrimination practiced in the public distribution system; forcing them to follow the existing social norms; forcing the *dalits* to vacate their seats in community transport when they see caste Hindus; restrictions imposed on the *dalits* in participating in common village functions; forcing the *dalits* to do some work without any wages; committing sexual harassment on the *dalit* women; restrictions imposed on *dalits* in purchasing lands or any property in caste Hindu settlements or area; using unparliamentary slang words with *dalits* with a view to wilfully degrading them and humiliating them; and dumping all the community wastes in the settlements of the *dalits*. The collected data are tabulated based on the nature of the discriminatory practices in each and every district. How these practices are in vogue in each district is narrated and explained.

Discriminatory Practices in the Gram Panchayats: District-wise Analysis

The existing discriminatory practices in the Gram Panchayat areas are classified district-wise. On each practice how many of the Gram Panchayats are presented in Table 10.1.

The collected data are analyzed separately for each district as problems and issues of untouchability and discriminatory practices vary from district to district. The form and the intensity of the problem also vary. Hence, the analysis is made district-wise.

Table 10.1: Types of Discrimination and Atrocities committed against *dalits* in the Panchayat Areas which are Governed by Dalit Panchayat Leaders in Tamil Nadu

Sl. No.	Name of the District	Total No.of Gram Panchayats Covered	No.of Gram Panchayats affected due to caste discrimination in tea and food stalls	No.of Gram Panchayats affected due to restriction on using the common roads and pathways	No.of Gram Panchayats affected due to restriction on entering into caste Hindu settlements	No.of Gram Panchayats affected due to restriction on using waterbodies	No.of Gram Panchayats affected due to restriction on using govt. and other public places	No.of Gram Panchayats affected due to restriction on entering into temples and participating in festivals	No.of Gram Panchayats affected due to discrimination inside and outside school	No.of Gram Panchayats affected due to restriction on using public toilets	No.of Gram Panchayats affected by abusing the Dalits who dress neatly	No.of Gram Panchayats affected due to discriminatory practices in health centres and hospitals
			(1)	(2)	(3)	(4)	(5)	(6)	(7)	(8)	(9)	(10)
1.	Madurai	83	77	75	80	79	77	79	70	81	80	36
2.	Sivaganga	80	48	38	45	54	34	64	5	20	37	8
3.	Erode	30	25	12	24	8	1	30	1	4	19	1
4.	Salem	27	6	2	5	0	2	11	0	5	3	5
5.	Perambalur	45	17	2	6	8	6	33	2	8	2	1
6.	Cuddalore	86	16	6	27	6	11	54	5	11	9	0
7.	Theni	20	10	7	9	0	2	13	0	1	6	0
8.	Dindigul	60	38	31	46	32	43	57	8	26	37	7

Table 10.1 (*Contd.*)

Sl. No.	Name of the District	Total No.of Gram Panchayats covered	No. of Gram Panchayats affected due to threats against contesting and participating in democratic elections (11)	No. of Gram Panchayats affected due to restriction on use of common burial ground / pathway to burial ground (12)	No. of Gram Panchayats affected due to forcing the Dalits to do scavenging work & removal of dead animals (13)	No. of Gram Panchayats affected by forcing Dalit to do menial services during death (14)	No. of Gram Panchayats affected due to problems created in cultivating their own lands (15)	No. of Gram Panchayats affected due to forced bonded labourers (16)	No. of Gram Panchayats affected due to compeling the children to be bonded labourers (17)	No. of Gram Panchayats affected due to judgments delivered by Traditional Panchayat leaders (18)	No. of Gram Panchayats affected due to punishment given to Dalits in the case of Dalit marrying a boy or girl from caste Hindus (19)	No. of Gram Panchayats affected due to discrimination while traveling in local buses (20)
1.	Madurai	83	80	76	78	82	70	50	46	63	80	76
2.	Sivaganga	80	53	58	48	44	22	14	33	29	73	20
3.	Erode	30	1	27	28	23	2	1	0	1	30	17
4.	Salem	27	10	18	22	26	0	0	2	5	26	0
5.	Perambalur	45	12	21	27	44	2	2	1	1	44	2
6.	Cuddalore	86	40	29	73	75	2	4	1	2	86	6
7.	Theni	20	11	8	20	20	0	1	0	1	20	0
8.	Dindigul	60	49	57	53	58	13	12	10	27	60	10

Table 10.1 (*Contd.*)

Sl. No.	Name of the District	Total No. of Gram Panchayats Covered	No. of Gram Panchayats affected due to discrimination in PDS shops (21)	No. of Gram Panchayats affected due to severe punishment meted out to Dalits violating social laws (22)	No. of Gram Panchayats affected due to threats, warning and attacks on Dalits by caste Hindus (23)	No. of Gram Panchayats affected due to restrictions imposed on Dalits to participate in common celebration and festivals (24)	No. of Gram Panchayats affected due to forcing to do jobs without wages (25)	No. of Gram Panchayats affected due to addressing elderly Dalits by their caste name (26)	No. of Gram Panchayats affected due to incidence of violence against Dalit women (27)	No. of Gram Panchayats affected due to violent insult and denigration of Dalits (28)	No. of Gram Panchayats affected due to restriction imposed on Dalits purchasing properties (29)	No. of Gram Panchayats affected due to dumping waste in the Dalits' settlement (30)
1.	Madurai	83	77	73	73	80	67	79	66	78	75	61
2.	Sivaganga	80	34	31	42	52	21	74	24	47	25	19
3.	Erode	30	1	12	5	26	2	30	2	27	1	2
4.	Salem	27	5	8	4	8	1	21	1	15	1	2
5.	Perambalur	45	6	4	5	25	3	42	3	32	2	2
6.	Cuddalore	86	18	13	26	37	0	79	5	47	5	1
7.	Theni	20	5	1	2	10	0	19	0	14	0	0
8.	Dindigul	60	33	18	28	53	25	57	24	54	14	7

Source: Computed.

In the 83 Gram Panchayats investigated in Madurai District, 22 Gram Panchayat Presidents confirmed the practice of untouchability and other forms of discrimination. In 77 Gram Panchayats two tumbler system is practiced; in 35 Gram Panchayats *dalits* are not permitted into the temples for worship, in 70 Gram Panchayats discriminatory practices are practised in schools, in 36 Gram Panchayats health institutions discriminate against the *dalits* while treating them for their ailments; in 46 Gram Panchayats *dalit* children are treated as bonded labourers; in 76 Gram Panchayats discriminatory practices are adopted while distributing essential things to *dalits* through the public distribution system. While going through Table 10.1, it is noted that all kinds of discriminatory activities were perpetuated in Madurai District. The maximum number of discriminations are practiced in this district compared as to other districts. Next to Madurai, Sivaganga is prominent.

In the 80 Gram Panchayats studied in Sivaganga District, 40 Gram Panchayat leaders confirmed discriminatory practices. In 48 Gram Panchayats two tumbler system is practiced; in 64 Gram Panchayats temple entry is not allowed for *dalits*; in 5 Gram Panchayats discriminatory practices are allowed in schools in different forms; in 14 Gram Panchayats *dalit* children are kept as bonded labourers; in 31 Gram Panchayats *dalits* are ill-treated in relationships and their due share of their entitlement is denied; in 24 Gram Panchayats caste Hindus exploit the *dalit* girls sexually. It is to be noted that Sivaganga district has maximum number of Traditional Panchayats still active and alive and it is one of the districts in Tamil Nadu regarded as models for management of irrigation canals with the active participation of the Community or Traditional Panchayats. Moreover, the Traditional Panchayats are active and vibrant and they invariably control the commons and the common property resources. The Traditional Panchayats have huge corpus funds and they are being used to manage the common property resources in the villages through a pucca management system. But all these Panchayats are not inclusive.

In the 45 Gram Panchayats studied in Perambalur District, the two tumbler system was in practice in 24 Gram Panchayats; in 35 Gram Panchayat areas *dalits* are not permitted to enter the temples of the caste Hindus; discrimination in school is in vogue in 3 Gram Panchayats; *dalits* are discriminated against in 8 Gram Panchayats when they get things in the public distribution system; in 30 Gram

Panchayats *dalits* are not permitted into the temples; *dalits* are not allowed to use the common properties and government properties in 12 Gram Panchayats; in 28 Gram Panchayats the *dalits* are asked to carry the dead animals and cremate the dead bodies; *dalits* are asked to perform certain funeral works in any caste Hindu family in 38 Gram Panchayat areas. Jeyamkondam and Andimadam areas are known for denial of hair dressing services to *dalits.*

In the 86 Gram Panchayats studied in Cuddalore District, 52 Gram Panchayat leaders confirmed the practice of untouchability by affixing their signatures in the document. In 16 Gram Panchayats the two tumbler system is practiced; in 54 Gram Panchayat areas *dalits* are not permitted to enter the temples of the caste Hindus; in 11 Gram Panchayats *dalits* are discriminated against in ration shops and public health centres in this district; Schools in 5 Gram Panchayats allow discriminatory practices; in 11 Gram Panchayats public toilets are not allowed to be used by the *dalits; dalits* are asked to perform funeral ceremonies in 75 Gram Panchayats; *dalits* are humiliated in all work places in 47 Gram Panchayats; and in 26 Gram Panchayats *dalit* women are harassed and sexually exploited.

In the 20 Gram Panchayats studied in Theni District, 11 Gram Panchayat leaders confirmed the existing practice of caste discrimination by submitting signed affidavits. 9 Panchayat Presidents confirmed the practice of the two tumbler system is in their areas; in 13 Gram Panchayat areas *dalits* are not allowed into the temples of the caste Hindus; in the same way commons and public places are restricted for *dalits*; in 6 Gram Panchayat areas *dalits* are not permitted to dress their hair in the saloons situated in their villages; in 20 Gram Panchayat areas *dalits* are compelled to perform the duties of burying and cremating the dead bodies; so also they are asked to perform the funeral duties; in 13 Gram Panchayat areas *dalits* are ill-treated.

In some of the districts many discriminatory practices are in vogue. Madurai, Theni, Dindigul and Sivaganga are the most affected as people have the memories of the caste clashes in the southern districts. It started from 1994 onwards. Later, it was intensified. Later it spread to the northern districts also. These kinds of problems are more acute in agricultural districts and backward districts. It is true, the discriminatory practices cannot be ended in a day or two. It requires a sea change in the altitude of the people belonging to dominant classes and castes. Wherever the societies are democratized, communities are politically mobilised the practice of untouchability has disappeared. To change the whole scenario, social movements have to help the State by doing social mobilization. The State has to work with a sense of commitment.

Problems faced by Gram Panchayat dalit Leaders

The following are the problems faced by the Gram Panchayat *dalit* leaders culled from the affidavits filed by them for the public hearing; in many places, when seats are reserved for *dalits,* the caste Hindus work out a strategy by which they sponsor a candidate from the same *dalit* community. The sponsored candidate has to affix his signature on the nomination paper and the rest of the things will be done by the Community Panchayats. In many Gram Panchayats, the sponsored candidate from the *dalit* community wins the election. Once he is declared elected, the candidate has to do his traditional work and the Panchayat activities will be looked after by the nominee of the Traditional Panchayat. Generally they are looked after by the Vice-President, normally from the dominant community.

In case the sponsored candidate of the Traditional Panchayat is defeated, the dominant community will find a person among the Ward Members for the Vice-President's post and that person will be selected as the Vice-President among the Ward Members of the Gram Panchayat. Once such a Vice-President is elected, Vice-President will try to usurp the power of the Gram Panchayat President. If the Gram Panchayat President is a *dalit* woman, the Vice-President will be from the caste Hindus. Once a Hindu male from among the Ward Members is elected for Vice-President, he will act as *de facto* President and the real *dalit* President has to sign on the dotted line. The women *dalit* leaders have formed their own federation to overcome such problems.

Based on this kind of experience the *dalit* Panchayat Presidents' Federation and Women Panchayat Leaders Federation repeatedly demanded of the government to reserve the President's and Vice-President's posts to women and *dalits.* In the same way when reservation is given to women in Gram Panchayat, the Vice-President's post should also be reserved for women. In all training programmes the *dalit* leaders used to lament that Vice-President being a caste Hindu representative, because they tend to dominate the whole body and marginalize the *dalit* leaders. Even at the Block level *Dalit* women leaders are not allowed to come to the office. Their husbands are attending to the office work and the officials also allow them into the office which is meant for elected women representatives.

There is another source of trouble from Traditional Panchayat leaders. In many Gram Panchayat areas, the common properties, especially natural resources, are with the Traditional Panchayats and the Traditional Panchayats have their own regulatory authority to use the commons and the commons are in the caste Hindu habitat areas. Hence, the *dalits* are not having access to the commons. Once the *dalits* become the Presidents, they want to have a legitimate hold over the commons which brings about conflict between the *dalits* and the caste Hindus.

There is yet another issue that destabilizes the *dalit* Panchayat leaders—the prevalence of social laws to regulate the social activities of the communities. Wherever the society is democratized the social laws are modified and the communities allow the *dalits* to perform their duties and responsibilities in Panchayats. Wherever communities are so rigid in adhering to established norms of social justice, the *dalits* find it very difficult to manage the Panchayats. *Dalit* leaders are not allowed to preside over the meeting, preside over the Gram Sabha. The *dalit* leaders are asked to follow the established social norms strictly. When they deviate they are punished.

Yet another source of trouble is the clerk. If the clerks belonging to the caste Hindus the entire office will be with the clerk. The elected *dalit* leaders will be made subservient to the Panchayat clerks who will be in the hands of dominant caste Hindus. Hence, *dalit* Panchayat leaders have been complaining against the clerks for the past one and half decades. Likewise the Women Panchayat leaders also make such complaints.

Officials who are dealing with Panchayats are not sensitive towards this kind of discrimination. Women leaders are elected and the elected leaders have to preside over the Gram Sabha meetings. The Traditional Panchayat leaders are asking the Vice-President to preside over the Gram Sabha meeting in front of the government officials who attend the meetings as observers. The observers have to object but they are not doing so. In the same way *dalit* Panchayat Presidents are not allowed into offices. Instead Vice-

Presidents belonging to caste Hindu are allowed to go to offices. These kinds of activities have to be opposed and should not be encouraged. But in reality the officials instead of discouraging, are encouraging the caste Hindu leaders to operate as proxies in Panchayats. The officials are the biggest obstacle in this process.

Gram Panchayat leaders have to work for economic development and social justice. When discriminatory practices are perpetuated, they are to be curbed and Panchayats have to work for it. Many Gram Panchayat leaders approach the officials when human rights are violated but their complaints are not taken into cognizance of. Even *dalit* Panchayat Presidents who are discriminated against complaint to the police no action is taken. In many places not even an FIR is filed. Even to file an FIR the *dalits* have to struggle. Normally, the officials have to support the *dalit* leaders to come out from all kinds of discriminatory practices. But it is not happening in the rural areas of Tamil Nadu.

In all offices excepting higher level offices, *dalit* Panchayat leaders are not allowed to sit in chairs. In the Gram Panchayat offices when non-dalits visit, the *dalit* Panchayat President has to give his seat and stand before them till the caste Hindus go out. *Dalit* Panchayat women leaders are not allowed to visit the Gram Panchayat office.

Moreover, in all beneficiary selections, the *dalit* leaders are not involved. They are all decided upon by the Vice-President who belongs to caste Hindu. In many of the Panchayat areas access to safe drinking water to *dalits* is a major issue. To overcome this issue *dalit* Panchayat leaders take steps to create such a kind of facility in their own area for which the *dalit* leaders seek the help of other members. But the caste Hindu leaders refuse to support the same. Some of the worst affected are given below as cases for understanding the gravity of the problems.

CASE – I
Koneripalayam Gram Panchayat
Perambalur District

K. Shanthadevi (32) wife of K. Kumar (35) is the President of Koneripalayam Gram Panchayat in Perambalur District. She belongs to Dravida Munnetra Kazhagam (DMK) party which is the ruling party at present. In her Gram Panchayat there are six

Ward Members and of them three are from Backward Class and the other three are from *dalits.* Of the six members three are men and the other three are women. She belongs to the *dalit* community. Her Vice-President is also a woman of the village. The clerk Mr. R. Kumar belongs to the same dominant community of the Vice-President. When she decided to contest in the election as it was reserved for *dalits,* the caste Hindus organized under the leadership of Mr. Karupaiah and found out a candidate from the Arundhadhiar community (a sub-caste of SC) and compelled him to contest in the election. Despite all their efforts she won the election. On the day of the election, after the declaration of the results, a gang of henchmen went to the house of the Panchayat leader and threatened her of dire consequences. She went to the police station and filed a case against them. A case was registered (FIR 541/06) and till date there is no action against them. All public utilities are in the dominant caste area. Whether it is a school, or ration shop, or health centre, or SHG building, or Panchayat Office, or Water tank, every facility is in their area only. For each and everything the *dalits* have to go to the area of the dominant caste. Hence, they have been teased, ill-treated, humiliated and harassed after this election. When she visits her office regularly, six to seven men of the caste Hindus join together, sat in front of the Panchayat office, and heckle her. She confirmed all those discriminatory practices in her affidavit submitted for public hearing. Whatever decision she takes, they are not implemented by her clerk as he belongs to caste Hindu and is working under the influence of the caste Hindu leader. When she was asked as to why her political party leaders (DMK) have not come to rescue her from this ordeal, she informed that the party will work only up to a certain level. But certainly it will not come up to community level. At the village level, communities are powerful and community practices are in vogue. Now it is a struggle between constitutional sanctions and community laws. She said that the *dalits* have to be prepared for a struggle for which fair minded citizens have to support them. She confirmed the discriminatory practices adopted in her Panchayat area by the caste Hindus. She also complained that to protect the common lands from encroachment she waged a relentless struggle against some influential individuals in this Village Panchayat. Totally the Gram Panchayat leader is in struggle for which she needs a support structure.

CASE – II
Ambalavanampatti Gram Panchayat
Cuddalore District

Ms. Sakunthala (45) wife of Kuppusamy, is the Gram Panchayat President of Ambalavanampattii Village Panchayat of Cuddalore District. Ambalavanampatti being reserved for *dalit* women, she was prompted by her own relatives and friends to contest in the election. Accordingly, she filed her nomination. After she filed her nomination without consulting the Hindu caste leaders, under the leadership of Mr. Ramachandran, former President of the same Gram Panchayat, all the caste Hindus joined and found another *dalit* woman of the same region and she was asked to contest in the election. Sakunthala mobilised the people and got victory in the election. She was offered Rs. 50,000 by the Traditional Panchayat leaders to keep away from Panchayat activities. In her Panchayat there are nine Ward Members, and of them three are from *dalits* and the others are from the Most Backward and backward communities. With the help of the Ward Members, the caste Hindus elected Mr. Selvakumar as Vice-President. He belongs to the dominant caste. Since the election he never helped the Panchayat leader to carry out any useful work. As Vice-President he has to work with her. But unfortunately he never cooperated with her as she reported in her affidavit. He demanded money to affix his signature in all the cheques to be passed. She further observed in her affidavit that the *dalits* in her village are not allowed to sit in the tea stall or to enter the temples of the Village Panchayat areas. *Dalits* are asked to perform all the low level jobs including burial and cremation of dead bodies of the caste Hindus. Even dead animals are to be removed only by the *dalits*. From day one of the election, the *dalits* whether they are school going children, or women or agricultural labourers are harassed by the caste Hindu leaders. The caste Hindus are not ready to recognize the *dalits* emerging as leaders. It is a mindset which has to be broken for which government officials have to help. *Dalit* women are sexually exploited by the caste Hindu leaders in this village. The *Dalit* women leaders never file complaints in the police stations as it will create a major conflict between *dalits* and non-*dalits*. Since one of her relatives is an educated person she is able to perform her duties and responsibilities. She feels that it is a relentless struggle; it is to be supported by the public.

CASE – III
Uthandiyur Gram Panchayat
Erode District

Mr. Marappan (47) who belongs to the Hindu Kuravar community (gypsies), is the President of Uthandiyur Gram Panchayat of Erode District. It has got 32 hamlets and twelve Ward Members. Of them five are women and seven are men. Of the 12 members three are from *dalit* community and the other nine are from the Backward Class. Mr. Ganakaraj (40) is the clerk of the Gram Panchayat. Mr. Nandakumar is the Vice-President of the Panchayat who belongs to dominant caste of the village. Marappan affirms the prevalence of caste discrimination in tea stalls, public places, transport, temples and other areas in his Panchayat. Since all resources are in the area of caste Hindus, they cannot be used by the *Dalits* and if they cross the limit, they are taken to task. He is not allowed to sit in his chair by the caste Hindu Ward Members. The Ward Members come to office only after consuming alcohol. He is always humiliated verbally by the males and females of the Panchayat Council. The Gram Sabha is not presided over by him. Gram Sabha meetings are conducted by the Vice-President. All records are with them. They carry out all activities of the Panchayat. He is being asked to sign the documents for which pressure is being built up by the Ward Members. In his Panchayat area discriminatory practices were observed and the President of Gram Panchayat confirmed them. He sent petition after petition to the District Collector but nothing came out of it.

CASE – IV
Chitrapattipudur Gram Panchayat
Salem District

Ms. Sahayammari (30), wife of Karuppanan, is the President Chitrapattipudur Gram Panchayat in Salem District. She unequivocally affirmed the existing practice of discrimination in her Village Panchayat area in tea stalls, ration shops and temples. In her Panchayat there are nine members and of them two women members are from the *dalit* community and the others are caste Hindus. Both the Vice-President and the clerk are non-*dalits*. It is a practice in this village that the *dalit* women and men are being treated very badly by using unparliamentary words. *Dalits* have tolerated so far. Now they feel it is a humiliation and hence something should be done about this. The former Panchayat President who belongs to the dominant caste, instigated all to work against her. They could not tolerate a *Dalit* woman to assume power in the Panchayat. The Vice-President is acting as President. The entire Panchayat Council has been oriented to ill-treat the Panchayat leader.

CASE – V
Padiganalam Gram Panchayat
Krishnagiri District

Ms. Gowramma (45) is the President of Padiganalam Gram Panchayat of Krishnagiri District informed that she is not allowed to sit in the chair. Her Panchayat has got eight hamlets. Ms. Mallechammal belonging to the caste Hindu, is the Vice-President of the Gram Panchayat. Gowramma is not allowed to sit during the Panchayat Council meeting. She has been asked to stand till the meeting is over. In the same way she is not allowed to preside over the Gram Sabha meetings. She is not even consulted by the Vice-President and other members. She is asked to come to the office and asked to affix her signature in the registers. She does it due to fear. Since she belongs to the tribal community she cannot mobilize the support of her people as they are in the hill areas. She was assaulted by a caste Hindu person, Mr. Nanjundappa, for her decision to create a water pond. Along with him other caste Hindu individuals joined together and beat her up in. Her husband was beaten with chappals by the same group. She was threatened by them and asked not to go to any place to complain. Srinivasan, a caste Hindu clerk is literally managing the Panchayat by the decision of the dominant caste group. Tribals are not allowed to organize themselves.

CASE – VI
Vakarai Gram Panchayat
Dindigul District

Mr. K. Chinnan (44) is the President of Vakarai Gram Panchayat in Dindigul District. He belongs to the Arundadiar community. It is one of the sub-castes of Scheduled Caste in Tamil Nadu. He is a daily wage earner. He is an unskilled labourer. Having got elected as President he carried out the activities of the Panchayat. In one of the hamlets (Pusarigouondan Valasu) a water tank was not functioning for some time and he took efforts to repair the same. He did it and ensured water supply for which he spent Rs. 25,000. Within a few days the whole pipeline was damaged by a group of miscreants with the intention of bringing bad name to the President. He went to the spot and inspected the same and complaint to the officials at the Block Development Office. The officials advised him to file a complaint in the police station. In the meanwhile when he visited the hamlets he requested the people who were sitting near the water tank to take care of the pipeline. Mr. Nataraja Gounder, a caste Hindu representative, argued that it is the responsibility of the Panchayat that too the responsibility of the Panchayat President to protect the properties of the Panchayat. People who were sitting along with him picked a quarrel with him and argued that a *dalit* is giving orders to a non-*dalit*. This was a point for further conflict with the Panchayat President. Based on this argument Nataraj Gounder picked a quarrel with the President and beat him up. He went to the police station and filed a complaint but it was not registered. The police advised him not to register a case against a caste Hindu. Everyone advised him not to file a case against him, but to reach a compromise with him. Otherwise it would become a law and order problem, observed the police officials. Later he submitted a petition to the Minister for Local Bodies. The Panchayat clerk Mr. Nachathan literally runs the Panchayat based on the advice of the caste Hindus in this Village Panchayat. So far no action was taken. All the time he was under duress and fear, yet he is waging a war against the tyranny of the dominant caste.

CASE – VII
Poyyalur Gram Panchayat
Sivagangai District

Ms. K. Tamilmani (45), wife of Kuppusamy, is the President of Poyyalur Gram Panchayat of Sivagangai District. There are eight hamlets in this Village Panchayat. Three are six Ward Members. Of them two belong to *dalits* and four others belong to caste Hindus. The Gram Panchayat clerk belongs to the dominant caste group.

All the four members along with the Panchayat clerk at the behest of the Traditional Panchayat are not allowing the President to discharge her responsibilities and duties. She submitted petitions to officials and the police but no action was taken in this regard. When she contested in the election, the caste Hindus sponsored a candidate, Ms. Nagarani, but she was defeated by her. The defeat of Nagarani was considered as the defeat of the caste Hindus. Hence, a group of caste Hindus started damaging the public properties as if they were damaging the Panchayat President's. Poyyalur Village does not have enough water to drink and no ration shop. To overcome the problem she took efforts to bring a ration shop and dig a bore well. When sanction was accorded it was disturbed by a group of people. She was threatened and abused by some of the caste Hindu leaders. She filed a complaint against them. When she conducted the Panchayat Council meeting and Gram Sabha meeting, she was insulted, humiliated and verbally abused. Her husband and her son were threatened by the caste Hindu leaders. She made complaints to District Officials and Police. No action was initiated. Instead of taking initiative to sensitise the caste Hindus, everyone is advising the dalit Panchayat leader to adjust with the caste Hindus. Everyone is developing fear over law and order problem.

Analysis

It was presumed before the introduction of the New Panchayati Raj System in Tamil Nadu through the Tamil Nadu Panchayat Act 1994 that the problems of untouchability and discrimination have gone down in Tamil Nadu because of the social transformation activities of the Dravidian Movement. In reality it is not so. After the election to Local Bodies in 1996 we have witnessed the Melavalavu murder of *dalit* Panchayat leader by the dominant community and subsequent refusal to conduct of election to four reserved Panchayats by the dominant communities in Pappapatti, Keeripatti, Nattarmangalam and Kottakatchiyenthal Gram Panchayats in Madurai and Virudhunagar Districts. Subsequently in many Panchayats elected *dalit* leaders are not allowed to govern and administer Panchayats. In many areas *dalit* Panchayat leaders are beaten up and physically tortured. They were all reported. In many Panchayats disputes arose between Constitutional

Panchayats and Traditional Panchayats over the management of common properties. But the conditions cf *dalit* Panchayat Presidents is not uniform. In some districts Traditional Panchayats are highly rigid and communal and they are very strict in adhering to community norms and laws. In some districts communities are socialized and politically oriented. They are flexible. The problems of the *dalits* are not so severe as we find in other districts. The *dalits* are not so rich and they have to rely on the others for each and everything in the rural areas. Moreover, their entire livelihood is based on the lands of the caste Hindus. The districts which are industrialized do not have much problem or as intensively as in non-industrialized districts. Districts which are agriculture based do have this problem very deeply. In the same way districts which are under the influence of the left parties do not have such problem.

There is yet another argument in this regard. Since Village Panchayats are free from party based electoral contest, Village Panchayat President's positions are viewed as non-party ones and hence communities have control over it. If it is done as in West Bengal or Kerala, this problem can be solved easily. Whenever the *dalit* Gram Panchayat leader is facing such problem at the community level, the political parties are not taking interest in it. In the left political parties, they view it seriously, if their party leader at Gram Panchayat level is attacked by the caste Hindus. After seeing the atrocities committed against the *dalit* leaders at the Gram Panchayat level, an argument has emerged from the intellectuals, media and the civil society organizations that Gram Panchayat should also be contested on a party basis.

Though the Gram Panchayat *dalit* leaders have political party affiliations, the parties are not coming forward openly to help them as they will lose the votes of other castes. One exception is the Communist Party of India (Marxist) and the Communist Party of India. They take care of their representatives belonging to the *dalit* community. At the Gram Panchayat level, when the President's post is reserved for *dalits,* the dominant communities find out one candidate from the *dalit* community who should be the proxy of the dominant classes. If the candidate is defeated, the caste Hindus will work out a strategy by which a caste Hindu male or female will be elected as Vice-President through this indirect election by managing the Ward Members. The clerk is always from a dominant community. By doing so, the *dalit* leaders are brought under the control of the community system. The leaders who want to act independently as per the provisions of the Act will be disturbed through the Vice-President, the clerk and the Ward Members. It is a well known practice in many places. *Dalit* leaders and women leaders face "no confidence motions" without any charge. In this way they are threatened. The officials who have to help the Panchayat leaders from the *dalit* community have let them down as they are insensitive to this issue of exclusion and gender. They always give advice to the *dalit* leaders to adjust with caste Hindus. The *dalit* Gram Panchayat leaders who take genuine interest in providing basic facilities to *dalits* are opposed by the caste Hindus. *Dalit* and women leaders need a specific orientation to handle power. Unfortunately they are not being given this. One is recognition of *dalit* to lead the Panchayat. The other is taking up the issues of untouchability by the Gram Panchayat *dalit* President. It is almost like abolishing slavery or apartheid. Once the untouchability issue is solved, a major problem in our society will be over. A poor *dalit* woman is harassed by a poor woman of caste Hindu. A poor woman of caste Hindus cannot be tortured by even a rich *dalit* woman. When the elected leader takes up the issue, he/she is cornered and disturbed. To solve this issue, the *dalit* Gram Panchayat leader has to broadbase his/her activities. It needs the support of civil society organizations, political parties, intellectuals and the media. The problems of the *dalits* are of different dimensions and intensities and are to be tackled with different strategies.

In some districts only a few problems are in practice. But their intensity may vary. In certain districts one will find more number of problems and with high intensity. For instance, in Madurai, Theni, Dindigul, Sivagangai, Ramanathapuram, Tuticorin, Thirunelveli, one will find more problems. Take the case of Erode, Salem, Coimbatore, Trichy. One will find lesser intensity of the issues, because the above districts are economically developed. Moreover, in urbanized and industrialized districts, the intensity of the problems will be less. In rural and agriculture based districts intensity of the issues will be very high. Again, even if they are rural and agri based, in those districts which are influenced by the Left will not find such intensity as we find in other districts.

As one can see the problems are many. But it is good that the Panchayati Raj System exposes the problems. Government and society cannot escape and solutions have to be found. The moment *dalits* come to power, they try to look at the issues of the *dalits*. First the *dalit* leaders try to provide basic facilities such as water supply, road, street lights, toilets and avoid dumping the waste of the entire village in the *dalit* settlements. By doing so visibly the *dalit* hamlets are getting a face-lift which cannot be digested by the other communities. The community leaders are not sensitized and hence they get angry with the *dalit* leaders. The *dalit* leaders by evolving a strategy through adequate training and with the help of a support structure, can transform the condition of the *dalits*.

Conclusion

It is obvious from the analysis of data that discriminatory culture in the rural areas has played havoc with governance at the grassroots under *dalit* leadership. The very purpose of reserving seats for *dalits* and women will yield results only when they are allowed to discharge their roles and responsibilities. At present, it is evident from the analysis that the leaders are facing a volley of problems because of the existing discriminatory practices. At every level they are facing the problems. The *dalits'* living conditions social and economic conditions have not improved despite the presence of *dalit* leaders as Presidents of the respective Panchayats. Since the Panchayat elections held during the period of clash between the dominant communities and the *dalits* in the southern districts, the animosity between two castes has not been decreased. The economic condition of the dominant communities is not high as other castes. The dominant communities are not always land owning communities barring a few families. So they are also agriculture based families with landholdings or agriculture labourers. With poor supportive structure, lack of training, insensitivity on the part of the officials, the *dalit* Panchayat leaders are groping in the dark. In many ways the cleavage in the community has been exposed. To overcome these problems a series of steps are needed.

Recommendations

Periodically the *dalit* Gram Panchayat leaders have to be organized and they are to be trained properly on how to attack the issue of untouchability. The *dalit* Gram Panchayat leaders should have a district level federation and a State level federation. To support this federation, a support structure has to be developed by the civil society organizations. Periodically they have to meet and share their problems and chalk out action programmes. Further, they have to connect themselves with political parties which are sensitive to the issues of the *dalits*. Periodically their issues have to be highlighted through media coverage and raised in the State Legislative Assembly. District Collectors should bring sensitive Panchayats under their scan in terms of discriminatory practices.

Independent research centres should be vested with the responsibility of investigating the problems of untouchability in the rural areas. The reports of research institutions should be viewed seriously by the District Administration for which the necessary instruction has to come from the State government. Periodical visits of the Human Rights Commission, SC Commission, ST Commission, Women Commission representatives to the districts will bring about sensitivity among the officials who are responsible for law and order in the districts. Simultaneously district level conferences have to be organized with the support of the political parties to bring about transformation on the part of the thought process of the dominant communities. Annually a social harmony prize is being distributed among the Gram Panchayats which bring about social harmony among the communities. Beyond that Panchayats should be given incentives for eradicating discriminatory practices.

Whenever public functions are organized in any village, the respective Gram Panchayat Presidents should be invited and they should be given seats on the dais as the other officials and representatives take seats and in this way they have to be recognized.

There is yet another need for *dalit* Panchayat leaders, namely, Capacity Building Exercise. Generally, Panchayat leaders are not trained properly and they are not provided with needed information to discharge their responsibilities. Hence, the Panchayat leaders are unable to carry out their main responsibilities of achieving economic development and social justice. The *dalit* leaders are the worst affected as they are not trained and they are not provided with the information related to Panchayat governance and administration. The existing practice of training in Tamil Nadu is organizing a two-day training programme at Block level in the Block Panchayat Office and the training sessions are handled by the Block level officials who are not well versed in Panchayati Raj. For all Panchayat leaders a minimum of five days training is an imperative need. For *dalit* Panchayat leaders, a separate training package is essential. They need a different kind of training. Further, they need a support structure to carry out their activities. *Dalit* leaders should have some kind of political affiliation preferably Leftist since the leftists are the only political parties extending all kinds of political support to *dalit* Panchayat leaders. Further, they need to have a media tie up for getting wider exposure and to expose the atrocities committed against *dalits* and *dalit* leaders.

Dalit Panchayat leaders should have contact with political parties which are pro-*dalit* and pro-Panchayat. By taking their problems to such political parties the *dalit* leaders can get the support of such parties and it will help proper policy advocacy. In Tamil Nadu, many *dalit* Panchayat leaders have joined left political parties that too the Communist Party of India (Marxist) when they face such problems in their Panchayats. On all occasions, the Left political parties extend such kind of support.

NOTES

1. I have used the term "*Dalit*" as used by the activists with the meaning oppressed because of caste. It includes all categories of the group called "*Harijan*" in the Constitution.
2. Nowhere are the *dalits* in isolation. Further, they are not coopted. They are elected and they are in the process of election. Wherever *dalits* occupy positions, they will be with *dalits* as their number is determined by their population strength. So they form a critical mass. This critical mass can assert and perform critical functions, namely providing basic facilities to the *dalit* areas to enable them to lead a decent human life. They can work for removing untouchability and other discriminatory practices.

REFERENCES

Ananthpur, Kripa, "Selection by Custom and Election of Statute: Interfaced in Local Governance in Karnataka" in Niraja Gopal Jayal, Amit Prakash and Pradeep K. Sharma (Eds), *Local Governance in India*, New Delhi: Oxford University Press, 2006.

Chattopadhyay, Raghabendra and Esther Dufflo, "Impact of Reservation in Panchayati Raj: Evidence from a Nationwide Randomised Experiment" in Satyajit Singh and Pradeep K. Sharma (eds.), *Decentralization: Institutions and Politics in Rural India,* New Delhi: Oxford University Press, 2007.

Chaudhary, S.N., *Dalit and Tribal Leadership in Panchayats,* New Delhi: Concept Publishing Company, 2004.

Palani, N., "Dalit Politics and Dravidian Movement in Tamil Nadu", Gandhigram Rural University, Unpublished Ph.D. thesis (May, 2004).

Palanithurai, G., *Capacity Building for Local Body Leaders,* New Delhi: Concept Publishing Company, 2001.

Palanithurai, G., *Process and Performance of Gram Panchayat Women and Dalit Presidents,* New Delhi: Concept Publishing Company, 2003.

Palanithurai, G., *Third General Election to Local Bodies in Tamil Nadu,* New Delhi: Concept Publishing Company, 2008.

Parthiban, T., "Caste and Political Mobilization in Tamil Nadu" in G. Palanithurai and R. Thandavan (eds.) *Ethnic Movement in Transition,* New Delhi: Kanishka Publishers & Distributors, 1998.

Rajiv Gandhi Chair, *Report of the Training Programme conducted for Dalit Block Panchayat Women Leaders of Tamil Nadu,* Gandhigram: Rajiv Gandhi Chair for Panchayati Raj Studies, 2002.

Sathyavanimuthu, *My Struggle,* Chennai: Chezhiyan Publications, 1981; Gnanaraj Xavier *et al., Outside the Caste (A Status Report on the Dalits of Tamil Nadu),* Chengalpattu: Educational Trust, 2002; and Hugo Gorringe, *Untouchable Citizens: Dalit Movements and Democratization in Tamil Nadu,* New Delhi: Sage Publications, 2005.

Shah, Ghanshiyam, "Dalit Politics: Has it Reached an Impasse?" in Niraja Gopal Jayal and Sudhai Pai (eds.), *Democratic Governance in India,* New Delhi: Sage Publications, 2001, p. 233.

Viswanathan, S., *Dalits in Dravidian Land,* Chennai: Navayana, 2005.

ANNEXURE

Annexure Table 10.1: Affidavit Filed by Gram Panchayat Dalit Leaders for Public Hearing

Sl. No.	*Name*	*Sex*	*Panchayat*	*District*
1.	K. Sandhadevi	Female	Koneripalayam	Perambalur
2.	R. Vanitha	Female	Veerananallur	Cuddalore
3.	S. Chandrakala	Female	Adhichanallur	Tuticorin
4.	N. Dhavamani	Female	Vadaku Melur	Cuddalore
5.	K. Sakundala	Female	Ambalavananpatti	Cuddalore
6.	A. Marappan	Male	Uthandiyur	Erode
7.	N. Ramalingam	Male	Aamavakkamthondi	Perambalur
8.	P. Ramalingam	Male	Nagampandal	Perambalur
9.	K. Sahayamari	Female	Chithirapadi	Salem
10.	K. Dhanam	Female	Ayyanapuram	Perambalur
11.	C.V.Sathya	Female	Asthinapuram	Perambalur
12.	M. Amirthavalli	Female	Sathiavadi	Cuddalore
13.	V. Mary	Female	Karkudal	Cuddalore
14.	V. Selvaraj	Male	Panikkanur	Salem
15.	S Kannan	Male	Vellarivelli	Salem
16.	V. Sabanayagam	Male	Thiraiyur	Cuddalore
17.	G. Thillaigoundan	Male	Velankkipattu	Cuddalore
18.	A. Sivaguruynathan	Male	Anaikudam	Perambalur
19.	P. Malarkodi	Female	Adhivaraganallur	Cuddalore
20.	M. Sasikala	Female	Nattarmangalam	Cuddalore
21.	S. Veeran	Male	Keelakuppam	Cuddalore
22.	K.P.Selvaraj	Male	Karthanam	Cuddalore
23.	M. Samayamuthu	Male	Thanjakur	Sivagangai
24.	K. Saraswathi	Female	Kulur	Erode
25.	K. Kannaiyan	Male	Periathukurichi	Perambalur
26.	C.Selvam	Male	Kurur	Perambalur
27.	N. Prema	Female	Plindikuzhi	Perambalur
28.	Selvaraj	Male	Thethampattu	Cuddalore
29.	V.Chitra	Female	Arasanur	Cuddalore
30.	Balaguru	Male	Santhirakillai	Cuddalore
31.	S.Jeganathan	Male	Okkaraipatti	Theni
32.	R.Palaniammal	Female	Natiyuthu	Theni
33.	L. Chandrasekaran	Male	Thirumanavayal	Sivagangai
34.	P. Gowravam	Female	Padiganalaur	Krishnagiri
35.	P. Nagaraj	Male	Kadamalaikundu	Theni
36.	K. Chinnan	Male	Vakarai	Dindigul
37.	K.Tamilmani	Female	Poyyalur	Sivagangai
38.	K.Lakshmi	Female	Morpatti	Dindigul
39.	T.Babiperumal	Male	Athikombai	Dindigul
40.	P. Vijayarani	Female	Viralimalaipatti	Dindigul
41.	M. Nagarajan	Male	Kullichettipatti	Dindigul
42.	S. Jeya	Female	Ethirode	Dindigul
43.	R. Velankanni	Male	Mangarai	Dindigul
44.	P. Manivannan	Male	Sirukudi	Dindigul

Source: Computed.

XI

Democracy, Development and Conflict at Grassroots

Introduction

India is a multi-ethnic society and it is always prone to conflict as diversities and disparities are vast. The presence of ethnic, lingual and cultural groups divides the society broadly and deeply on a variety of socio-cultural conditions into groups (Basu and Kohli, 1993:3). All the conflicts organized in any society are based on resource sharing and power sharing. When the aspired for demands are not met it is natural that people organize themselves with some identity and exert pressure on the state (Palanithurai, 1993). The available economic resources and political spaces are inadequate to meet the aspirations, needs and demands of the existing population in many countries in the world. As a result, one witnesses conflict among collectivities. Despite the presence of all such conflicts and crises, democracy survives in the world. But there is a limit to such conflicts. If the conflicts cross the manageable limit, they will destabilize democracy. Theoretically speaking, the existing level of conflicts will not allow democracy to function. Democracy cannot survive and flourish amidst conflicts. Many countries which had committed themselves to practicing representative democracy have slipped and moved away from democracy (Sau, 2008: 28-37). But in India democracy survives despite a high level of social and political conflicts. So India is regarded as a paradox (Weiner, 1989). In India democratic institutions are functioning above the community level. India is a country of one billion people for whom we had only six thousand representatives of the people (Both in the Indian Parliament and the State Legislatures). It is a well known fact that in India still 72 per cent of the people live in rural areas and they are predominantly engaged in agriculture. Further, they are living a feudal culture. In all the villages, one cannot find equality, equity and modern democracy. For the first time in India a new system of governance has been established through the Constitution (the 73rd Amendment to the Constitution of India) in Indian villages, which, in my opinion, will create basic changes in the villages by altering the social relations in some places and will create conflicts in many villages (Palanithurai, 2007). Because, even after sixty years of democratic governance, villages are still under the framework of community laws (Palanithurai, 2007). Democracy has not been practiced as a culture, a value and a way of life in Indian Society. In India polity alone is democratized and that too limited to elections. Democracy is equated with elections. As a result, people have developed a perception that election is democracy. One finds feudal elements in the functioning of the political parties in India (Palanithurai, 2008:61-67).

The 73rd Amendment to the Constitution of India has come with the potential of transforming the socio–economic life and politics of the people at the grassroots. For the first time in India after Independence, democracy has been deepened and restored at the grassroots as a culture with more representatives and with an inclusive character of accommodating all social groups in the process of governance and development. The new institutional mechanism created at the grassroots through the 73rd Amendment has the basic objective of establishing a participatory culture in governance and administration. A people centric governance and administration will be established up to the lowest unit of the human habitat. This was the general expectation of all when the historic amendments were introduced. The powers of decision making, evolving micro plan for development and allocating resources for activities have been devolved to these institutions through this new dispensation constitutionally (Palanithurai, 2002:3-5). Apparently it gives a feeling that it will enhance the scope for people's participation in the process of development and deepening of democracy. It is to be noted that the new institutional mechanism has to work in a social settings which are highly fragmented and hierarchical because of the social and economic inequality in Indian society (Srinivas, 1996). It is already a proved fact that many of the fine provisions of Constitution have not been implemented and as a result state is in a state of guilt. The social groups which are going to be benefited are not in a position to claim the entitlements as rights. That is why many of the academics argue in favour of giving the right to the people to resist and protest against the state when it fails. There is yet another issue associated with the devolution of powers. People who are enjoying power at present are devising strategies to keep power with them and those who are going to gain benefit out of reservation of seats under the new dispensation are not aware of the new opportunities and they do not have the skill and capacity to claim their legitimate benefits. Further, they do not have the needed support structure to claim their entitlements also (Palanithurai, 2001). In this context one has to visualize a condition theoretically whether the democracy envisaged at the grassroots will solve many of the problems hitherto unsolved.

Theoretically speaking, democracy has the potential to solve conflicts provided society has got the requisite maturity, understanding and skill on the part of the leadership (Palanithurai, Thirunavukkarasu, Uma, 2008:288). But, in reality, it has triggered intensive conflicts among the communities as this new democracy at the grassroots starts with the electoral process. The electoral process in India creates conflicts among contenders and contending parties. On many occasions it is explicitly demonstrated that democracy is practiced at the cost of development. It seems that India paid a heavy price for democracy. Sometimes it is argued that in India democracy is practiced at the cost of development. Yet it is a needed instrument. It is also true that it is the only available instrument of the poor to fight against the injustice done to them socially, economically and politically. For the first time the new Panchayati Raj System goes to the community with constitutional provisions for governance. The moment the constitutional provisions go to the communities, they have to interact with community provisions and practices. Communities follow social norms which prevent equality and equity being followed as the social hierarchy has been accepted and internalized. Along with social hierarchy, patriarchy too has been accepted and internalized. But now the new provisions of the constitution negate the social norms and community practices. The new provision negates patriarchy. When the state takes steps to make the communities follow the provisions of the Constitution and allow the marginalized and oppressed to occupy the space legitimately through the electoral process for governance and administration, the social groups which have been in control of the community develop conflicts (Palanithurai, 2008:101).

It is to be noted that conflict arises out of fear of the coming of the oppressed to the power centre and their getting control over the resources and changing the social relations. Till date resources in the rural areas have been controlled by the dominant communities (Palanithurai and Ragupathy, 2007). But now it has been changed because of the introduction of the New Panchayati Raj System. Indian conditions and experiences have projected an argument that this creates more of conflict. Even the conflicts will also have to be solved only through the democratic process. In a society like India it is natural that democracy is an instrument by which society is oriented. Social and political conflicts are resolved only through this process. The whole exercise of deepening of democracy starts with elections. At present the electoral process will certainly create conflict. The presence of more number of players are in electoral contest at the micro level intensifies the political conflict. As a result, community cohesion is thwarted. Community cohesion means the social order created by the dominant groups and universally accepted and internalized. The reservation of seats for women and *dalits* has further deepened the divide between the *dalits* and the other dominant communities. One has to understand that communities at the grassroots are organized on caste lines and they live together without having any friction in many places as people generally have accepted the social norms. Wherever society becomes mature, the communities live together and understand the process of social transformation. The dominant communities do not act as a barrier to the progress of the *dalit* communities (Palanithurai, 2004). *Dalits* are not ill-treated either. Wherever there is no such understanding among the communities communal conflict persists. When election was declared, in many places the positions were auctioned, sold and the persons for positions were arbitrarily decided upon, because of the dominant communities' "dictated decisions" were imposed on the communities. In a few Panchayats the dominant communities rejected the proposal for conducting election itself as the President's positions were reserved for *dalits*.

In many places *dalits* and women were allowed to file their nominations and they were allowed to contest in the election. Once they were elected, they were not allowed to go to office and perform their duties. In all those places the community leaders have taken a conscious decision that one could not stop the election as it was mandated by the Constitution. But, after the election, the *dalit* and women leaders were not allowed to perform their duties and responsibilities. By allowing *dalit* and women candidates to contest in the election, the communities have operationalised the constitutional provision. After the election, the *dalits* and women elected to the positions were not allowed to go to their offices and discharge their responsibilities by the dominant communities through their organizational structure by which constitutional provisions are undermined and community laws are upheld. It is expected that at this juncture the state has to act firmly by supporting the elected leaders to take on power and discharge their responsibilities. What is going on at present at the grassroots is a kind of proxy. In certain places women and *dalits* are allowed to contest, and allowed to perform their duties, but they are not supported effectively by the communities. The *dalit* and women leaders have to face all kinds of the problems in the system without having any support structure (Palanithurai, Uma, Vanishree, 2008). Here the community leaders felt that it would be very difficult to keep the elected leaders away from office and power when the Constitution has granted them. Hence, they have evolved a new device by which the elected leaders' activities are not supported by the communities. It is a kind of non-cooperation practiced in certain places.

Over a period of time representative democracy not only in India but also in many countries has intensified the conflicts between and among political parties to capture positions. The political parties which contest in the elections for the National Parliament and the State Legislative Assemblies trigger the conflict to the level of treating each other as an arch enemies in a very acrimonious way. Once the election is over the ruling party uses all official machinery to suppress the opposition party and files cases against the opposition party. Defaming each other and maligning each other is the normal phenomenon in Indian politics. This kind of syndrome has started at the State Level and now it has gone up to the national level. Political parties are fighting in such a way that the party cadres are also taking positions and fighting against each other.

Moreover, even within the party intra-party rivalry has picked up to the maximum to capture party positions and to seek tickets to contest in the Parliament and Assembly elections. Those who are not accommodated leave the party, levelling charges against the party leadership. Even in the party elections one finds murderous attacks on the candidates who contest. In Tamil Nadu above more than 800 cases have been registered against the candidates who contested in the election for party positions in a single party. The internal conflict within a party is also a factor in determining the quality of democracy. Further, all these positions carry economic and political value. As long as the public space is meant for serving and not for making profit, the positions are not keenly contested by the candidates. Once it is perceived that the public space is meant for private benefits while serving the people intense conflict arises to capture positions. All these political conflicts are basically triggered by the economic interest.

There is another issue one has to take note of. Many political parties have not conducted elections. For several years positions were given by mere nomination. Several positions were kept by some individuals for decades. Elections are even managed and not allowed to happen. There is no free will in the manufactured will.

Theoretically speaking electoral representative democracy has to orient the citizens and the leaders for governance. It provides opportunity for the people to understand others, respect others, and value the opinion of others while taking decisions on a consensual basis. The explicit objective is to achieve maturity. Democracy is an instrument for perfecting individuals and groups in resolving their own affairs through an institutional process in a mutually acceptable way from the lowest level to the highest. Over a period of time, by protecting this through a dialogue process by recognizing the positions and standpoints, decisions are taken and policies formulated. The assumption is that this kind of practice will enhance the maturity of the people by which the quality of the democratic practice will also be enhanced (Mill, 1976). In India it has moved in a different way. Instead of moving higher, it has receded to lower levels. Why does it move in a retrograde way instead of progressing? It was believed in the formative years after

Independence that politics is for service and one has to spend one's own money. So it was the rich men's space. Moreover, the value profile developed during the freedom struggle was in the memory of people and the politicians. At that point of time positions were offered to individuals. People were identified and compelled to go over to the public space. The concept of Trusteeship was the basis for occupying public positions. Whether rich or the poor, politics would not allow them to earn profit. Politicians of the first generation in India after Independence retired from politics and led a simple life till their death. For their basic needs they approached only public institutions and never went to private institutions and agencies. But now politics is treated as a process where decisions are taken, policies are formulated and resources are allocated. To whose advantage, how much is allocated and how they are enabled through policy options determine the mode of politics. Since the shifting of the thrust from well–being of people to individual economic prosperity, the whole process and perspective has shifted from service to profit.

Now it has become a space for intense competition. Politicians consider that corruption is nothing but transaction or service cost. Knowingly or unknowingly, in our representative democracy, the political parties have been made to play a role. In a society where disparities are vast among the social collectivities, it is natural, that more number of political parties' spring up to addresses the unique problems of the district's social groups. Thereby the political parties emerge in large numbers. The political parties have to be managed and elections have to be managed and for everything money is required. Thus, the leaders have to manage the party, elections and governance. To perform the above, cost is involved and the cost is received from the development brokerage done by the parties and party functionaries and representatives. The same syndrome has percolated into the grassroots institutions also. There are two issues involved in the process at the grassroots. In a hierarchical society based on the caste system and patriarchy, now steps are taken to transfer power from the dominant class to the oppressed and from men to women. Since it is power transfer, it will happen only through a conflict and it will not be done smoothly. Hence, for proper transfer of power, the stakeholders have to be ready for the struggle by which the oppressed will gain power. Collectivities which are going to gain benefits from this new dispensation have to work for it and struggle for it.

The common impression gained by the people is that the state will support those leaders who have hailed from the marginalized communities to empower themselves. With this assumption they contest in the election but, after coming to power, they realize the problems in the space as created by the dominant communities. It is to be noted that, to empower the marginalized and the depressed, a support structure is an imperative as the forces who oppose this process are many. There are many leaders who have come to this new space with the determination to keep the space and work for the poor in the space provided to them. They struggle for their empowerment. Wherever the dominant communities have extreme mobility and are politically mobilized, they never act against the leaders who hail from marginalized communities. They get along with them. The dominant communities will do the same conscientiously. One cannot expect the same behaviour from all the social, caste, lingual or religious groups. The moment seats are reserved for women and *dalits,* the communities get a feeling of shock as they are not sensitive towards the issues of women and *dalits.* Communities which know about the implications of the act will allow the people from the suppressed and marginalized communities to contest in the election. But it is mere tokenism. Up to capturing the position, the dominant class will allow them and beyond that the representatives have to rely on the community which is dominant in that area. The practice varies from area to area. Depending on the level of maturity of the community, harmony and conflict will prevail in the areas where the leaders from the marginalized communities are elected. Further, the leadership plays an important role in maintaining the relationship with the communities. Against this background how conflict arises in the rural areas due to the process of reservation of seats for *dalits* and women and how those conflicts are resolved will be analyzed in this article.

Methodology

In order to understand the intensity of the issues and the nature of conflicts it was decided to conduct intensive case studies in the places where the leaders work with the community as elected representatives. Further, for this study, case studies conducted by the media are also taken as the perspective of the media could also be understood. Moreover, in many places, public hearings were organized. Views expressed by the elected women representatives and *dalit* representatives were taken into account for the analysis.

It is based on the intensive fieldwork done by our scholars and the case studies covered by the media over a period of time. The data generated over a period of ten years from newspapers and magazines are also used. The Rajiv Gandhi Chair has got a resource centre and a documentation unit. In the documentation unit we collect and preserve all the reports of the case studies done by the media and other agencies both in print and electronic form in the past one decade. Apart from the above we were ourselves involved in collecting data from the field about the cases. In the resource centre we keep all the records in published form either as reports or books. Apart from the above, through websites, we collect pertinent details related to grassroots governance and administration in the form of reports, monographs, and books. From all those records, cases are culled narrated, analyzed and explained.

Case Studies

There were a large number of cases of conflicts at the grassroots reported in the media in connection with the Local Body elections. Conflict starts from the decision to file nomination to contest in the election and goes on up to going the office and performing their role and responsibilities by themselves. Conflict arises only in those places where seats are reserved for *dalits* and women. As long as the institutional mechanisms created for governance are far away from the community, the social hierarchy in the society is by and large undisturbed and, hence, powers and resources are with the dominant community leaders. The moment resistance comes from the oppressed against the dominance of the dominant communities, the traditional leaders try to militate and establish their control which results in conflict. Yet the established traditional dominance seems weakened. So, the dominant communities start their stiff resistance and they mobilize the people to show their strength which ultimately weakens the case of the marginalized as the state machinery cannot do much. Representative democracy ultimately rests on votes. The factor "Vote" really acts as a stumbling bloc to apply the rule of law. The entire law enforcing machinery is with the two higher level governments. Of the two the provincial government is solely responsible and the feudal government comes to the rescue of the state government only if it is asked for by the State government. The State government knows fully well the social hierarchy and social dominance but it cannot act forcefully in enforcing the rule of law, because the ruling party has to look at its own future also. It has to rely on the votes of the dominant groups and castes. In this context what will the State government do? Thus, the social transformation of the society may not help pace with the political transformation. Thus, those who want to contest in the election for the positions reserved for women and *dalits* have to decide whether to wage a relentless struggle to keep the space for themselves or to keep away. Once they have decided, they have to face the challenges and struggle for their honourable existence in power.

Case – I: K. Rasu, a Gram Panchayat President of Sivaganga District, filed a complaint against K. Subbaiah from the same place with the District Collector. K. Rasu hails from the *dalit* community. He was elected President of Sottathatti Gram Panchayat. He hoisted the national flag in a school and presided over the Gram Sabha. K. Subbaiah, who belonged to a dominant community, quarrelled with him on the ground that a *dalit* has hoisted the National flag and presided over the Gram Sabha meeting, which is unacceptable to the community. K. Subbaiah beat the Panchayat President with a chappal and threatened him. Since Rasu had no support in that village he sought the help of the Communist Party of India (Marxist). The Marxist party leader took him to the District Collector for redressal. The District Collector ordered an official inquiry. It is to be noted that the village allowed the *dalit* to contest in the election and voted for him. He got elected and when he faced social ill-treatment, the community could have responded. But unfortunately it did not do so (Dinamani, 2003).

Case – II: Elavarasan (42) was the President of Shenbagaraman Nallur Gram Panchayat in Thirunelveli District. He belonged to the *dalit* community. V. Perachi belonged to a dominant caste and became Vice-President of the same Gram Panchayat. The President brought to notice the encroachment of land in the centre of the village by the Vice-President of the same Gram Panchayat. As the Panchayat President, Elavarasan issued a notice to the Vice-President and asked him to vacate the encroached land. The Vice-President started his quarrel with the President of the Gram Panchayat. The Vice-President had not only encroached on the lands but also used the public drinking water tap to water his plantation. He had planted plantain and coconut trees. For the entire farm he took water from the public tap. Till the Gram Panchayat President raised the question nobody in the village had raised this question. Since the Vice-President did not pay heed to the notice of the President, he filed a complaint against the Vice-President with the District Collector. The Sub-Collector inspected the site and confirmed the illegal encroachment. As a result, the Vice-President threatened the President of dire consequences. On June 29th the Vice-President and his brother went to the President's house and abused him and attacked him physically. He was admitted to hospital. Subsequently, the encroachment was removed and the plantain, coconut and other trees were felled. For removing the encroachment the President constantly got threats from the Vice-President who is a member of a dominant community (Marava). The Vice-President had kept the common lands of the Panchayat with him for long and it was being well maintained with the water supply provided by the public tap. Till the Panchayat President raised the issue, no one had raised it because the Vice-President was a dominant caste person. The President did a good job for the Panchayat. But the community did not support the President when he was attacked. It was only a member of the Communist Party of India (Marxist) that supported him. Thus, the community is always a mute spectator. Only a few dominate the community affairs (Viswanathan, 2001).

Case – III: Thadiyanpatti, is a Gram Panchayat in Thirunelveli District reserved for the *dalit* community. Hence, a *dalit* has been elected as the President of the Gram Panchayat. The Panchayat office building was constructed in the *dalit* hamlet. The Councillors belonging to the dominant communities asked the Panchayat President, who is from the *dalit* community, not to conduct the Panchayat Council meeting in the Panchayat building as it was located in a *dalit* community area. This was brought to the notice of the District Administration. As per the instructions of the District Administration, twice the meeting was held in the building and subsequently it was abandoned. The Panchayat building is not being used because it is located in a *dalit* hamlet which created a rift between *dalits* and non-*dalits*. Simply because the Panchayat office building is located in a *dalit* area the Panchayat President has been asked to conduct the meeting elsewhere. It is an issue which created a rift between the Panchayat President and the Councillors. The community is watching the entire episode (*The Hindu*, 2003:).

Case – IV: Ms. Mangalam Kutty, a *dalit* Panchayat President of Melamayanur Gram Panchayat in Kancheepuram District, filed a complaint against the Thiruporur MLA Ms. Kavitha Sampath for her involvement in murdering her husband Kutty on 27th May, 2002 because she contested in the Gram Panchayat election as a *dalit* representative against the wishes of Kavitha Sampth. It is not only that Kavitha Sampath also contested in the election, but Managalam Kutty also won the election. As a result, the popularity of Kavitha Sampath was curtailed. So Mangalam Kutty was asked to resign her post but she refused to do so. Hence, her husband was murdered. An FIR was filed. Kavitha Sampath, being a popular politician, believed that everyone from the *dalit* community would obey her orders. When it was defied things went to the extreme. The Panchayat President filed a complaint and based on it, an FIR was filed. The matter is in court (*The New Indian Express*, 2001:).

Case – V: Ms. P. Vanathi, (36) the President of Venkatachalam Gram Panchayat in Uppiliapuram Panchayat Union in Trichy District, resigned from her President's position and handed over her papers to the District Collector because anti-social elements continuously disrupted her and worked against her. The District Collector and the people of the Gram Panchayat said that she was a good and efficient Gram Panchayat President. She performed very well, officials claimed. The District Collector listed all the activities of the Gram Panchayat President. There were a few anti-social elements who created all kinds of troubles in the village and they were being reported to the police as complaints. But the police did not act and she filed complaints against them to the District Collector. There was no action against them. Total non-cooperation of the District Administration and police officials made her quit the post. The anti-social elements were instigated by some of the Ward Members who were not happy with the emergence of Vanathi in the public space.

Three Ward Members were involved in all kinds of illegal activities in the village. Yet she managed to perform her role and responsibilities despite all the hurdles. Beyond a certain stage she was not able to tolerate this kind of torture. It was an irony that neither the public nor the officials supported her even though she was a good performing Panchayat President. She left the village in search of another place to have peace. It is all the more important to understand that communities will act only at the initiative of the community representatives or the opinion makers. The District Administration is not in a position to interfere in the affairs of the community as it feels that it will create a law and order problem. The police will act only if driven either from political circles or from public pressure. In the absence of the above it will not work. In this context one can imagine the plight of the *dalit* and women leaders (*The Hindu,* 2003).

Case – VI: J. Menaka (35), the President of Oorapakkam Gram Panchayat, was murdered in her office on 29th March, 2001 by a gang of three men. She belonged to the *dalit* community and she is a party worker and office bearer of the DMK party. She was known for her views against encroachment of public lands. This Gram Panchayat is in Kancheepuram District. It is very near to Chennai. Hence, the land mafia is powerful. She was responsible for many development activities of the village. But she was very firm in liberating the common lands from encroachment, which created a conflict between the land mafia and her. There was yet another issue for her. She wanted to contest in the Assembly Election on behalf of the DMK party. She sought the ticket for which she filed an application with the party office. Since Thiruporur constituency is reserved for SC, she wanted to contest in the election. She was asked to withdraw her application and she refused. As a result, it was stated, she was murdered. She was determined to remove encroachments by which she created enmity. The encroachers were powerful and influential individuals and they earned a profit out of it. Secondly, she ventured to move up on the political ladder. There also one has to face challenges. It is an irony that when a Panchayat President was able to remove the encroachment, the community did not support her. The community was silent (*The New Indian Express,* 2001).

Integrated Analysis

All are events and are derived from the narration of the respondents and media representatives. Here we are not venturing into an analysis of the merits of the issues but we are analyzing the sources of this kind of conflict in grassroots institutions. This conflict is more acute when *dalits* and women come to these positions and perform their roles and responsibilities.

The above cases clearly demonstrate that society still lives in a social hierarchy, following set social norms. The rule makers in India do not evince any interest in implementing the rule. Hence, it is being left to the individuals and groups who are gaining benefits out of the laws and rules enacted by the rule makers. Further, the authorities who enact the laws and rules gauge the perception and receptivity of the community. By doing so the state becomes soft and flexible. There is yet another reason for this softness. In a representative democracy votes decide the fate of governments. In this context, the government may not be strong enough against the communities. Unless the society is transformed, it is very difficult to impose the will of the state on the people. It requires courage to lose power. Further, political transformations are fast in our society. But social transformation is not that fast and there is a perceptible gap between political transformation and social transformation. While observing the process of the deepening of democracy, the communities feel that their culture will be disturbed. In our society democracy is identified with election. Even the electoral process is not properly perceived by the people. It is also being looked at from the perspective of social conditions and social norms. Never is democracy perceived as a culture. Many of the provisions of the Constitution are not implemented, because the social conditions are so protective and preventive of change. Instead of implementing the provisions of the Constitution, the implementing agencies are allowing the social norms to be followed at the grassroots (Kishwar, 2005). But the 73rd Amendment brings a compulsion on the part of the state to implement it. As a result, the new constitutional norms drive out the community norms. The conflict between constitutional provisions and community norms continues and on many occasions the community norms dominate over the constitutional provisions. To deal with this problem political will is needed on the part of the leadership. In India we find only noisy democracy. All the time noise is heard but it is not converted into voice and taken into account for decision–making. Down below the district, people are not organized institutionally to raise their voice and solve their problems. Hence, people are to be mobilized to raise their noise to draw the attention of the decision makers. People have been oriented to receive benefits as beneficiaries and submit petitions if they are not able to get benefits. People have been oriented to follow the social norms and to be submissive to the government to claim their benefits. As a result, people have lost their self-respect. They are not assertive. They never claim their rights and entitlements. Empowering the people and the marginalized is the imperative step to redeem the situation. But no one is interested in empowering the people. Everyone wants the people to be either beneficiaries or petitioners not assertive empowered citizens. Empowered and assertive citizens will pose challenges to the existing governing and administrative system. When people are not provided with an institutional mechanism to resolve their issues naturally they have to rely on the official machinery. The existing institutional arrangement does not cope with the growing demands of the people and the new aspirations of the marginalized. So the existing conditions have compelled us to think of an alternative to the existing representative democracy (Kothari, 2005). Against this background, in the name of social justice, the official machinery does not want to break the social order. So the social order is maintained by the officials. Even the just demands of the marginalized communities are not looked into sensitively and as a result they indulge in violence and conflict. But, to provide such opportunity, reservation of seats has been given to women and *dalits.* But, when they are in a position, they are not allowed to function independently and a battery of barriers are created and as a result they are unable to perform their role. The problems of women and *dalits* are not projected and properly deliberated upon for decision making at the grassroots. So the new democracy has created a whole lot of problems and conflicts at the grassroots. The women and *dalit* leaders need backup and a support structure for their struggle. The state has to support the struggle for deepening democracy.

Conclusion

Indian democracy is paradoxical as it always produces contradictory propositions to the postulates of representative democracy. Indian democracy generates conflicts all the time and it is being managed by the intervention of the state. The grassroots democracy which has been created through the 73rd Amendment to the Constitution of India triggered the social conflict further in an intensified way. Instead of looking into the problems of *dalits* and women, it created problems for *dalit* and women leaders. The marginalized, though they emerged successfully in the electoral process, could not perform their role and responsibilities. There are a few leaders who are able to manage the system and perform their roles but, even for in their case, the community fails to extend its support to them. In a few places they struggle and come out successfully and emerge as models. But conflict remains and is intensified. The whole conflict is not on the issues of development. The social base of democracy is the basic question. Democracy resolves conflicts, but only in a few societies. In many societies it creates conflict and, by evolving a mechanism, they are resolved. Democracy brings maturity to the society through the dialogue process. Democracy is not election alone. It is a culture by itself. Deepening of democracy has triggered conflict and it has intensified while making democracy inclusive. The whole conflict is not over development but over democracy. To make the provision work, a strong support structure is needed for women and *dalit* leaders. They will overcome all problems if they get support from various quarters.

REFERENCES

Basu, Amrita and Kohli Atual (ed.). 1998. *Community Conflicts and State in India.* New Delhi: Oxford University Press.

Dinamani, 2003. (17th August).

Kishwar, Madhu Poornima. 2005. *Deepening of Democracy: Challenges of Governance and Globalisation in India.* New Delhi: Oxford University Press.

Kothari, Rajni. 2005. *Rethinking Democracy.* Hyderabad: Orient Longman.

Mill, J.S. 1976. *Considerations on Representative Government.* London: Fontana.

Palanithurai, G. 1993. *Management of Ethnic Conflict in India and Canada:*

A Comparative Analysis. New Delhi: Kanishka Publishers and Distributors.

Palanithurai, G. 2001. *Empowerment of Women: Problems Faced by the Elected Women Representatives. Experience from Tamil Nadu* (Monograph). Gandhigram: Rajiv Gandhi Chair for Panchayati Raj Studies.

Palanithurai, G. 2002. *Dynamics of New Panchayati Raj System in India, Vol. I.* New Delhi: Concept Publishing Company Pvt. Ltd., New Delhi.

Palanithurai, G. 2004. *Leadership Matters in Grassroots Governance Pathfinders Series – I* (Monograph). Gandhigram: Rajiv Gandhi Chair for Panchayati Raj Studies.

Palanithurai, G. 2007. "Panchayats: Relevance and Potentials". In: T.M. Joseph (ed.). *Local Governance in India: Ideas, Challenges and Strategies*. New Delhi: Concept Publishing Company.

Palanithurai, G. 2007. "Constitutional Laws Vs. Community Laws in India: Conflict and Synergy" *The Grassroots Governance Journal, 5* (1).

Palanithurai, G. and Ragupathy, V. 2007. *Communities Panchayats and Governance at Grassroot's* New Delhi: Concept Publishing Company.

Palanithurai, G. 2008. "Democratizing Society and Governance", *Gandhi Marg* 30(1).

Palanithurai, G.; Thirunavukkarasu M.A. and Uma, G. 2008. *Change Makers at Grassroots*. New Delhi: Concept Publishing Company Pvt. Ltd., New Delhi.

Palanithurai, G. 2008. *Third General Elections to Local Governments in Tamil Nadu: Expectations and Shocking Realities Third General Elections to Local Governments in Tamil Nadu: Expectations and Shocking Realities*. New Delhi: Concept Publishing Company Pvt. Ltd., New Delhi.

Palanithurai, G.; Uma G. and Vanishree J. 2008. *Networking of Elected Women Representatives at Grassroots*. New Delhi: Concept Publishing Company Pvt. Ltd., New Delhi.

Palanithurai, G. 2008. *Status of Dalit Gram Panchayat Leaders in Tamil Nadu* (Monograph). Gandhigram: Rajiv Gandhi Chair for Panchayati Raj Studies.

Sau, Ranjit. 2008. "Towards Transition to Democracy", *Bharatiya Samajik Chintan*, 7(1).

Srinivas, M.N. 1996. *Village, Caste, Gender and Method*. New Delhi: Oxford University Press.

The Hindu, 2003. (April 20th).

The Hindu, 2003. (6th August).

The New Indian Express, 2003. (30th December).

The New Indian Express, 2001. (30th March)

Viswanathan, S. 2001. *Frontline* (October).

Weiner, Myron. 1989. *The Indian Paradox: Essays in Indian Politics*, New Delhi: Sage Publications.

XII

Local Governance as a Factor in Centre-State Relations in India

Introduction

Ministry of Panchayati Raj, Government of India, organised a National Convention of District and Block Panchayat leaders of India at Delhi in April 2008 to celebrate the 15th year of the introduction of the new Local Governance in pursuance of the 73rd Amendment to the Constitution. The convention adopted a declaration and presented the document to the Prime Minister on the concluding day of the conference. The PM declared that the State Governments have to do more for Panchayati Raj in order to strengthen local governance because the existing distribution of powers is inadequate. The Convention was not attended by the leaders of Tamil Nadu local bodies and the Minister fcr Local Governance saying that the document prepared by the Ministry of Panchayati Raj contained some objectionable statements which affect the Centre-State relationship. At the insistence of the Tamil Nadu CM, certain portions of the document were dropped. Yet neither the Minister for Local Governance nor the local body leaders attended the Convention, which ultimately created an issue in Tamil Nadu politics. Further, it has given an impression that there is a misunderstanding between the Government of Tamil Nadu and the Government of India on this issue. It is to be noted that the ruling party of Tamil Nadu is part of the Central Government and the same ruling party of Tamil Nadu is getting the "outside" support of the Indian National Congress. Further, the Minister for Panchayati Raj, Government of India, who hails from Tamil Nadu, could not convince the Minister for Local Administration, Government of Tamil Nadu, on this issue. Tamil Nadu is the only State to keep out of the Conference. Is the issue worth making such a row? If so, why the other States in the country did not protest? All of them could not be insensitive to the rights of the State in the Union! There are many critical issues, which deserve to be raised as factors affecting the Centre-State relations. But, they are not raised as the ruling party of the Government of Tamil Nadu is a part of the coalition Government at the Centre. Instead, the Government of Tamil Nadu picked a small matter and made it a big issue, which is in no way beneficial either to the State or Centre or the local bodies. An unnecessary misunderstanding was created between the Ministry of Panchayati Raj, Government of India, and the Ministry of Rural Development and Local Administration, Government of Tamil Nadu. To dispel the cloud surrounding the issue is the objective of this article.

THE ISSUE AND THE ANTECEDENTS

Weakening of the System

In Tamil Nadu, both the Dravida Munnetra Kazhagam (DMK) and the All India Anna Dravida Munnetra Kazhagam (AIADMK) oppose each other on all issues. However, the two agree on one issue, i.e., opposing the federal government's initiatives to strengthen local bodies as institutions of self-governance. It is evident from their activities since the beginning of enacting of the Constitutional amendments during the period of the late Prime Minister Rajiv Gandhi and subsequently when the 73rd and the 74th Amendments were introduced in Parliament during the Prime Ministership of Narasimha Rao that both the parties are not in favour of a strong local governance as envisaged by the Central Government. The overall argument is that creating a strong local government as envisaged in the 73rd and 74th Amendments without giving adequate powers to the State will amount to weakening the State Government.[1] On all occasions both the DMK and the AIADMK opposed the move for creating vibrant local bodies as a system of governance with the argument that it is a State subject, which cannot be touched by the Central Government. They always held that the Central Government directing the State Government with regard to the functioning of the Panchayati Raj is equivalent to interference of the Central Government in matters of State Government. Moreover, both the parties want a two-tier Panchayati Raj System, and not a three-tier one with the district government under Panchayati Raj. When the 64th and the 65th Amendment bills were introduced earlier, they were opposed and defeated because of these two parties. The second time, when the 73rd and the 74th Amendments were passed unanimously in Parliament, these two parties raised an objection to the inclusion of the District Panchayat. It is to be noted that the vibrant Panchayati Raj System created by Shri K. Kamaraj was weakened in Tamil Nadu (as elsewhere in India) only during the periods when these two parties were in power. For nearly fifteen years (from 1971 to 1986) the Panchayati Raj System was kept inoperative in the State. More than fifteen times elections to local bodies were postponed and the reasons were well documented.[2]

Procrastination

Even after the enactment of the Amendments to the Constitution of India, the conformity legislation that had inbuilt weaknesses, and it did not reflect the spirit of the 73rd Amendment. The AIADMK Government slept over the file for over eleven months and engaged in drafting the bill in a hurry during the final two weeks. Though outwardly the Panchayati Raj System in Tamil Nadu was in place, the spirit of self-governance, which is the foundation of the two historic Amendments, was missing. Though the State law was enacted in 1994, Panchayats came into being only in 1996. The AIADMK, which was in power at the time of enacting the law, did not evince any interest in conducting the elections.[3] But the DMK picked up the issue and put it in its election manifesto and assured the people that it will conduct the local bodies' election, if it came to power. After the DMK came to power, Panchayat elections were conducted. However, the Panchayat system was not strengthened as envisaged in the Constitution. Tamil Nadu is known for its commitment to honouring the Constitution. But, when it comes to the Panchayati Raj System, something is amiss.

Comply to Constitution Spirit Lost

Tamil Nadu will seemingly fulfil all Constitutional formalities, whether it is enacting conformity legislation, conducting election to local bodies, constituting committees for power devolution, formation of district planning committee. But if one analyses the status of Panchayati Raj in terms of its functioning and autonomy, one will find the paradoxes.[4] Panchayat finance has not improved beyond eight or nine per cent over a period of fifteen years. It is a well known fact that the Panchayati Raj System was diluted and weakened by reducing the financial flow to Panchayats. To forestall such an eventuality, consisting a State Finance Commission was made mandatory. Yet, in Tamil Nadu even this is a ritual. Three State Finance Commissions submitted reports and yet finances of local bodies have not improved. District Planning Committees have been functioning over a period of fifteen years, Planning Committee meetings are being held regularly and a Planning Secretary was also appointed in every district. But not even a single district plan has been prepared by the District Planning Committees. The leaders are in office keep on asking why the State government wastes money on conducting elections, electing leaders, and providing infrastructure facilities to the District Panchayats without assigning them substantial roles and responsibilities.

Governance Reduced to Contract

The annual grants given are mechanically divided among the various District Panchayat Councils and corks are given to contractors. The disease has spread to the Block Panchayat also, as they are also weak. Many Departments which worked integrally with Block Panchayats are pulled out and are now under the control of the respective Department hierarchies. The Block Panchayats do not enjoy power as they did during the Kamaraj period. The two-tier system, as introduced by Kamaraj, was no doubt ideal.[5] But the two-tier system being talked about by these two political parties now is weak. Like the MPLAD and the

MLALAD, the District Panchayat Ward Members and the Block Panchayat Councillors have funds. It is nothing but sharing the total amount received from the State and giving the same to the contractors to carry out activities. It is always presumed that, by entrusting such kind of works to the contractors, the persons who have given works will get a minimum of 10 per cent to 15 per cent of benefits in cash from the contractors. The system has been developed in such a way that even a honest leader or representative cannot survive. They have to fall in line. Furthermore, the elected leaders are not getting money from the contractors. This kind of common practice is a problem only for the representatives of the left parties as they oppose sharing of such funds and getting money from the contractors. But they are a minority in all places and hence they are struggling for survival in the system.

After seeing such a pervasive practice, the Ward Members of Gram Panchayats are demanding similar "allocations" for themselves. At the Gram Panchayat level activities are carried out by the Gram Panchayats. Allocations are for specific activities and works. They cannot be shared among the members. In many places the Vice-Presidents of the Gram Panchayats refuse to sign the cheque as they are not aware of the activities carried out by the Panchayats and many openly demand money for signing cheques. The assumption is that somehow or other the Panchayat President will take money and hence he or she has to give a share to the Vice-President. Such a sharing practice has penetrated into the system at all levels. Already the local bodies are being treated as implementing agencies and now the leaders are treated as contractors. Consequently, principle of subsidiarity has become the casuality.

Only Committees not Devolution

In practical terms Panchayats are treated as implementing agencies. They are being put under the control of the officials. Three committees have been constituted to devolve powers to local bodies. Of the three committees, one was headed by L.C. Jain, a reputed Gandhian and noted development economist and the other two were headed by the Local Administration Minister himself. All the committees were constituted by the DMK government. Of all the committees, the L.C. Jain Committee has produced the best report with minute details as per the spirit of the 73rd Amendment. Had the government been committed to implementing the report in letter and spirit, Tamil Nadu would have been number one in the devolution of powers to local bodies. It would have been the model State in India. It is unfortunate that this did not happen. In an interview to the press the then Law Minister of Tamil Nadu, late Aladi Aruna, said that Delhi does not devolve powers to State capitals but it expects the State Governments to devolve powers to local bodies. The State Government feels that it needs more powers. At this juncture, the Centre takes away the power of the State by enlarging the scope of the Concurrent List. In this context, how can the Central Government expect the State to devolve powers meaningfully to local bodies? Unless the ruling party in the State is ideologically committed, devolution of powers will always remain a problematic, citizens are unlikely up to a demand for responsibility and power.

New Initiative

After the installation of the UPA Government at the Centre, a new Ministry has been created to push the devolution further as promised in its manifesto. The new Ministry of Panchayati Raj has been given to Shri Mani Shankar Aiyar, who has established a command over the subject and also because of his close interaction with Rajiv Gandhi. He wanted a new Panchayati Raj system as the institution of governance in a totally revolutionary way by giving power to all and particularly to the *dalits,* women and *adivasis.* Rajiv Gandhi emphatically argued that in the absence of women and other marginalised groups from governance and development, we cannot claim that we are a true democracy. The administration which is being established through the Amendments should be responsive, responsible and representative in character. For the first time in independent India, a governing structure is created constitutionally at the grassroots with an all-inclusive character. The new Ministry has taken several steps of which one is the conduct of Round Tables by involving the State Ministers and Secretaries of Panchayati Raj to take stock of the process of devolution of powers. Seven Round Table meetings were attended by the Local Body Ministers and the Secretaries of local bodies of various States. Within 150 days from the first Round Table to the last, 150 resolutions were passed unanimously with the active participation of Panchayati Raj Ministers and Secretaries of all other States.[6] During the Round Table meetings themselves, it was found that the exercises in devolution of powers are done in a half hearted way. It was felt that some monitoring mechanism is needed to track the devolution process. The exercises carried out during the Round Table brought about a consensus among the State governments about the steps to be taken to strengthen the Panchayati Raj System.

Indifference

However, not even a single meeting of the Round Tables was attended either by the Minister or by the Secretary of Panchayati Raj, Government of Tamil Nadu. Lower level officials were deputed and the officials were instructed not to open their mouth and express any opinion at the Round Table meeting. This was the practice adopted by the AIADMK Government. The Government of Tamil Nadu never objected to any of the resolutions contained in the document even though time was given to do so. There was no response at all from the Government of Tamil Nadu. The silence of the Government of Tamil Nadu on the resolutions gave an impression that it approved of all the resolutions. If committed to the resolutions, the State government has to prepare an activity mapping. The Tamil Nadu Government did not concur with this proposal of preparing an activity mapping stating that it had already done so. Activity mapping is nothing but clarifying responsibilities for Gram Panchayat, Block Panchayat and District Panchayat. There is a subtle difference in the perception of "activity mapping" between the Government of Tamil Nadu and the Government of India. The Government of India insists that the subsidiarity principle is the basis on which activity mapping has to be done. There should not be any overlapping responsibility among the three tiers of the Panchayats. Further, the concept of power has been clearly defined through the Round Table meetings. Many of the States for the first time admitted that of the 29 items listed only a few had been given to the Panchayats. Till then, it was presumed that the State Governments had given powers to local bodies on all the subjects mentioned in 11th Schedule. Normally, transfer of power from one level to another and from one group to another requires an authority to advise and clarify. The Tamil Nadu Government insists that since devolution is a State subject, what powers are to be given to local bodies and how they are to be given are to be decided upon by the State and not the Centre. It should not be decided by the Central Government. Why does the Central Panchayati Raj Ministry insist that the State has to prepare an activity mapping? The Central Government should not interfere in power devolution to local bodies. It is equivalent to interfering in the domain of the State by the Centre, Tamil Nadu argues.

Misleading Arguments

There is a general argument that Panchayati Raj is a State subject, no doubt, but it does not mean that the State should not be questioned when it is not honouring its own commitment to the Constitution of India. Panchayati Raj is covered in Article 40 of the Constitution. If it is a State subject, how has the Centre brought in an amendment? It is not a simple amendment. It was approved by two-third majority in the Parliament and more than fifty per cent of the States agreed to the proposal. Then only it became an Amendment. Now putting up the same argument does not hold good. Scholars who argue that Panchayati Raj is a State subject have an altogether different purpose and point of view. They argue that State is responsible for strengthening Panchayati Raj as Panchayati Raj is closer to the people, community and culture and it knows the local conditions much better than the Federal Government. Moreover, the State has to devolve powers from its pool to the local bodies. The weaknesses and strengths of Panchayati Raj are attributed to the State government. But now the condition of the State is that it has to face pressures from below and from above. The Central Government is directing the State Government by imposing conditions on the State government and the local bodies are exerting pressure on the State government for more powers, resources and finance from the State Government. Local bodies are not putting up such a demand to the Federal Government to devolve powers from the Central Government to the State Government. The difficulty arises when operationalising the whole scheme of decentralisation of powers. The Centre and the State do not concur on the definition of the concept of "power".

The State Government says that it has given more than 721 powers to local bodies. The Central Government has defined power as authority to take decision. The State Government presumes that the involvement of local body in any activity in any form is power. Most of the powers entrusted to local bodies are advisory and recommendatory and they are not powers in real terms. To make a plea, petition, recommendation and advice, one requires no power. Any citizen can give advice and make recommendation. It cannot be construed as power. The State Government perceives that giving advice is power, making recommendations is power, assisting the officials to carry out works is also power. Both the Centre and the State have different perceptions of the concept of power. If one accepts the argument of the Central Government, the Tamil Nadu Panchayat system has got only limited powers. As per the accepted definition of power, the Tamil Nadu Government has given limited powers to local bodies. In Tamil Nadu the local bodies are engaged with entrustment of certain responsibilities to carry out or implement schemes of both the Central and State Government. But as per the definition of the State Government, the Tamil Nadu Panchayat enjoys powers.

Non-Compliance

The State Government perceived that after the creation of the Ministry of Panchayati Raj in the Government of India at Delhi, a lot of stipulations came to State Government with regard to the handling of Panchayats. All Central Government schemes to be implemented through Panchayats have not provided any role for the State Government. Moreover, the State Government cannot even withhold the money which is due to Panchayats. Supposing the State Government withholds the money for more than one month, the State Government has to pay the interest to the Panchayats. To get some of the specialised programmes, the Central Government stipulates the condition that unless the State Government completes certain formalities through Panchayats the grant will not be given. For example, the Backward Regions Grant Fund (BRGF) is a scheme introduced by the Central Government to provide assistance to backward districts. This grant will be provided only after getting the district plan prepared by the District Planning Committee as stipulated by the Ministry of Panchayati

Raj.[7] Tamil Nadu has not taken up this project as it will strengthen the District Planning Committee. It is to be noted that the District Planning Committee is the creation of the Constitution. Here both the Dravidian Political Parties the All India Anna Dravida Munnetra Kazhagam and the Dravida Munnetra Kazhagam have approached this issue from their ideological stand point. From their perspective strengthening the District Panchayats and District Planning Committees amounts to weakening the position and powers of the State Government. Hence, they argue from the beginning for two-tier panchayat system up to Block Panchayats. At the district level the whole system of administration should be under the control of the District Collector. Hence, in Tamil Nadu the District Planning Committee has been constituted but it has not been provided with adequate facilities to prepare a district plan. But it is almost a violation of a provision of the Constitution.

Moreover, the Ministry of Panchayati Raj, Government of India, has enabled the Panchayat leaders to interact with the Panchayat leaders of other States and compare themselves with those of other States. This has empowered them to argue against the State Government and demand more powers to Panchayats on par with the Panchayats of other States. This kind of enabling is perceived as a ploy to work against the State Government through Panchayats. There is yet another problem that the State faces with regard to Panchayats in Tamil Nadu. The leaders who are elected to local bodies and are already oriented in politics will put up a powerful show against MLAs and MPs. The Tamil Nadu political culture is anti-democratic as members of the opposition are treated as opponents. Further, the relationship between the two major political parties, the DMK and the AIADMK, is so acrimonious and they treat each other as enemies. The cadres have been oriented in this way. It is against this background, that both the political parties are looking at the Panchayati Raj System. An empowered Panchayati Raj System will not permit the present culture of adoration of leaders. Just like a monarch, the leaders are enjoying respect among the public and this will be challenged if the Panchayati Raj system is strengthened. The District Panchayat is looked at from this perspective. This is always in the back of their minds. Against this background this issue has to be looked into and analysed.

An Important Event

The Ministry of Panchayati Raj, Government of India, decided to hold a celebration of the 15th year of the new Panchayati Raj System after the enactment of the 73rd Amendment to the Constitution of India at Delhi. It was planned to conduct a meeting in the month of December 2007. Somehow or the other it got postponed to April 2008 and limited to District Panchayat and Block Panchayat leaders of India excluding the Gram Panchayat leaders. To discuss the matters relating to the strengthening of Panchayats in the conference scheduled from 22nd to 24th April, 2008, a consultative committee was constituted with the elected representatives of local bodies from different States including Tamil Nadu. They met in Delhi from 13th to 15th March, 2008 and drafted a document of recommendation covering several important aspects of local bodies which according to them were so important that they were to be handed over to the Prime Minister on 24th April, 2008. Panchayat leaders wanted to remind the Prime Minister that the Central Government's responsibility does not rest with passing of legislation and it has to go further in implementing the legislation also. So they wanted to hand over a copy of the document to the Prime Minister. The draft contains a letter from the Panchayati Raj Minister Shri Mani Shankar Aiyar to Panchayat leaders.

Content of the Draft

The draft provides a detailed analysis of the existing situation of power devolution and institutionalising Panchayati Raj in India against the backdrop of the framework given through the 73rd Amendment to the Constitution of India. Issues relating to powers, functions, finance, capacity building, micro-planning, Panchayats Extension to Scheduled Areas (PESA), people's participation, Rural Business Hub, incentives for Panchayat performance and formation of a national network of local body leaders have been incorporated in the sixteen page document. It is a draft prepared for presentation to the Prime Minister after a thorough discussion in the conference to be held from 22nd to 24th April, 2008. It is a draft prepared by the Panchayati Raj leaders. While preparing the document, the Ministry facilitated simultaneous translation for the advantage of the Panchayat leaders coming from different States.

The draft is full of the views of the Panchayat leaders to strengthen the Panchayati Raj System as per the 73rd Amendment to the Constitution of India. This step was perceived by the Government of Tamil Nadu as an instigation of the Panchayat leaders by the Ministry of Panchayati Raj to rise against the State Government. There is yet another view prevailing among the intellectuals that the Ministry of Panchayati Raj is playing the activist's role to strengthen Panchayati Raj by doing the work of the civil society. There is a justification for doing so as the civil society in India has failed to mobilise a mass movement from below for empowering the people by strengthening the Panchayats.

State Government's Apprehension

The Tamil Nadu Government has picked up an argument that the drafted document declaration contains some objectionable recommendations which are against the State's rights and they have to be removed. Tamil Nadu Government has taken a position that unless they are removed, the Government of Tamil Nadu will not send the local body leaders to the conference at Delhi. Further, the Chief Minister of Tamil Nadu has written a letter to the Prime Minister in this regard and asked him to direct the Ministry of Panchayati Raj to drop such objectionable points from the charter of recommendations. The contentious issue raised here is that the draft makes a recommendation that Panchayati Raj should be removed from the State List and included either in the Central List or the Concurrent List. It further recommends that a Panchayat code has to be prepared for Panchayats by the Ministry of Panchayati Raj. The question here is how can the Government of Tamil Nadu impose a condition against the expression of views by the stakeholders. It is against fundamental rights. Secondly, the Government of Tamil Nadu has decided against the rights of participation of the Panchayat leaders. In normal circumstance it has to make a declaration that it is the decision of the Panchayat leaders whether they participate or not. How could the government take such a decision? It is a total violation of fundamental rights. Further, if the government has certain views they are to be discussed in the conference and the government could have forcefully defended the State's rights in front of the Prime Minister. Instead, it asked the Prime Minister to drop that point from the draft prepared by the Panchayat leaders. The Prime Minister of India has also asked the Ministry of Panchayati Raj to drop it and the Ministry of Panchayati Raj has also dropped it. Here, there is yet another issue which is very serious but is treated very lightly. What right has Prime Minister in this matter to ask the Ministry to drop it? It is a draft of the Panchayat leaders. How can the Chief Minister writes a letter to the Prime Minister to delete a portion in the draft of the Panchayat leaders? How can the Prime Minister also asks the Ministry of Panchayati Raj to drop it, without getting any explanation and how can the Ministry drop it all of a sudden from the document of the Panchayat leaders? Subsequently, an argument was developed that the State Government has acted in the best interests of the State's rights. The Tamil Nadu Chief Minister thanked the Prime Minister for his letter informing Tamil Nadu about the decision of the Ministry to drop that statement. Some of the members of the Tamil Nadu Legislative Assembly appreciated the Government of Tamil Nadu for its prompt action in defending the State's rights but it is nothing but infringing on the rights of Panchayats and the fundamental rights of the people.

Even after dropping of the objected items in the draft nobody either the representatives of the local bodies or the officials attended the conference at New Delhi from Tamil Nadu. This part of the episode is ignored in Delhi circles. Had the Tamil Nadu contingent attended along with the Ministers and argued at Delhi, either the Tamil Nadu Government could have gained the support of the other States or cut a sorry figure as the Tamil Nadu Government is working against Panchayat autonomy in the name of working for State autonomy. Further, arguments have been built up over a period of time that like the Central List, the State List and the Concurrent List local bodies should have a list called "Fourth List". So keeping the Panchayati Raj as subject in concurrent list is not anti-India or anti-Constitution or anti-people. It is the wisdom of the practitioners to hold such a view and they can work for it. In a democracy, we have to respect ideas.

Elusive Task

The Tamil Nadu Government treated this event as defending the State's Rights. Tamil Nadu could have done much more substantially in certain areas for which it can fight. Education was a State subject and it has been transferred to the Concurrent List. Through the Central Finance Commission, the States have really been dictated to and through centrally sponsored schemes the discretion of the States has been completely removed. Even in the recently constituted Centre-State Relation Commission the terms of reference are indicative of the centralizing tendencies of the Central Government about which the Tamil Nadu Government has to act. But, it is silent or just issue some press statements beyond which there is no action. The recent action of the State Government is really not for protecting the State's rights but it firmly acts in curbing the power of Panchayats.

The West Bengal Government has also written an objection letter to the Central Government. It does not say that it won't send its representatives. The West Bengal Government participated in the Round Table Conferences organized by the Ministry of Panchayati Raj, Government of India to arrive at consensus among the state governments to strengthen Panchayati Raj System in India and expressed its opinions on each and every resolution. Even in the April convention of this year Panchayat leaders attended and participated and argued that Panchayat should be in State List. The West Bengal Minister attended the ministerial conference held on 25th April 2008 at Delhi despite the Panchayat elections in West Bengal. Similarly the elected representatives of Panchayats of Kerala also asked to keep Panchayat as a State subject. It is clear that the left parties have devolved powers to Panchayats not because of pressure from the Central Government. They have political will to empower the people and hence they are doing it with a sense of commitment. Tamil Nadu wants middlemen or development brokers to be empowered and hence it wants to keep local bodies as implementing agencies. There is another tendency prevailing in Tamil Nadu, namely, converting the elected representatives into contractors carrying out the activities and implementing the schemes and programmes for the State Government. One finds such a change in the leaders' perception in Tamil Nadu.

There is yet another issue raised by the Government of Tamil Nadu which is so contentious. After the Round Table discussions were over and resolutions were adopted with the concurrence of the State Governments, the Ministry of Panchayati Raj took a decision to draw a road map for strengthening Panchayati Raj.

The State and the Ministry of Panchayati Raj have to sign a memorandum of understanding about the status of devolution in the respective States and the activities to be done by both the State and the Central Governments to strengthen Panchayati Raj. The Government of Tamil Nadu is considering it a sensitive area not to be touched by the Central Government. This issue is perceived from the perspective of 'states' rights or State autonomy. These kinds of memorandums were signed by many State governments including the Government of Kerala and the Government of West Bengal. Have they surrendered the 'states' rights to the Central Government? Are they afraid of the Central Government? Any Government which respects the people will find ways and means to strengthen local government. They understand the potential of the Panchayati Raj System and hence, even without the bill, powers have been given to the people.

Delivery of services will be very effective, people's needs will be attended to immediately, wastages will be reduced, people's participation will be enhanced, corruption will be reduced, botheration and workload of higher level governments will be reduced, faith confidence and respect of the people for the State and the Central Governments will be enhanced, the menace of anti social elements will be curtailed by strengthening local bodies. When people are entrusted with responsibilities, the frustration of the people with regard to governance and administration will be reduced. In a federal state, at present, we have three governments instead of two. The new phenomenon is always missing in the Centre-State relationship. Inter-governmental relationships are always perceived between the central and the states and not between the states and local governments. Even intellectuals fail to recognize the relationship between the State and Local Governance.

Conclusion

Tamil Nadu is known for its vociferous demand for State autonomy and State's rights. It is a pioneer in projecting this demand. It appointed the Rajamannar Committee to study Centre-State relations. The recommendations are still valid. But now the States have lost substantial autonomy in administrative federalism. Yet, the State Government could not do much as it got into power sharing in the federal government. But at the same time, the State Government looks at the grassroots democracy in the same old way as an implementing agency. The same State Government looks at globalisation in a new perspective and it works for it vigorously despite opposition. But the decentralisation of powers is new in the context of globalisation. It is also an opportunity to empower and mobilise the people. It looks at globalisation as an opportunity to increase its revenue and is willing to provide doles to the poor to keep them permanently as poor beneficiaries. In this process, power brokers will get a substantial share in the development activities and they will help the political parties to mobilise votes as mediators.

Against this background, the government wants to fight on a non-issue by which it can easily escape from the process instead of going into the substantive issues of Centre-State relationship. The State Government needs a new approach which is beneficial to the people and the State. West Bengal served as model for the enactment of an amendment and Kerala served as model for effective implementation of the 73rd Amendment to the Constitution of India. Kerala is far ahead of many other States. They have demonstrated to the world that, for devolution of powers and empowerment of people, political will is needed more than a constitutional bill. Now, after the passing of the constitutional bill, everyone is arguing that political will is needed to empower people through strengthening Panchayats. In many of the States this political will is missing. In the absence of political will, people will shall prevail.

NOTES

1. K.C. Sivaramakrishnan, *Power to the People?* (New Delhi: Konark Publishers Pvt. Ltd., 2000).
2. Malcolm S. Adiseshaiah, "The Need for Constitutional Safeguards", in George Mathew, ed. *Panchayati Raj in Karnataka Today* (New Delhi: Concept Publishing Company, 1986).
3. G. Palanithurai, *Emerging Dimensions in Decentralization* (New Delhi: Concept Publishing Company Pvt. Ltd., 2005), pp. 2–3.
4. G. Palanithurai, *Evolving Grassroots Democracy* (New Delhi: Concept Publishing Company Pvt. Ltd., 2007).
5. S. Sarasvathi, *The Madras Panchayat System: A Historical Survey,* Vol. I

(Delhi: Impex India, 1973); Dharampal, *The Madras Panchayat System: A General Assessment*, Vol. II (New Delhi: Impex India, 1972).

6. Ministry of Panchayati Raj, *A Compendium of Resolutions of the Seven Round Tables of Ministers In-Charge of Panchayati Raj*, conducted during July-December 2004 (New Delhi: Ministry of Panchayati Raj, 2005).
7. Ministry of Panchayati Raj, *BRGF Guidelines* (New Delhi: Ministry of Panchayati Raj, 2007).

XIII

Restructuring Local Governance in Globalization

Introduction

Globalization and IT revolution have prompted countries to reposition and alter the government and governance at every level and more particularly at the grassroots level with adequate powers, responsibilities and resources with a view to making use of the opportunities and combating the threats and the ill effects of globalization for the benefit of the people more specifically the poor and the marginalized. All over the world leaders are in search of good instruments to establish responsive governance to tide over the existing crises in governance. The rising aspiration for development and democracy among the hitherto marginalized groups have prompted the countries to think of alternative paradigms. Thereby for local development and local democracy, institutional mechanisms have been created at local level for governance and development.

Global Scenario

Thus, local self-governments have gained attention and importance in the world where the economy is globalised. It is being looked upon as an instrument to deepen democracy and empower people.[1] Throughout the world local bodies are being given due recognition at varying levels. Brazil, Denmark, France, India, Italy, Japan and Sweden have given constitutional status to local governments. Australia and the United States of America have given due status in the state or provincial constitutions. New Zealand, the United Kingdom and a large number of countries have enacted ordinary legislation in the Central Parliament of the respective countries to recognize local governments. Canada and Pakistan have enacted legislation through the provincial legislature to accord recognition to the grassroots institutions. China is an exception and it has accorded status only through an executive order. In whatever way the country has accorded recognition to local government, local governments have reached a stage of attracting due attention of the researchers.[2] It does not mean that all over the world local bodies are strengthened and have perfectly carved out a framework for their functioning in the federal and unitary governments as State and Central Governments created through the Constitution.

Even while recognizing the local governments, the countries have adopted different modes and strategies as central leaders perceive local bodies differently. Perceptions vary from country to country. India is a classic example: even after passing the 73rd and the 74th Amendments to the Constitution of India and making the local bodies institutions of governance State governments still treat the local bodies as only implementing agencies to carry out the schemes and programmes of the State and Central governments. So perceptions vary widely. One set of countries have recognized the local bodies through the basic document of the countries, namely the Constitution another set of countries have created local governments through the Provincial Constitution. A third set of countries have recognized the local governments through a simple legislation of the respective National Parliament. A fourth group of countries have enacted legislation through Provincial Legislature by which local bodies are recognized. The fifth not a set of countries but China alone, which has recognized local bodies through an executive order.

While going through the recognitions one should not be under the impression that simply because the local bodies are recognized through Constitution, the institutions of local governance have been given vast powers. For example, China had created and given powers to the local bodies only through an executive order. But the powers are decisive and fifty per cent of the resources are spent on development activities through local bodies. But, in India, local bodies in many of the provinces are not given such decisive powers and resources despite Local Governments being recognized through the Constitution.[3] The US has accorded legitimacy through the State Constitution and which have given specific powers to local bodies. Denmark has given constitutional status and perfectly devolved needed powers also. But discourse is on among the academics, researchers, activists and practitioners to push an item of agenda in reforming governance,[4] especially strengthening the grassroots institutions and this process has to be done through recognizing the local institutions by the respective constitution of the country. To tide over the mounting pressure from below the more democratic and developed countries are in a compelling condition to install a legitimate governance mechanism with needed powers, functionaries and resources to take decisions and implement the same. Against this background, all over the world, activities are on to strengthen the local institutions. In many countries, the federal government itself wants vibrant local institutions to reduce its stress and burden of delivering services and goods. Even the socialist countries have also wanted such a kind of arrangement to combat the micro movements. China is the best example.[5]

Context

One cannot hide the context in which the local bodies gain primacy. It is to be noted here that the existing form of governance and governments at higher levels in all democratic countries in the world have been losing their primacy and, as a result, people lose confidence and faith in the system and the leaders.[6] It has been unequivocally demonstrated through studies that voting percentages in democratic countries are steadily decreasing, participation of youth in politics has been dwindling and the people's participation in civic affairs has also been decreasing.[7] People's perception of politics, governance and administration has been changed. In the same way their expectations have increased enormously.[8] To meet the new requirements of the people our governance and administrative mechanism does not have the capability. When the market is satisfying the new aspirations of the people (consumers) constantly through its research and innovation, government does not improve, innovate and reform its machinery to meet the increasing needs and aspirations of the people. Moreover, the government machinery is involved in corrupt practices which further degraded the image of the mechanism.[9] The political system, political leaders and bureaucracy have been losing their credibility and image among the people. Everyone is looking for efficient government which may be an alternative to the existing one.[10] In this context decentralization of powers is thought of as one of the strategies to combat the crisis in governance. There is yet another issue, namely, strains and stress on federal governments due to unprecedented market activities and, to overcome the same, restructuring of local governance was considered. Hence, this restructuring of local governance is in the neo-liberal agenda. While advocating reinventing governance in general from the federal institutions to grassroots institutions the neo-liberals advocated restructuring of local governments and putting them in proper framework to deliver services effectively to the public and create a market linkage for the economic development of the local populace. Moreover, it was considered that people have to be empowered and they must be made to participate in governance. Even the neo-liberals have set this agenda on the popular dissent and discontent over the performance of the State and the bureaucracy.[11]

Models and Perspectives

According to the neo-liberal ideology global economic challenges require a flexible, down sized local government, responsible for the integration of a locality into the world economy.[12] While liberating the local bodies from the control of the higher level institutions and empowering the same for the benefit of the market and the citizens, the higher level governments enable local politics to control over resources. As a result, the local bodies will emerge as power centres to mobilize people and function as economic units. It all depends on how the new paradigm of power shift is being perceived and handled by the leaders of local bodies. There are a variety of models of local governance that have emerged in the world. They are the Nordic model, the Swiss model, the French model, the German model, the British model, the Indian model, the Chinese model, the Japanese model, the North American model, the Australian model, and so on. While analyzing the models of governments at the local level a number of perspectives emerge. They are traditional fiscal federalism, new public management, public choice, new institutional economics and network forms of local governance. Fiscal federalism and new public management perspectives are concerned with market failures. Public choice and new institutional economics perspective is concerned with institutional arrangements to overcome both market and government failures. But one thing has been accepted all over the world. Though there are several theories on governance, all accept a strong rationale for decentralized decision making and a strong role for local governments on the grounds of efficiency, accountability, manageability and autonomy.[13] The local bodies in unitary governments create new kinds of political problems and solutions contradictory to the federal government. In the new context when local bodies are created with adequate powers for governance, it induces the participation of the people and the community in decision making. In the whole process one will find the empowerment and engagement of the people and the community. Continuous engagement will bring about enlightenment on the part of the citizens. In the new dispensation institutional space is found for citizens' engagement. In India, the 73rd Amendment to the Constitution of India has created such a space through the Gram Sabha. An informed community can be created through a continuous process of engagement. An informed community and citizens may not always work for the market as they know the positive and the negative implications of the market. One cannot expect a mad support for the market. It can handle the market very effectively for the benefit of the community and the society.

Issues in Question

Some countries find the emerging local governments a fine solution to the problems created by the provincial governments to the federal government. When provincial governments are exerting pressure on the national government constantly, the national governments are compelled to find a way to manage the State governments. Creation of local government statutorily at the grassroots will make the State governments face the demands of the local governments. It is considered a strategy to mitigate the pressure of the State Government over the Central Government by empowering the local governments through recognizing the local governments with adequate powers and resources. Take the case of India: when 63rd Amendment was introduced in the Parliament, the argument was projected that the powers of the State Government would be eroded if the amendment was allowed to pass in the national parliament. The proposal was criticized and it was considered a ploy against the State governments. The arguments were projected from a narrow federalistic theory: the federal government wants to build up the grassroots institution with the aim of weakening the State governments and it wants to bypass the State governments. In a true federal set-up both governments should be strong and equally the grassroots government also. As a result, the 64th Amendment Bill was defeated and subsequently a weak framework was evolved for local governance through the 73rd Amendment to the Constitution of India. The Parliamentary Committee removed the controversial clauses from the 64th Amendment Bill and the same was passed. Yet another issue which is being talked of is the emergence of the new federalism. Fiscal federalism is foremost and most important in determining the strength of local bodies. The Nordic countries have paved way for a strong fiscal federalism. In the same way China is also allocating 50 per cent of the resources for development to local bodies. Against this background, it is to be seen that federalism in the world has undergone a change.

No theory prevents the creation of a new tier of governance. It is a dynamic concept and it is evolving in character. Harmonizing diversities and differences is the main function of federal governance. When diversity is more the society requires different levels of governance. In a diversified and divisive society, multiplicity of governance mechanism will strengthen the federal government at the top. It will be strengthened only through the diversified governance mechanism. When grassroots institutions are strengthened, automatically the pressure exerted on Central Government and State governments will be reduced.[14]

New Leadership

At present, the emergence of vibrant local leaders through the new local government—both urban and rural—created a lurking fear among the representatives of Provincial Legislatures and the National Parliament that their power base would be eroded by the emergence of the new leaders.[15] Yet another argument projected is that for negotiating the power base of the MLAs and the MPs in certain areas the cooperation and the support of local body leaders are needed as they emerge as their representatives to safeguard the interests of the people. The political parties look for some vibrant leaders emerging through local bodies to strengthen the base of the party. They are the strength of the political parties. This is not unique in India. In many countries a new kind of leadership is emerging and they are called transformative leaders who bring about transformation among the people. In many places the grassroots leaders are the models for regional and national leaders. In the same way in Canadian politics, the local body leaders are powerful individuals carrying the support of the communities despite reduced powers and resources. It was noticed in a recent study visit done by me in Canada where I interacted with local body leaders that the provincial leaders have to necessarily get the support of local body leaders to get the support of the people for any political task. Facing them is a difficult task for the provincial leaders. As a result, the provincial governments such as Ontario have reduced the number of Municipalities from 800 to 400. It was perceived by the leaders of local bodies as a strategy of the State government to reduce the strength of the local body leaders. Local body leaders of Canada have a federation at national and regional levels. The argument projected by the State government is that the size of the municipalities has to be decided from the management perspective and hence the State government has reduced the numbers. To reduce the cost of services, economy of scale is considered. The local body leaders are not claiming provincial identity. Provincial leaders want a provincial identity to bargain with the federal government but it reduces the local community identities.

Service Delivery and Development

Since the local body leaders do not want to antagonize both federal government and provincial government leaders they do not want to indulge in intensive political activities and they develop a perception that they are development leaders. Local bodies are totally involved in delivering basic services to the people in which there is no ideology involved. There is no ideological difference in delivering services to the people and hence local body leaders need not entertain politics. This is the perception of local body leaders of many countries. There is yet another argument that the local bodies are the seed bed and nursery of democratic political culture. All over the world arguments are projected that a strong federal government can protect the country and work for development. To support the endeavour of the federal government the local government can play a major role and hence both at the top and at the bottom the base should be strong. There is another argument that the provincial government should be the powerful instrument to mitigate the pressure from the bottom to the federal not the grassroots institutions as political aspirations and development aspirations cannot be effectively handled by the grassroots institutions but they can be handled by the provincial governments effectively.

Clash of Interest

There is yet another question persisting in the minds of researchers as to why the US, the UK and Canada have not given constitutional status to local bodies even though they give adequate powers to manage local bodies. In India local bodies are recognized constitutionally but powers are not given even to the minimum level in many States. The best known reason is that down below the State the provincial political leaders do not want institutions for governance as the powers enjoyed by the State governments are limited. That is why the State governments have talked about State autonomy.[16] They also bring in an argument that the local bodies will work against larger development proposals of the provincial government and that, moreover the State will have to lose its sovereignty. When an argument is projected on the loss of sovereignty by the Central and State governments while giving power to the local government constitutionally it is to be remembered that people are sovereign and they give power to the State. While giving power to the State, it includes the three governments, namely, the federal government, the provincial government and the local government. The problem arises only when national interest and provincial interest are disturbed by the actions of local government. There are events and incidents in India to posit that national interest is at stake due to the activities of the many of the States. There are evidences that the State governments have acted unilaterally against the national interest with a narrow mind with the intention of protecting the regional interest. Nobody argues that we do not want provincial government as they are acting against national interest. Everyone wants a mechanism to resolve it and hence there is an inter State council.

In the same way local governments' demands have to be seen. When the local bodies are acting with a narrow interest by negating the public interest of the province and the nation, steps have to be initiated to resolve such tangles. It is not a problem and it can be solved very easily by demarcating the powers and the functions of local government. When there is a dispute between and among the State governments and between the State and the Central Government, an institutional mechanism is in the Constitution. Similarly, the dispute between the State government and the local government can be resolved through an institutional device which could be evolved. But unfortunately nobody has thought of this. In many States in India local government leaders have formed federations to deal with the State governments. This is so in many of the developed countries also. Unfortunately this relationship between the State government and the local government is not being studied and researched. The USA is the best example to demonstrate that even though powers are not given constitutionally, adequate functional clarity is given as to the powers and the functions of the local bodies.

The whole problem lies not in giving constitutional status but in demarcating the powers, functions and responsibilities of the local bodies. In the absence of functional clarity and overlapping powers, normally the higher level government will take the upper hand and this will become a problem in the relationship between the State government and the local government. In India many States are facing problems because of the confusion in delineating the powers and the responsibilities of each tier of the local bodies even though the local bodies are recognized through the Constitution of India. There are a few States which have done power devolution scientifically.[17] The State governments are bringing in an argument that these local bodies will look at even large development issues from the narrow perspective of local interest by which they will make use of the devolved power to stop the development initiative. Against this background the federal and provincial governments have to act against such initiatives of the local bodies. As the capacity of the local governments is very low, managing them in the development context is not very tough. When they are constitutionally recognized, the capacitated local bodies will be a powerful political force to reckon with. But in the case of Indian local bodies, the leaders' capacity is poor and hence they have not realized the sovereign power of the local bodies and, as a result, both the Central Government and the State Government manage the local bodies very easily. There are events and incidents in India to prove that national interest is at stake due to the activities of many States. A forceful argument was generated by a group of advocates that the right of Local Self Government is implicit and inherent in the principles of liberal democracy. Even arguments have been projected that if the local bodies are given such constitutional status the local parochial authorities might stand in the way of economic advancement, delivery of efficient services at an affordable cost, protecting the natural resources, safeguarding human rights and promoting efforts to bring people together under wider public authorities.

Judicial Interpretation

While recognizing the status and the position of local bodies in the political system of countries as institutions of governance, the role of the judiciary is important through its interpretation. While interpreting the provisions of the Constitution of the countries and the activities of the federal and provincial governments towards local bodies the judiciary takes different positions depending on the nature of the political system in the respective countries. We cannot find a uniform interpretation across the world. It is to be noted here that the Indian judiciary is positive[18] and fair in pronouncing judgments in favour of the local bodies in the context of disputes between the provincial governments and the local governments by invoking the constitutional provision by which the judiciary recognizes the self-governing nature of the local bodies. The judiciary protects the local bodies from the encroachment of the State governments in the domain of Panchayati Raj. It is only the local body leaders who have not made the local bodies self-governing because of their poor skill, capacity, and capability in managing the institutions. This is also because of the poor initiative of the higher level governments in building the capacity of the local body leaders. Even the capacity building exercise is also being done only by the street bureaucracy which is totally inefficient. In the absence of proper perspective on the part of the lower level officials, what kind of training will be given to the local body leaders by the officials at the grassroots? Absolutely the local body leaders are not aware of the full potential and implications of the new dispensation. But in the UK, the USA and Canada, the local body leaders have brought to count several arguments through their cases against the provincial governments to strengthen local bodies constitutionally. But the judiciary, given the capacity and capability of the grassroots leaders, develops an apprehension that the local bodies will work effectively in challenging the initiative of the provincial governments if they feel that their interests are not protected. Hence, the judiciary refuses to recognize the local bodies as self-governing sovereign power.[19]

Implications of Restructuring

The agenda for restructuring governments promoted by the neo-liberal groups is with the aim of restructuring of local governance with two perspectives: one is to link the local economy with the wider market economy and the next one is to deliver service and goods effectively with the wider participation of the people and the private sector. Adequate literature is available to prove that the local bodies are vibrant after the restructuring of the delivery of services and public goods. But literature is scanty to portray that due to the poor linkage of the local economy with the wider economy, community economy has not been developed. One cannot argue that, in the new economic linkage, the poor have gained profit or any advancement. There is yet another argument that the poor have lost their endowments and livelihoods due this new linkage of connecting the rural economy with the wider market economy.[20] As a result, the empowered citizens started protesting against the new dispensation of linking the local economy with the wider economy. Previously local politics was confined to local areas, provincial politics was confined to the province alone. But now it has all gone to any level by breaking the boundaries. When the environmentalists organized a civil disobedience movement in Canada, the environmentalist mobilised not only the local population, but also from different countries and leaders from different countries participated in the movement. They were arrested and the problem became complicated.[21] Since people from all over the world participated, the arrested people were to be dealt not with the same laws. Arguments were posited that the citizens of other countries cannot be treated as citizens of Canada. It created lot of problems to the Central Government. Now the local problems go global. Now the local body leaders have formed local, regional, national, continental organisations to express their problems and to solve the same. In such a way Local Bodies are empowered to make use of the opportunity, if any that comes from globalization and if there is any threat it can be avoided or resisted through their solidarity. But it is possible in the developed countries because the people are well informed and they are not beneficiaries and petitioners. They claim their rights and entitlements. Well informed people can have control over the institutions and the leaders are responsive to the people. In the developing countries people are not much empowered. As a result, local bodies may not be able to resist. Moreover, the local bodies are not having the capacity to make use of the opportunity unless they are specifically oriented, trained and capacitated. One thing is obvious from the literature generated out of research in the developing countries. The new dispensation has started the exercise of deepening democracy and achieving downward accountability in a phased manner with limited powers devolved to local bodies in developing countries. As a result, local bodies are emerging as institutional structure to address the question of democratic deficit.[22]

System's Failure

There is yet another argument that the local governments have to address the issues of government failures and market failures. Having seen the market failures in addressing the issues of the poor, donor institutions have started advocating a citizen centred local governance which includes a citizen empowerment through a rights-based approach, bottom up accountability for results and evaluation of government performance as the facilitator of a network of providers by citizens as governors, tax payers and consumers of public services. The above proposal came out after the evaluation of the performance of the local bodies. It is further attributed that if the local bodies have not delivered the goods to the level of the expectation it is due to the failure on the part of the State governments in empowering people.[23] When a drive is initiated for decentralizing powers to grassroots institutions, the funding agencies who fund democracy promotion and development provide funds to create more of parallel bodies which challenge the local bodies. The donor agencies do not shed adequate clarity on the process of decentralization of powers.

Quota System

The quota system brings in a new wave of enthusiasm for this democracy. Women have been brought into the system. Yet their barriers and obstacles do not permit them to perform their role and responsibilities. Against this background a support structure has been created in the form of networking of the leaders and, the barriers and obstacles are dismantled.[24] There is yet another action vigorously being pursued. Decentralization of powers is intended to empower people and more particularly the marginalized. It is a proven statement that many of the legislations in many of the countries are well conceived and well prepared but, after passing the same, they are not vigorously implemented as they are conceived and prepared. The reason is that path breaking legislations will always meet challenges and those challenges have to be overcome by the leaders of the government. In the absence of such initiative on the part of the government, the civil society organizations have to prepare the groups which are going to gain benefits to raise their voice to implement the legislations. In such a context only these initiatives will sustain the process of strengthening local governance. Decentralization of powers having the potential of transforming the paradigm of governance in many of the developing countries, those who are in power will not allow the existing arrangement to be changed. To change the condition a movement has to be formed at the grassroots. At present, it is the felt need and considered opinion among the people who are concerned about deepening democracy that a movement has to be launched to protect the local self-government. It is not intended to ensure delivery of services alone and it has to go beyond the service delivery. It has the capacity and capability to alter the paradigm of accountability from upward to downwards, transform the people and community from the position of beneficiaries and petitioners to citizens with responsibility, power and authority. It will also address the main problem of democratic deficit by which it will work for deepening democracy. In the developing countries it has to address the issues of equity and inclusion. By building up the local capacity the local body will address the above issues. Over a period of time a new participatory empowerment culture will emerge which will alter the existing feudal culture in politics.

Poor Capacity and Skill

There is yet another argument to undermine the local bodies. It is the incapacity to govern, manage and administer development through the institutions. The poor capacity for management and governance is not only the problem of local bodies, it is also the problem of the provincial government and the federal government. We have witnessed steady growing of literature on poor governance ability where the scholars question the capacity and capability of the federal and provincial governments.[25] Local bodies, historically speaking, have been viewed with different emphasis over a period of time. Now it is not for delivering of services alone or implementing the schemes and programmes of the federal and provincial governments. It is for governance. The service providing role can be given to even a private organization. There is yet another argument that the local bodies should have adequate resource mobilising power either through tax or through service or grant. But it is a known fact that the local bodies have lost the power over a period of time. The argument is that it is to be decided by the provincial government by considering the paying power of the people and the regional variation. To overcome this problem a tax reform initiative has to be done.

Conclusion

While analyzing all the factors for and against the Local Self Government, it is necessary that a world level initiative has to be taken to empower the local bodies restructuring the local bodies to emerge as the third stratum of government in federal states and the second stratum of government in unitary states. In the context of globalization the neo-liberals are advocating restructuring and it has to be viewed positively to empower the local governments and people to make use of the advantages if any they see from globalization and avoid threats and ill effects if they find any in the process of analysis of globalization. For both the people need power and facilitating institutions.

NOTES

1. James Manor, *Political Economy of Decentralization of Powers,* (Washington D.C: The World Bank, 1999).
2. Warren Magnusson, "Protecting the Right of Local Self Government", *Canadian Journal of Political Science,* Vol. 38, No. 4, (December, 2005), pp. 897–922.
3. Ministry of Panchayati Raj, *Status of Panchayat Mid-term Appraisal,* (New Delhi: Government of India, 2006).
4. Bidyut Chakrabarty and Mohit Bhattacharya (eds.), *Administrative Change and Innovation: A Reader,* (New Delhi: Oxford University Press, 2005).
5. Pallavi Aiyar, "China's Experiment with Village Elections", *The Hindu,* (Chennai) (24th July, 2007).
6. Susan J. Pharr, Robert Putnam and Russell Dalton, "A Quarter Century of Declining Confidence", *Journal of Democracy,* Vol. 11, No. 1, (2000), pp. 5-25.
7. M. Gray and M. Carel, "Declining Voter Turnout in Advanced Industrial Democracies 1950 to 1997: The Effects of Declining Group Mobilization", *Comparative Political Studies,* (2000), Vol. 33, No. 4, pp. 1091–1122.
8. G. Palanithurai, *Peoples Perception of Politics,* (New Delhi: Kaniska Publishing House, 2002).
9. Ajit Mishra, *The Economic of Corruption,* (New Delhi: Oxford University Press, 2005).
10. Margart Levi, "Why we need a New Theory of Government" *Perspectives on Politics,* Vol. 13, No. 2, (June 2005), pp. 235-252.
11. Geoffrey Lawrence, Murray Kneuttila and Ian Gray' "Localization, New Liberalism and Rural Decline in Roger Epp and Dave Whitson (eds.), *Writing off the Rural West: Globalization Governments and the Transformations of Rural Communities,* (Edmonton: The University of Alberta Press and Parkland Institute, 2001), pp. 89–108.

12. Warren Magnusson, "Protecting the Right of Local Self Government" *Canadian Journal of Political Science,* Vol. 38, No. 4, (December, 2005), pp. 897–922.
13. Anwar Shah (ed.), *Local Governance in Industrial Countries,* (Washington D.C: The World Bank, 2006); and Anwar Shah (ed.), *Local Governance in Developing Countries,* (Washington D.C.: The World Bank, 2006).
14. Balveer Arora's presentation on "Federalism in India" in the Regional Round Table organised by the Inter-State Council, Ministry of Home Affairs, Government of India in Goa on 30th and 31st July, 2007.
15. G. Palanithurai, *Process and Performance of Dalit and Women Panchayat Presidents.* (Concept Publishing Company Pvt. Ltd., New Delhi, 2005).
16. G. Palanithurai, *New Panchayati Raj System at Work: An Evaluation,* (Concept Publishing Company Pvt. Ltd., New Delhi, 2002).
17. Ministry of Panchayati Raj, *A Mid-term Review of Panchayati Raj in India,* (Government of India, 2007), New Delhi.
18. Institute of Social Sciences, *The Jurisprudence of Panchayati Raj Institutions,* Institute of Social Sciences, 2005, New Delhi.
19. Amasa M. Eaton, "The Right to Local Self Government", *Harvard Law Review,* Vol. 14, No. 1, (1900), pp. 20–38.
20. A Study has been conducted in seven sectors with the support of the Ford Foundation to assess the impact of Globalization. Following are the reports: G. Palanithurai, *Handloom Sector under Globalization,* (Gandhigram: Rajiv Gandhi Chair for Panchayati Raj Studies, 2006); G. Palanithurai, *Water Sector under Globalization,* (Gandhigram: Rajiv Gandhi Chair for Panchayati Raj Studies, 2006); G. Palanithurai, *Agriculture Sector under Globalization,* (Gandhigram: Rajiv Gandhi Chair for Panchayati Raj Studies, 2006); G. Palanithurai, *Food Security Sector under Globalization,* (Gandhigram: Rajiv Gandhi Chair for Panchayati Raj Studies, 2006); G. Palanithurai, *Rural Artisan Sector under Globalization,* (Gandhigram: Rajiv Gandhi Chair for Panchayati Raj Studies, 2006); G. Palanithurai, *Fishing Sector under Globalization,* (Gandhigram: Rajiv Gandhi Chair for Panchayati Raj Studies, 2006); G. Palanithurai, *Plantation Sector under Globalization,* (Gandhigram: Rajiv Gandhi Chair for Panchayati Raj Studies, 2006);
21. Geoffrey Lawrence, Murray Kneuttila and Ian Gray, "Localization, New Liberalism and Rural Decline in Roger Epp and Dave Whitson", (eds.). *Writing off the Rural West: Globalization, Government and Transformation of Rural Communities,* (Edmonton: University of Alberta Press and Parkland Institute, 2001), pp. 89-108.
22. Jesse C. Ribot, Representation, Citizenship and the Public Domain

in Democratic Decentralization, *Development*, Vol. 50, No. 1, (March 2007), pp. 43-49.

23. Anwar Shah and Furhawn Shah, Citizen Centred Local Governance: Strategies to Combat Democratic Deficits, *Development*, Vol. 50, No. 1, (March 2007).
24. Michael Clalow, Women's Organizations and Local Democracy: Promoting Effective Participation of Women in Central America, *Development*, Vol. 50, No. 1 (March, 2007), pp. 86–89.
25. W.A. Johnston, Harvey Krafin and Trevor Harrison, "Democracy, Political Institutions and Trust: The Limits of Current Electoral Reform", *The Canadian Journal of Sociology*, Vol. 31, No. 2, (Spring 2006), pp. 166–167.

XIV

Conclusion

From the analysis and conclusion of all the articles in this book there are certain striking features emerging which are serving as guide posts to make certain key recommendations for governance, Politics, administration and decision making at the grassroots. Primarily our politics has moved away from development and keeping a sizeable section of the mass away from Governance and Development. As a result, our polity and governance are elite centric and people are made as onlookers. Our governance and administrative mechanisms are so complicated and complex which will keep the ordinary citizens away from them. They are to be simplified and reformed by keeping the people at the centre.

Corruption in Public life is pervasive and negative to the just governance and people are deeply engaged by media on this issue.As a result, a negative trend has emerged in Political System which is so dangerous to our democracy and development. There is absolute a leadership crisis in India. In this context India needs more number of transformative leaders at the grassroots to transform the rustic folk in the rural areas. We have alternative path as shown by M.K. Gandhi not only for India but also for the whole world. In our governance system accountability is weak. There is no transparency in our administrative system. They are to be dealt with through the New Panchayati Raj System. For any decision making accurate data basis is needed. At present there is no scientific data generation. At Gram Panchayat we have governance unit and administration unit but neither are they entrusted with the task of data generation nor data maintenance for decision making. There is much scope for RTI to reduce corruption in development works at grassroots but its utility is very limited.

As per the studies conducted the entry of *dalits* in local governance has not shown much impact on the life of the *dalits* as they are facing volley of problems handling power at the community level. We have organizations to support *dalits* at National and Regional levels, but there is no strong and active organizations at the grassroots level to support and facilitate *dalit* local body leaders. In the context of globalization, local bodies have to be contextualized. Reforming governance at grassroots in the context of globalization is imperative. Yet actions are slow.

Bibliography

Aiyar, Pallavi, "China's Experiment with Village Elections," *The Hindu*, Chennai, 24th July, 2007.

Andrews, Matt; Connell Mc Jesse and Wescott Alison, *Development as Leadership – Led Change – A Report for the Global Leadership Initiative and the World Bank Institute*, Harvard Kennedy School, 2010.

Appleby, Paul, *Public Administration in India: Report of a Survey*, Delhi: Mangal Publications, 1953.

Arora, Balveer, "Federalism in India", Regional Round Table, Inter-State Council, Ministry of Home Affairs, Government of India in Goa, July 2007.

Banarjee, M. Ajit and Chandrasekaran, K.A., *Reviewing Governance*, New Delhi: Tata McGraw Hill, 1996.

Banerjee, V. Abhijit, and Pande Rohini, *Parochial Politics: Ethnic Preferences and Politician Corruption*, Faculty Research Working Papers Services, Harvard Kennedy School, 2007.

Basu, Amrita and Kohli Atual (ed.), *Community Conflicts and State in India*, New Delhi: Oxford University Press, 1998.

Baviskar, B.S. and Mathew George (eds), *Inclusion and Exclusion in Local Governance* New Delhi: Sage Publications, 2009.

Baviskar, B.S. and Patel Tulsi (eds), *Understanding Indian Society: Past and Present*, New Delhi: Orient Blackswan, 2010.

Bhardhan, Pranab and Mookherjee Dilip (eds), *Decentralization and Local Governance in Developing Countries: A Comparative Perspective*, New Delhi: Oxford University Press, 2007.

Bhaskaran, S. and Sumathi B.S. (eds), *Human Development in India: Initiatives and Experience*, Hyderabad: The Icfai University Press, 2009.

Chakarbarty, Bidyut and Bhattacharya Mohit (eds) *Administrative Change and Innovation: A Reader*, New Delhi: Oxford University Press, 2005.

Chakrabarty, Bidyut and Bhattacharya Mohit (eds.), *The Governance Discourse: A Reader*, Delhi: Oxford University Press, 2008.

Chandrasekar, C.P., "Changing Priorities", *Front Line*, Vol 28: No. 21 Oct. 21, 2011.

Chaudhary, S.N., *Dalit and Tribal Leadership in Panchayats*, New Delhi: Concept Publishing Company Pvt. Ltd., New Delhi, 2004.

Chief Minister Special Division, *Central Government Schemes,* Chennai: Government of Tamil Nadu, 2008.

Chief Minister Special Division, *Welfare Schemes of Tamil Nadu Vols. I, II & III,* Chennai: Govt. of Tamil Nadu, 2008.

Chief Minister Special Cell, *Welfare Schemes of the Government of Tamil Nadu,* Chennai: Govt. of Tamil Nadu, 2007.

Chopra, Kanchan and Rao Hanumantha C.H. (eds), *Growth, Equity, Environment and Population,* New Delhi: Sage Publications, 2008.

Clalow, Michael, *Women's Organizations and Local Democracy: Promoting Effective Participation of Women in Central America,* Development, Vol. 50: No.1, March, 2007.

Dharampal, *The Madras Panchayat System: A General Assessment, Vol. II,* New Delhi: Impex India, 1972.

Drug, Cooper A., Kricckhans Jonathan and Lerzting Michael, "Corruption, Democracy and Economic Growth", *International Political Science Review,* Vol. 27: No 2, 2006.

Eaton, Amasa M., "The Right to Local Self Government", *Harvard Law Review,* Vol.14: No.1, 1900.

Epp Roger and Whitson Dave (eds), *Writing off the Rural West: Globalization Governments and the Transformations of Rural Communities,* Edmonton: The University of Alberta Press and Parkland Institute, 2001.

Ganev, V., *Preying on the State: Political Capitalism after Communism* (Ph.D. Dissertation), Department of Political Science, University of Chicago, 1999.

Godbole, Madhav, "Unending Struggle for Right to Information", *Economic and Political Weekly,* 12, August, 2000.

Gorringe, Hugo, *Untouchable Citizens: Dalit Movements and Democratization in Tamil Nadu,* New Delhi: Sage Publications, 2005.

Gorwala, A.D., *Report of Public Administration and Efficient Conduct of State Enterprises,* Govt. of India, 1951.

Gray, M. and Carel M., "Declining Voter Turnout in Advanced Industrial Democracies 1950 to 1997: The Effects of Declining Group Mobilization", *Comparative Political Studies,* Vol. 33: No. 4, 2000.

Harrison, Elizabeth, "Corruption", *Development in Practice,* Vol. 17: No. 4 & 5, Aug. 2007.

Institute of Social Sciences, *The Jurisprudence of Panchayati Raj Institutions,* New Delhi: Institute of Social Sciences, 2005.

Jain, L.C. (ed), *Decentralization and Local Governance,* New Delhi: Orient Longman, 2005.

Jayal, Gopal Niraja and Pai Sudha (eds), *Democratic Governance in India,* New Delhi: Sage Publications, 2001.

Jayal, Gopal Niraja, Prakash Amit and Sharma Pradeep K., (Eds.), *Local Governance in India,* New Delhi: Oxford University Press, 2006.

Jenkins, Rob and Goetz Marie Anne, "Accounts and Accountability:

Theoretical Implications of the Right to Information Movement in India", *Third World Quarterly,* 2003.

Johnston, W.A., Krafin Harvey and Harrison Trevor, "Democracy, Political Institutions and Trust: The Limits of Current Electoral Reform", *The Canadian Journal of Sociology,* Vol. 31: No. 2, 2006.

Joseph, T.M. (ed.), *"Local Governance in India: Ideas, Challenges and Strategies",* New Delhi: Concept Publishing Company Pvt. Ltd., New Delhi, 2007.

Kabeer, Naila, Kabir Hag Ariful, *"Citizenship Narratives in the Absence of Good Governance: Voice of the Working Poor in Bangladesh",* IDS Working Paper, 2009.

Kashyap, C. Subash, *Basic Constitutional Values,* New Delhi: Ajanta Publications, 1994.

Kishwar, Purnima Madhu, *Deepening Democracy: Challenges of Governance and Globalisation in India,* New Delhi: Oxford University Press, 2005.

Kohli, Atul (ed), *The Success of India's Democracy,* Cambridge: Cambridge University Press, 2001.

Kohli, Atul, *Democracy and Development in India,* New Delhi: Oxford University Press, 2009.

Kohli, Atul, *Democracy and Discontent: India's Growing Crisis of Governability,* Cambridge: Cambridge University Press, 1990.

Kothari, Rajni, *Rethinking Democracy,* New Delhi: Orient Longman, 2005.

Kumar, Krishna, "Cleaning the State", *Economic and Political Weekly,* Vol. XLV1:No 48, Nov. 26th, 2011.

Levi, Margaret, "Why we need a New Theory of Government" *Perspectives on Politics,* Vol. 13: No. 2, June 2005.

Magnusson, Warren, "Protecting the Right of Local Self Government" *Canadian Journal of Political Science,* Vol. 38:No. 4, December, 2005.

Manor, James, *Political Economy of Decentralization of Powers,* Washington D.C: The World Bank, 1999.

Mathew, George, (ed), *Panchayati Raj in Karnataka To-day,* New Delhi: Concept Publishing Company Pvt. Ltd., New Delhi, 1986.

Migdal, Samuel Joel, Kohli Atul and Shue Vivienne (Eds), *State Power and Social Forces: Domination and Transformation in the Third World,* New York: Cambridge University Press, 1994.

Mill, J.S., *Considerations on Representative Government,* London: Fontana. 1976.

Ministry of Panchayati Raj, *A Compendium of Resolutions of the Seven Round Tables of Ministers in-charge of Panchayati Raj,* (July-December 2004), New Delhi: Ministry of Panchayati Raj, 2005.

Ministry of Panchayati Raj, *A Mid-term Review of Panchayati Raj in India,* New Delhi: Government of India, 2007.

Ministry of Panchayati Raj, *BRGF Guidelines,* New Delhi: Ministry of Panchayati Raj, 2007.

Ministry of Panchayati Raj, *Status of Panchayat Mid-Term Appraisal*, New Delhi: Government of India, 2006.

Mishra, Ajit, *The Economics of Corruption*, New Delhi: Oxford University Press, 2005.

Myron, Weiner, *The Indian Paradox: Essays in Indian Politics*, New Delhi: Sage Publications, 1989.

Narayanasamy, N.; Boraiyan M.P.; Jeyaraju M.A (Eds), *"Corruption at the Grassroots: The Shades and Shadows"*, New Delhi: Concept Publishing Company Pvt. Ltd., New Delhi, 2000.

Nayar, Baldev Raj, *The Myth of the Shrinking State: Globalisation and the State in India*, Delhi: Oxford University Press, 2009.

Nelbo, A. Michael *et al.*, *Who Wants to Deliberate – And Why?*, Faculty Research Working Papers Services, Harvard Kennedy School, 2009.

Oldfield, Adrian, Citizenship and Community: Civic Republicanism and the Modern World, London: Routledge, 1990.

Palani, N., *"Dalit Politics and Dravidian Movement in Tamil Nadu"* Gandhigram Rural University, (Unpublished Ph.D. thesis) May, 2004.

Palanithruai, G. (ed.), *Rajiv Gandhi's Vision on Local Governance*, New Delhi: Concept Publishing Company, 2009.

Palanithurai, G., *"Containing Corruption at Grassroots"*, Paper presented in International Policy Dialogue, 1st to 3rd October, 2009 at Senegal.

Palanithurai, G., *"Democratizing Society and Governance"*, Gandhi Marg, 30 (1), 2008.

Palanithurai, G., "Governance and Administration: Reforms at Grassroots", *The ICFAI University Journal of Public Administration*, Vol. 4:No. 4, October, 2008.

Palanithurai, G., "Grassroot Level Corruption: A Cursory Analysis" in G. Palanithruai (Ed.), *New Panchayati Raj System: Status and Prospects*, New Delhi: Kanishka Publishers and Distributors, 1996.

Palanithurai, G., *"Report on the Study of Market and Democracy in Tamil Nadu"*, Gandhigram: Rajiv Gandhi Chair for Panchayati Raj Studies, 2009.

Palanithurai, G., *Agriculture Sector under Globalization*, Gandhigram: Rajiv Gandhi Chair for Panchayati Raj Studies, 2006.

Palanithurai, G., and Thandavan R., (eds), *Ethnic Movement in Transition*, New Delhi: Kanishka Publishers & Distributors, 1998.

Palanithurai, G., *Committee System in Gram Panchayat* (in Tamil), New Century Book House, 2006.

Palanithurai, G., *Containing Corruption: A Micro Experiment*, Gandhigram: Rajiv Gandhi Chair for Panchayati Raj Studies, 1998.

Palanithurai, G., *Critical Issues in Decentralisation of Powers in India*, Concept Publishing Company Pvt. Ltd., 2009.

Palanithurai, G., *Emerging Dimensions in Decentralization*, New Delhi: Concept Publishing Company Pvt. Ltd., 2005.

Palanithurai, G., *Evolving Grassroots Democracy,* New Delhi: Concept Publishing Company Pvt. Ltd., 2007.

Palanithurai, G. *Fishing Sector under Globalization,* Gandhigram: Rajiv Gandhi Chair for Panchayati Raj Studies, 2006.

Palanithurai, G., *Food Security Sector under Globalization,* Gandhigram: Rajiv Gandhi Chair for Panchayati Raj Studies, 2006.

Palanithurai, G., *Handloom Sector under Globalization,* Gandhigram: Rajiv Gandhi Chair for Panchayati Raj Studies, 2006.

Palanithurai, G., *How Some Panchayats Becomes a Model? Actionable Agenda to Become a Model,* Gandhigram: Rajiv Gandhi Chair for Panchayati Raj Studies, 2009.

Palanithurai, G., *Indian Polity: Myth and Reality,* New Delhi: Kanishka Publishers and Distributors, 1993.

Palanithurai, G., *New Panchayati Raj System at Work: An Evaluation,* New Delhi: Concept Publishing Company, 2000.

Palanithurai, G., Panchayati *Raj System in Tamil Nadu* (Monograph), Gandhigram: Rajiv Gandhi Chair for Panchayati Raj Studies, 2002.

Palanithurai, G., *People's Perception of Politics,* New Delhi: Kanishka Publishing House, 2002.

Palanithurai, G., *Plantation Sector under Globalization,* Gandhigram: Rajiv Gandhi Chair for Panchayati Raj Studies, 2006.

Palanithurai, G., *Process and Performance of Dalit and Women Panchayat Presidents,* New Delhi: Concept Publishing Company, 2005.

Palanithurai, G., *Rajiv Gandhi's Vision on Local Governance,* New Delhi: Concept Publishing Company, 2009.

Palanithurai, G., *Role and Responsibilities of Gram Sabha* (in Tamil), Chennai: New Century Book House, 2006.

Palanithurai, G., *Rural Artisan Sector under Globalization,* Gandhigram: Rajiv Gandhi Chair for Panchayati Raj Studies, 2006.

Palanithurai, G., Vallinayagam K., Chidambaram N.S., Subramaniam K., *Handbook of Panchayati Raj Administration (Tamil Nadu),* New Delhi: Concept Publishing Company, 2006.

Palanithurai, G., *Water Sector under Globalization,* Gandhigram: Rajiv Gandhi Chair for Panchayati Raj Studies, 2006.

Palanithurai, G. and Ragupathy V., *Functional Efficiency of Gram Sabha in Tamil Nadu,* New Delhi: Concept Publishing Company Pvt. Ltd., 2006.

Palanithurai, G., "Constitutional Laws *Vs* Community Laws in India: Conflict and Synergy", *The Grassroots Governance Journal, 5* (1), 2007.

Palanithurai, G., *Management of Ethnic Conflict in India and Canada: A Comparative Analysis",* New Delhi: Kanishka Publishers and Distributors, 1993.

Palanithurai, G., *"Third General Elections to Local Governments in Tamil Nadu: Expectations and Shocking Realities,"* New Delhi: Concept Publishing Company Pvt. Ltd., 2008.

Palanithurai, G., and Ragupathy, V., *"Communities Panchayats and Governance at Grassroots,* New Delhi: Concept Publishing Company, 2007.

Palanithurai, G., *Capacity Building for Local Body Leaders,* New Delhi: Concept Publishing Company, 2001.

Palanithurai, G., *Process and Performance of Gram Panchayat Women and Dalit Presidents,* New Delhi: Concept Publishing Company, 2003.

Palanithurai, G., *Status of Dalit Gram Panchayat Leaders in Tamil Nadu* (Monograph), Gandhigram: Rajiv Gandhi Chair for Panchayati Raj Studies, 2008.

Palanithurai, G., Thirunavukkarasu M.A. and Uma, G., *Change Makers at Grassroots,* New Delhi: Concept Publishing Company, 2008.

Palanithurai, G., Uma G. and Vanishree J., *Networking of Elected Women Representatives at Grassroots,* New Delhi: Concept Publishing Company, 2008.

Palanithurai, G. *Dynamics of New Panchayati Raj System in India* (Vol. I), New Delhi: Concept Publishing Company Pvt. Ltd., New Delhi, 2002.

Palanithurai, G. *Empowerment of Women: Problems Faced by the Elected Women Representatives. Experience from Tamil Nadu* (Monograph), Gandhigram: Rajiv Gandhi Chair for Panchayati Raj Studies, 2001.

Palanithurai, G. *Leadership Matters in Grassroots Governance Pathfinders, Series – I* (Monograph), Gandhigram: Rajiv Gandhi Chair for Panchayati Raj Studies, 2004.

Palanithurai, G., *Panchayati Raj System, Act, Rules, Government Orders and Schemes and Programmes* (in Tamil), Chennai: South Vision, 2009.

Pande, Rohini, *Understanding Political Corruption in Low Income Countries,* Faculty Research Working Paper Series, Harvard Kennady School, 2007.

Parekh, Bhikhu, "The Crisis in Indian Democracy", Jawaharlal Nehru Memorial Lecture in Trinity College, 21st November, 2011.

Patnaik, Prabhat, "Things, not people", *Front Line,* Vol. 28: No. 21, 2011.

Pharr, J. Susan, Putnam Robert and Dalton Russell, "A Quarter Century of Declining Confidence", *Journal of Democracy,* Vol. 11:No. 1, 2000.

Poornima, Madhu Kishwar, *Deepening of Democracy: Challenges of Governance and Globalisation in India,* New Delhi: Oxford University Press, 2005.

Prior, D., Stewart J. and Walsh K., *Citizenship, Rights and Community Participation,* London: Pitman, 1995.

Rajagopal, Arvind, Visibility as a Trap in the Anna Hazare Campaign *Economic and Political Weekly,* Vol. XLV1: No. 47, Nov. 19, 2011.

Rajiv Gandhi Chair, *Report of the Training Programme conducted for Dalit Block Panchayat Women Leaders of Tamil Nadu,* Gandhigram: Rajiv Gandhi Chair for Panchayati Raj Studies, 2002.

Rama Krishnan, Venkatesh, "Neoliberal Plan", *Front Line,* 28: No. 21, Oct. 21, 2011.

Ranjit, Sau, "Towards Transition to Democracy", *Bharatiya Samajik Chintan*, 7 (1), 2008.

Ribot, C. Jesse, "Representation, Citizenship and the Public Domain in Democratic Decentralization", *Development*, Vol. 50, No. 1, March 2007.

S.N. Chaudhary, *Dalit and Tribal Leadership in Panchayat*, New Delhi, Concept Publishing Company Pvt. Ltd., New Delhi, 2004.

Sarasvathi, S., *The Madras Panchayat System: A Historical Survey, Vol. I*, New Delhi: Impex India, 1973.

Sathyavanimuthu, *My Struggle*, Chennai: Chezhiyan Publications, 1981.

Shah, Anwar (ed.), *Local Governance in Developing Countries*, Washington D.C.: The World Bank, 2006.

Shah, Anwar (ed.), *Local Governance in Industrial Countries*, Washington D.C: The World Bank, 2006.

Shah, Anwar and Shah Furhawn, Citizen Centred Local Governance: Strategies to Combat Democratic Deficits, *Development*, Vol. 50: No. 1, March 2007.

Shore, C. and Haller D. (eds), *Corruption: Anthropological Perspectives*, London: Pluto Press, 2005.

Shylendra, H.S., (ed), *New Governance and Development: Challenges of Addressing Poverty and Inequality*, New Delhi: Academic Education, 2009.

Singh, Rajesh, "Performance Impediments in Government: Some Suggestions for Reform", *The Indian Journal of Public Administration*, Vol. LV. : No. 2, April – June, 2009.

Singh, Satyajit and Sharma K. Pradeep (eds), *Decentralization: Institutions and Politics in Rural India*, New Delhi: Oxford University Press, 2007.

Sisodia, Singh Yatindra (ed), *Indians Development Scenario: Challenges and Prospects*, New Delhi: Rauht Publications, 2009.

Sivaramakrishnan, K.C., *Power to the People?*, New Delhi: Konark Publisher's Pvt. Ltd., 2000.

Solomon, Lester M., *The Tools of Government: A Guide to the New Governance*, New York: Oxford University Press, 2012.

Srinivas, M.N., *"Village, Caste, Gender and Method"*, New Delhi: Oxford University Press 1996.

Tavits, Margit, "Clarity of Responsibility and Corruption", *American Journal of Political Science*, Vol. 51 : No. 1, Jan. 2007.

The Catalyst Trust, *Citizens' Audit of Basic Services in Tamil Nadu*, Chennai: The Catalyst Trust, 2008.

Venkataraman, R., *My Presidential Years*, New Delhi: Harper Collins, 1995.

Venkatasubramaniam, A.K., *Participant or Petitioner* (in Tamil), Chennai: Catalyst Trust, 2001.

Viswanathan, S., *Dalits in Dravidian Land*, Chennai: Navayana, 2005.

Vittal, N., *Corruption in India*,New Delhi: Academic Foundation, 2003.

Vohra, Kashyap C. Subash, (ed), *Eradication of Corruption and Restoration of Values* New Delhi: Sterling, 2001.

Weiner, Myron, *The Indian Paradox*, New Delhi: Sage Publications, 1989.

Weisskopf, E. Thomas, "Why worry about inequality in the Booming Indian Economy", *Economic and Political Weekly*, Vol. XLV: No. 47, Nov, 19, 2011.

World Bank, *Governance and Development*, Washington DC: World Bank, 1992.

World Bank, *The World Development Report, 1999 – 2000, Vol. I*, Washington DC, World Bank, 2000.

Xavier, Gnanaraj *et al.*, *Outside the Caste (A Status Report on the Dalits of Tamil Nadu)*, Chengalpattu: Educational Trust, 2002.

Index

Abdul Kalam, A.P.J., 33
Abusive attacks, 36
Academic institutions, 135
Accountability, 3, 88, 89, 90, 96, 97, 98, 108, 110, 112, 114, 115, 132, 134, 218
  downward, 97, 98, 134, 225
  macro, 97
  micro, 97
  upward, 19, 97
Accountability and Transparency in Development Activities, 3, 96
Accountability Mechanisms, 19, 27
Activity mapping, 203, 204
Administration, 3, 7, 22, 50, 82, 96, 97, 98, 108, 109, 111, 116, 135, 137, 181
Administration domain, 43
Administrative control, 20
Administrative cost, 112
Administrative federalism, 211
Administrative institutions, 134
Administrative mechanisms, 134, 216, 231
Administrative models, 97
Administrative Reforms Commission of India, 26
Administrative system, 7, 18, 73, 74, 116, 117, 132, 194, 231
Adult Education, 65
Agriculture and Animal Husbandry, 143
AIADMK Government, 203
Animal Husbandry, 68, 143
Anna Dravida Munnetra Kazhagam, 198
Anna Hazare's Anti Corruption Movement, 30, 39, 44, 56
Anti-Constitution, 209
Anti-corruption, 32, 74
Anti corruption movement, 2, 30, 45, 47, 50, 54
Anti-state groups, 20
Assembly elections, 185
Australian model, 217

Backdrop, 3, 4, 66, 143, 152, 155, 207
Backward Regions Grant Fund (BRGF), 205
Basic Education, 65
Beneficiary selections, 166
Bio-Diversity Act, 126
BJP, 92, 93
Bonded labourers, 158, 162
British model, 217
British Rule, 97
Bureaucratic elites, 47
Bureaucratic system, 79

Canadian politics, 220

Capitalism, political, 76, 88
Caste clashes, 163
Caste discrimination, 157, 163
Caste system, 10, 186
Caste violence, 153
Catalyst Trust in Chennai, 84
Centralization, 112
Centralized administration, 98
Centre-state relationship, 197, 198, 211, 212
Ceremonial functions, 91
Charitable trusts, 46
Child development, 69
Chinese model, 217
Citizen empowerment, 225
Citizen information centre, 147
Civil disobedience movement, 225
Civil society groups, 56, 84
Civil society organizations, 46, 50, 146, 147, 155, 156, 173, 174, 176, 226
Cleansing operations, 49
Climate change environment degradation, 25
Coalition Government, 51, 52, 88, 90, 198
Coalition partners, 51
Coalition politics, 3, 90
Colonial Administration, 97
Colonial characteristics, 132
Colonial days, 100
Colonial society, 7
Colonial state system, 62
Colonial yoke, 7
Common pool money, 78
Communal conflict, 183
Communal Unity, 65
Communication development, 22
Communication revolution, 43
Communist Party of India, 173, 177
Communitarian order, 66
Communitarian society, 12
Community cohesion, 183
Comptroller and Auditor General of India, 48
Computerization, 122
Conceptualization, 2, 43, 61
Concurrent List, 202, 208, 209
Confrontationist approach, 54
Congress Party, 38, 44, 92
Constitutional Amendment, 198
Constitutional Bill, 212
Constitutional compulsions, 155
Constitutional design, 91
Constitutional formalities, 200
Constitutional provisions, 19, 133, 182, 184, 193, 223
Constitution Amendment Bill, 199, 219
Consultative committees, 207
Continental organisations, 225
Controversial clauses, 219
Controversial decisions, 93
Corporate company politics, 23
Corpus funds, 162
Corruption
  at grassroots, 2
  in Public life, 231
  justification, 78
Corrupt
  politicians, 34, 37, 53
  practices, 31, 34, 49, 51, 53, 56, 73, 74, 134
Credible leadership, 53
Criminal
  politician, 40
  wastage, 122
Cultivable land, 150
Cultural groups, 180
Culture of Demand, 114

Dalit
  communities, 151, 154, 156, 164, 173, 174, 183
  families, 156
  girls, 162
  gram panchayat, 150

grassroot leaders, 155
hamlets, 175
leaders, 150, 152, 153, 154, 155, 156, 164, 165, 166, 173, 174, 175, 176, 177, 194
leadership, 153, 156, 175
Panchayat, 154, 156, 166, 177
population, 150
representatives, 188
settlements, 175
votes, 153
woman, 158, 164, 174
Data generation, 3, 120, 122, 123, 124, 131, 231
Data Generation Mechanism, 125
Data Management System functions in India, 123
Data manipulation, 123
Data preservation, 131
Data validation, 131
Decentralisation, 116, 204, 212
Decentralized decisions, 218
Decentralizing powers, 68, 154, 226
Decisive powers, 215
Delivery mechanism, 134
Demand money, 201
Democracy
deepening, 71, 194, 225, 226, 227
destabilize, 180
local, 214
modern, 155, 181
parliamentary, 26, 35, 45, 47, 152
Democracy votes, representative, 193
Democratic countries, 22, 23, 74, 216
Democratic deficit, 225, 227
Democratic mechanism, 24
Democratic practices, 185
Democratic voice, 38
Democratization, 3, 44, 116
Denmark, 214, 216
Department activities, 86
Departmental Administrative System, 123
Deprivation, 152
Developmental tasks, 115
Development aspirations, 14, 221
Development brokerage, 85, 186
Development brokers, 18, 19, 74, 85, 107, 114, 145, 147, 210
Development displacement, 31
Development domain, 147
Development engagement, 17, 18, 20, 25, 27, 65, 67
Development finance, 18
Development framework, 60, 61
Development indicators, 21
Development management activities, 122
Development mechanism, 17
Development methodology, 11
Development mobilization, 2
Development Politics, 2, 49
Development schemes, 19, 21, 73, 107, 133
Devolution of powers, 182, 202, 203, 212
Devolution process, 203
Dialogue process, 54, 56, 185, 195
Discretionary powers, 46, 93
Discriminatory practices, 150, 152, 157, 158, 163, 166, 176
Dissemination of information, 43
District level federation, 176
District National Informatics Centres, 122
District Panchayat Councils, 200
Documentation units, 188
Donor institutions, 225
Dravidian movement, 151, 172
Dravidian parties, 151, 152
Dravidian Political Parties, 206
Drinking Water, 68

Economic development, 50, 151, 166, 176, 217

Economic inequality, 10
Education in Health and Hygiene, 65
Election Commission, 23, 48, 73, 88, 89
Election Commissioner of India, 89
Election manifesto, 199
Election process, 50
Electoral contest, 183
Electoral reforms, 16
Empowered citizens, 224
Empowered communities, 64
Empowerment process, 62
External forces, 90

Farmers Development, 65
Farm land, 158
Federal institutions, 217
Federalism, 219
Federalistic theory, 219
Feudal characteristics, 24
Feudal culture, 24, 181
Feudal elements, 181
Feudal government, 189
Feudalism, 23
Feudal society, 146
Finance Commission, 210
Fiscal Federalism, 218, 219
Fishery, 68
Fodder, 68
Ford Foundation, 84
Freedom movement, 27
Freedom struggle, 7, 16, 17, 26, 50, 69, 186
French model, 217
Fundamental rights, 208, 209
Funding agencies, 226
Funeral ceremonies, 158, 163
Funeral duties, 163

Gandhi, Indira, 51
Gandhi, Rahul, 18, 19, 22, 33, 38, 44, 45, 48, 51, 74, 79, 89, 90, 122, 202
Gandhi, Rajiv, 32, 45, 198
Gandhi, Sonia, 40
Gandhian Framework, 2
German model, 217
Global economic challenges, 217
Globalization of economy, 116
Globalization opportunity, 51
Governance
  accountable, 19
  bad, 6, 96
  colonial, 135
  crisis, 43, 58
  decentralized, 20
  design, 11
  federal, 219
  framework of, 61, 66, 67, 71, 97
  institution of, 98, 202
  mechanism, 3, 6, 21, 56, 64, 216, 219
  order, 64
  reforms, 16
  representative, 32
  responsive, 214
  shaping, 89
  social, 71
  strong, 62
  units of, 79, 121
Gram Panchayats, multi-caste, 143
Grassroots
  institutions, 131
  bureaucracy, 116
  democracy, 195, 212
  mobilization, 38
  organizations, 61
  politics, 45
Happiness index, 58

Hazare, Anna, 2, 31, 32, 33, 34, 35, 36, 40, 42, 45, 46, 52, 53, 54, 55
Health Department, 121, 130
Historic welfare schemes, 39
House arrest, 53
Human Resource Information System, 112

Human Rights Commission, 176
Hunger Project, 82, 83

Ideological commitment, 24
Inclusive development, 11, 12, 21
Inclusive growth, 11, 12, 137
Inclusive society, 133
Indian Administrative system, 20
Indian model, 217
Indian National Congress, 38, 39, 40, 41, 42, 44, 45, 50, 51, 54, 55, 56, 89, 92
Indirect elections, 173
Industrialized districts, 174
Information Act, 32, 35, 39, 43, 50, 83, 85, 109, 137, 143
Informational distance, 111
Information Bill, 133
Information Commission, 136, 137
Information
  centre, 84
  channel, 75
  conversion, 108
  gap, 85, 109, 116, 147
  package, 80
Infrastructure development works, 81
Institutional arrangement, 194, 218
Institutional mechanism, 11, 12, 26, 188, 194, 214, 222
Institutions mockery, 40
Inter-governmental relationships, 211
Internal conflicts, 185
International media, 42
Intra-party rivalry, 185

Japanese model, 217
Judicial Interpretation, 223
Judiciary and Election Commission, 73

Key elements, 2

Labour Department, 123
Labour Development, 65
Land consolidation, 68
Land reforms, 68
L.C. Jain Committee, 201
Leadership crisis, 33, 231
Leadership style, 82
Leadership vacuum, 40
Legislations, 22, 132, 133, 207, 215, 226
  breaking, 50, 226
  conformity, 199
  strong, 41
Legitimate powers, 98
Liberal democracy, 223
Liberalization, 11, 115
Local governance
  constitutional, 32
  models of, 217
  strengthening, 226
Local self-governments, 214, 223, 227
Local Self Help Group, 131
Lokpal, 32, 41, 42, 45, 46, 48, 49, 53

Mahatma Gandhi, 25, 26, 32, 35, 48
Mahatma Gandhi Rural Employment Guarantee Act, 50
Malgovernance, 53
Management models, 24
Manpower planning, 112
Marginalization, 152
Marginalized communities, 154, 187, 194
Market exploitation, 114
Mass deprivation, 1, 31, 74
Mass movement, 58, 208
Master-servant relationship, 134
Media corruption, 85
Mediation, 18
Methodological nuances, 47
Micro development actions, 32
Micro movement, 216
Millennium Development Goals, 25, 69, 70

Ministry of Rural Development and Local Administration, 198
Minor Irrigation, 68
Mobilization, 16, 17, 22, 33, 69
  activist, 147
  huge resource, 27
  political, 2, 22, 38
  popular, 49
  silent, 33
  social, 164
  wider, 16
Model Code of Conduct for Elected Representatives, 112
Model State, 202
Modernization process, 7
Money power, 34, 53
Moral crises, 94
Moral laws, 65
Multi-ethnic society, 180
Multinational companies, 27, 46
Municipal Corporation area, 124
Mutual benefits, 85

Narayanan, K.R., 33
National Advisory Council, 39
National Convention of District and Block Panchayat, 197
National Parliament, 12, 70, 152, 184, 215, 219
Nehru, Jawaharlal, 27
Neo-liberal agenda, 217
Neo-liberal groups, 224
New development paradigm, 70
Non-Brahmin communities, 151
Non-dalits, 166
Non-formal education, 69
Non-industrialized districts, 173
Non-party movement, 49
Nordic model, 217

Operational framework, 3
Oppression, 152, 153
Organic individuals, 67
Organizational backup, 55
Organizational strength, 54

Packaged information, 109, 110
Panchayat Act, 116
Panchayat administration, 83, 155
Panchayat autonomy, 209
Panchayat code, 208
Panchayat Council, 130, 153
Panchayat elections, 175, 199
Panchayat elections in West Bengal, 210
Panchayati Raj Department, 139
Panchayati Raj System, 64, 84, 150, 154, 156, 174, 199, 200, 203, 206, 208, 211
Panchayat performance, 207
Parliamentary Committee, 219
Parliamentary Election
  Eleventh, 92
  Ninth, 91
Party coalition, 92
Peaceful protests, 43, 53
Personalized verbal attacks, 54
Police department, 152
Political
  affiliation, 177
  aspirations, 221
  brokers, 85
  business, 23
  compulsions, 37
  conflicts, 180, 183, 185
  controversies, 93
  crises, 92
  culture, 206, 221
  development, 30
  discourse, 39
  elements, 56
  elites, 47
  forces, 52
  institutions, 16
  leader, credible, 33
  organizational structure, 24
  party system, 49
  performance, 38

protests, 43
reforms, 16
value, 185
Postal Bill, 93
Poverty alleviation, 69, 75, 123
Power brokers, 212
Power corridor, 14
Power devolution, 155, 200, 204, 207, 222
Power hungry government, 62
Procedural formalities, 77
Procedural reforms, 111
Processing charges, 77, 78
Procrastination, 199
Pro-development initiatives, 135
Professional institutions, 22
Professionalism, 99
Pro-poor policies, 40, 135
Pro-poor welfare schemes, 40
Provincial Constitution, 215
Provincial Legislatures, 215, 219
Public distribution system, 69, 122, 147, 158, 162
Pucca management system, 162

Rajamannar Committee, 211
Rajiv Gandhi Chair for Panchayati Raj Studies, 83
Rao, Narasimha, 92
Rational Governance Model, 63
Ration card, 122, 131
bogus, 122
Ration shops, 163
Reform initiatives, 27, 111
Reform measures, 24
Regional governance actions, 32
Religious groups, 187
Religious institutions, 46
Remedial actions, 99
Representative democracy, 6, 10, 11, 26, 42, 46, 47, 48, 49, 56, 59, 180, 184, 185, 186
Rights reforms, 116
RTI Act, 116, 136
Rule of laws, 77, 111, 189
Ruling party middlemen, 78
Rural Development, 100, 116, 144
Rural Development and Panchayati Raj Department, 146
Rural development schemes, 74, 85
Rural society, 79, 99

Sanitation culture, 17
Sarvodaya, 17
School education department, 122
Scientific analysis, 31
Scientific data management system, 123, 131
Scientific evaluation, 39
Sectoral departments, 116
Self Help Group, 124, 130
Self-regulation, 64, 65
Sensitization, 17
Service Delivery and Development, 220
Sharma, Shankar Dayal, 3, 92
Singh, Manmohan, 51, 56
Social Audit, 74
Social audit system, 27
Social conditions, 193
Social conflict, 21, 150, 195
Social discrimination, 151
Social elements, 211
Social harmony, 176
Social hierarchy, 182, 188, 189, 193
Socialist countries, 216
Social laws, 165
Social movement, 152, 164
Society democracy, 193
Socio-economic life, 181
Socio-economic problems, 31
Socio-political actions, 12
Socio-political activities, 151
Sovereign power, 223
Sovereignty, 34, 40, 61, 221
State Finance Commissions, 200
State Information Commission, 136
State regulation, 64

State Society Market Relationship, Dynamics of, 60
ST Commission, 176
Strong civil society interventions, 23
Subsidiarity principle, 201, 203
Supreme Court of India, 51
Supreme powers, 39
Sustainable development, 60
Swiss model, 217
Systematic generations, 120
Systematic knowledge, 76

Tamil Nadu Panchayat Act, 172
Tamil society, 154
Tax reform initiatives, 227
Technological advancement, 21, 22
Theoretical framework, 11
Tihar prison, 53, 55
Tracking information, 147
Training mechanism, 22
Transfer of powers, 186, 203
Transfer powers, 154, 186
Transformation, 1, 59, 66, 67, 155, 176, 220
- economic, 79
- political, 189, 193
- social, 150, 183, 189, 193

Transformative methodology, 71
Tribals Development, 65

UPA, 38, 50, 51, 53, 55

Vajpayee, A.B., 92
Venkataraman, R., 33, 89, 90, 94
Village nurse, 122
Village Panchayats, 80, 138, 173
Vituperative verbal attacks, 36
Vocation education, 69
Voluntary associations, 66

Water conservation, 17
Watershed development, 68
Welfare programmes, 8, 50
Welfare schemes, 74, 76, 80, 110, 135, 137, 146
Western model of development, 61
Women Commission, 176
Women Development, 65
Women Panchayat, 165
Women Panchayat Leaders Federation, 164
World Bank, 74, 97